CHICKEN SOUP FOR THE FATHER AND DAUGHTER SOUL

CHICKEN SOUP
FOR THE FATHER AND
DAUGHTER SOUL

Stories to Celebrate the Love Between Dads and Daughters Through the Years

Jack Canfield
Mark Victor Hansen
LeAnn Thieman
Patty Aubery
Nancy Autio

Health Communications, Inc.
Deerfield Beach, Florida

www.hcibooks.com
www.chickensoup.com

We would like to acknowledge the many publishers and individuals who granted us permission to reprint the cited material. (Note: The stories that are in the public domain or that were written by Jack Canfield, Mark Victor Hansen, LeAnn Thieman, Patty Aubery and Nancy Autio are not included in this listing.)

Amanda. Reprinted by permission of John St. Augustine. ©2004 John St. Augustine.

Love in a Box. Reprinted by permission of Nancy J. Kopp. ©2004 Nancy J. Kopp.

Just Between Us. Reprinted by permission of Janet Lynn Mitchell. ©2004 Janet Lynn Mitchell.

I Love You, Pilgrim. Reprinted by permission of Aletheia Lee Butler. ©2003 Aletheia Lee Butler.

On the Nose. Reprinted by permission of Dierdre Dizon. ©2004 Dierdre Dizon.

(Continued on page 378)

Library of Congress Cataloging-in-Publication Data

Chicken soup for father & daughter soul : stories to celebrate the love
   between dads and daughters through the years / [compiled by]
   Jack Canfield . . . [et al.].
      p. cm.
   ISBN 0-7573-0252-1 (trade pbk.)
   1. Fathers and daughters. 2. Conduct of life. I. Title: Chicken soup for
   father and daughter soul. II. Canfield, Jack, 1944-

HQ755.85.C47b 2005
306.874'2—dc
                                                          2005040432

©2005 Jack Canfield and Mark Victor Hansen
ISBN 0-7573-0252-1 (trade paper)

Publisher: Health Communications, Inc.
         3201 S.W. 15th Street
         Deerfield Beach, FL 33442–8190

Cover design by Andrea Perrine Brower
Inside formatting by Dawn Von Strolley Grove

To our dads, Terry Mitchell,
Paul Duello and Kenneth Autio who we will
remember forever for what they said, what they
didn't say and how they lived.

*To a father waxing old,
nothing is dearer than a daughter.*

Euripides

Contents

Acknowledgments...xi

Introduction..xv

Share with Us...xvii

1. BEING THERE

Amanda *John St. Augustine*...2

Love in a Box *Nancy Julien Kopp*..6

Just Between Us *Janet Lynn Mitchell*..9

I Love You, Pilgrim *Aletheia Lee Butler*...12

On the Nose *D. B. Zane*..15

We Are Dragon-Slayers *Timothy P. Bete*..19

Understanding Dad *Marianne L. Vincent*...23

The Camping Trip *Laura M. Stack*..27

Outstretched Arms *LaDonna Gatlin*..30

Sour Pickle *Isabel Bearman Bucher*...33

Run for Gold *Ruth Barden*...37

Love's Lance *Margaret Lang*..40

2. A MATTER OF PERSPECTIVE

Safe Harbors and Sailing Ships
    Cynthia Fonk with Linda Evans Shepherd.......................................46

Daddy's Dance *Louise Tucker Jones*...48

The Adventure *Suzanne Eller*...52

Fired from the Peanut Patch *Louise Tucker Jones*................................56

Man of Few Words *Elaine Ernst Schneider* 59
Retirement Plan *Bettye Martin-McRae* 62
Father Meets Cat *Harriet Cooper* 66
The Artist *Janet Hall Wigler* 70
Finding Lost Love *Marna Malag Jones* 74
A Father's Gift from a Daughter *Raymond L. Morehead* 79
Dirt Cheap *Lynn Dean* 82
My Father's Hands *Dena Smallwood* 84
The Obituary *Carol Haynes* 88

3. LIFE LESSONS

The Great Candy Bar Debate *Naida Grunden* 94
"Yes, Daddy, I Promise" *Nancy C. Anderson* 98
The Lesson *Jean Stewart* 102
How to Trust, Dad-Style *Sylvia Duncan* 105
Of Wings and Strings *Carol McAdoo Rehme* 108
Just a Walk in the Park *Steven H. Manchester* 112
The Fifty-Cent Sewing Machine *Brenda K. Stevens* 118
Lessons from a Teenager *Courtney Soucy* 121
Hidden Wings *Joyce L. Rapier* 126
Questions *Danny Dugan* 129
Bullfrogs, Butterflies and Dads
    Joe Strube as told to Marilyn K. Strube 133
What I Learned at the Outhouse Races *Patricia Lorenz* 137

4. SPECIAL MOMENTS

The Dad He Planned to Be *Stephanie Welcher Thompson* 144
Dad's Right Hand *Lana Brookman* 148
Trust Me *Lanny Zechar* 151
Papa's Gift to Kelsey *Sonja Walder* 154
Humor Me *Lynn Dean* 156
Baseball Game Plan *Larry Bodin* 160
Who Giveth? *S. Maitland Schrecengost* 163
Long-Distance Vitamins *Emily Chase* 165
The Best "Father-Daughter Date" Ever! *Carol McClain Bassett* 167

I'm Confessin' That I Love You *JoAnn Semones* 171
Father of Fortune *Ted Bosley*...174
Daddy's Little Tomboy *Sally Kelly-Engeman* 177
Father's Secret *Betty Stanley*.......................................180
Two Fathers and a Bride *Janelle Breese Biagioni*..................183
Roadside Rescue *Christie Rogers* 186

5. ON GRATITUDE

Father Christmas *Steven H. Manchester*.............................190
Solemn Images *Ron Gold*..194
Spelling L-O-V-E *Bonnie Compton Hanson* 197
The Painted Tractor *Bobbie Wilkinson* 201
Ethyl *Isabel Bearman Bucher* 205
Memorial Day Flags *Arthur B. Wiknik Jr.* 210
Struggle and Celebration *Jerry Snider*.............................213
A Decent Thing to Do *Isabel Corr Rizzo*............................217

6. FROM THE MOUTHS OF BABES

She Calls Me Daddy *John Cox* 223
Anna's First Cubs Game *Louis Schutz* 225
Owed to Joy *Ted A. Thompson* 227
Be Slow to Anchor *Dan DeVries*....................................230
Moonshine *Debra Ann Pawlak* 232
A Forkful of Humor *Kimberly A. Ripley* 236
The Price of a Child *Debi Stack*....................................240
Black and White *Al D. Luebbers* 243
Dear Daddy . . . *Linda Saslow*......................................244

7. ON HEALING

Tearing Down the Wall *Patti Davis* 248
Advice from a Tree *Ilan Shamir*.....................................251
Taken for Granted *Donna Pennington*..............................255
Letter to a Stranger *Karen L. Cooper*...............................258
The Haircut *Margaret J. Wasilewski* 263
Peela *Donna J. Gudaitis* 267

Father Knows Best *Abigail R. Gutierrez*......................................269
A Piece of Chalk *Holly Smeltzer* 272
Unpaved Roads *Linda Poehnelt*..275
Apology to a Child *Ron Wutka* 280
I Want My Daddy Back *Deb Haggerty* 282
Daddy's Story *Ruth A. Hancock*..284
Time to Forgive *Tracy Ryzan Ross* 288
Closer and Closure *Carol McAdoo Rehme* 291
Secret Tears *Nancy B. Gibbs* 295

8. TRADITIONS

Smeared Ink *Amy Adair* 300
Across the Pond *Linda Bryant* 303
Christmas in a Nutshell *Bobbie Bonk*...307
Slow-Dance *Stephani Marlow James* 309
Eat Dessert First *Judith Marks-White* 314
My Father's Chair *Susan Wales* 318
Donuts *Gail Eynon* 322
Wedding Day *Pamela G. Smith*...325

9. ACROSS GENERATIONS

Apa's Motto in Life *Renie Burghardt* 328
Punch Lines *Deborah Shouse*..332
Like Riding a Bike *Linda Ferris*..336
Reel Event *B. J. Taylor* 338
Connected by Love *Linda Apple*...341
Cash Rewards *Michelle Bazan Reed* 344
That Dang Horse *Ann Clarke*..348
In My Dad's Boots *Margaret Lang* 351
Daddy's Gift *Wanda Rosseland*..354

More Chicken Soup? 359
Supporting Others..360
Who Is Jack Canfield?...361
Who Is Mark Victor Hansen? 362
Who Is LeAnn Thieman? 363
Who Is Patty Aubery?...364
Who Is Nancy Autio? 365
Contributors...366
Permissions *(continued)* 378

Acknowledgments

The path to *Chicken Soup for the Father and Daughter Soul* has been made all the more beautiful by the many "companions" who have been there with us along the way. Our heartfelt gratitude to:

Our families, who have been chicken soup for our souls!

Inga, Travis, Riley, Christopher, Oran and Kyle for all their love and support.

Patty, Elisabeth and Melanie Hansen, for once again sharing and lovingly supporting us in creating yet another book.

Mark, Angela, Brian, Dante, Christie, Dave, Mitch, Jeff, Kirk, Molly, JT and Chandler, who hearten our efforts.

Our publisher, Peter Vegso, for his vision and commitment to bringing *Chicken Soup for the Soul* to the world.

Russ Kamalski for being there on every step of the journey, with love, laughter and endless creativity.

Barbara Lomonaco, for nourishing us with truly wonderful stories and cartoons.

D'ette Corona, for being there to answer any questions along the way.

Patty Hansen, for her thorough and competent handling of the legal and licensing aspects of the *Chicken Soup for the Soul* books. You are magnificent at the challenge!

Laurie Hartman, for being a precious guardian of the *Chicken Soup* brand.

Veronica Romero, Teresa Esparza, Robin Yerian, Jesse Ianniello, Jamie Chicoine, Jody Emme, Debbie Lefever, Michelle Adams, Dee Dee Romanello, Shanna Vieyra, Lisa Williams, Gina Romanello, Brittany Shaw, Dena Jacobson, Tanya Jones, Mary McKay and David Coleman, who support Jack's and Mark's businesses with skill and love.

Bret Witter, Elisabeth Rinaldi, Allison Janse and Kathy Grant, our editors at Health Communications, Inc., for their devotion to excellence.

Terry Burke, Tom Sand, Lori Golden, Kelly Johnson Maragni, Tom Galvin, Sean Geary, Patricia McConnell, Kim Weiss and Paola Fernandez-Rana, the sales, marketing, and PR departments at Health Communications, Inc., for doing such an incredible job supporting our books.

Tom Sand, Claude Choquette and Luc Jutras, who manage year after year to get our books translated into thirty-six languages around the world.

The art department staff at Health Communications, Inc., for their talent, creativity and unrelenting patience in producing book covers and inside designs that capture the essence of *Chicken Soup*: Larissa Hise Henoch, Lawna Patterson Oldfield, Andrea Perrine Brower, Anthony Clausi and Dawn Von Strolley Grove.

All the *Chicken Soup for the Soul* coauthors, who make it so much of a joy to be part of this *Chicken Soup* family.

Our glorious panel of readers who helped us make the final selections and made invaluable suggestions on how to improve the book: Jean Bell, Michelle Blank, Helen Colella, Heather Cook-Lindsay, Bernice Duello, Nancy B. Gibbs, Donal Gurley, Kristine Harty, Tony Jaworski, Sally Kelly-Engeman, Mary Kieler, Karen Kilby, Renee King, Karen Kishpaugh, Charlotte A. Lanham, Terry LePine, Mary McMahon, Colleen Moulton, Mary Panosh, Christie

Rogers, Wanda Rosseland, Duane Shaw, Irene Sheehan, Wendy Stanton, Mary and Rich Streit, Terry Tuck, Suzanne Vaughan and Sue Wade.

And, most of all, we are grateful to everyone who submitted their heartfelt stories, poems, quotes and cartoons for possible inclusion in this book. While we were not able to use them all, we know that each word came from your heart and soul. Thank you for all you shared. Because of the size of this project, we may have left out the names of some people who contributed along the way. If so, we are sorry, but please know we appreciate you very much.

Special thanks to Amy Williams, LeAnn's marketing assistant, who so masterfully manages LeAnn's speaking business while she travels and writes.

And to LeAnn's husband, Mark, who could write the book on how dads love their daughters.

And mostly to God, for his divine guidance.

Introduction

Few of life's relationships compare to that of a father and daughter. From the first time she grasps his finger to the day he lets her go, their bond deepens. Those dads and daughters who enjoy a close relationship will happily identify with these stories. For others, miles, and sometimes even memories, separate them more than they'd like. These stories of inspiration, hope and healing will rekindle their bond and strengthen their love. *Chicken Soup for the Father and Daughter Soul* can be a fun and loving tool to increase communication, "saying" what may have gone unspoken.

Chicken Soup for the Father and Daughter Soul inspires dads and daughters to embrace these stories and each other, evoking their own memories and deepening their love— proving that none can liken that of a daddy and his "little girl."

Share with Us

We would like to invite you to send us stories you would like to see published in future editions of *Chicken Soup for the Soul.*

We would also love to hear your reactions to the stories in this book. Please let us know what your favorite stories are and how they affected you.

Please send submissions to:

Chicken Soup for the Soul
P.O. Box 30880
Santa Barbara, CA 93130
fax: 805-563-2945

You can also visit the *Chicken Soup for the Soul* Web site at:

www.chickensoup.com

We hope you enjoy reading this book as much as we enjoyed compiling, editing and writing it.

1

BEING THERE

*Children want to feel instinctively that
their father is behind them as solid as a
mountain, but, like a mountain, is
something to look up to.*

Dorothy Thompson

Amanda

It is the very essence of love, of nobleness, of greatness, to be willing to suffer for the good of others.

Spence

She looks like all the rest of them on the volleyball court with her gold number "12" on the purple jersey. Tall, blonde, with incredible blue eyes and a slim athletic build, my fifteen-year-old daughter Amanda, the kid who gets good grades and works her tail off at everything she does, could easily be the cover girl for any teen magazine. My wife, Jackie, and I watch in amazement as she dives for another dig on the court, slides across the floor headfirst until she reaches the ball and sends it flying back over the net as the crowd claps its approval. As the coach calls time-out and the girls hurry to the sidelines, Amanda uses her jersey to wipe her face, like any other kid, but at that moment you can see the scar that runs down the right side of her abdomen and across her belly. She is not like all the rest of them. She has my kidney inside her.

As they huddle off-court, my mind drifts back to September 20, 1988, and the little girl who came into our lives. "Bubs" was her nickname, short for "Bubba Girl," a name tagged by Jackie's sister Kim when she first saw the ten-pound, two-ounce infant. At first everything was normal with Amanda, but a few months into her life she developed searing fevers, and every visit to the doctor left us more confused. Still, Amanda's toothless grin and shining blue eyes comforted us. Even after throwing up in the doctor's office, she would raise her head and smile as if to say, "Don't worry, be happy!" Her joy was contagious, but our fear was enormous.

Shortly after her first birthday, Amanda was diagnosed with kidney reflux, a common condition that often reverses itself, but without treatment can be very harmful. Her doctors decided, with our approval, to perform a simple outpatient procedure to correct the problem. Surgery was scheduled just before Amanda's fifth birthday. Not long before we were to go to the hospital, the phone rang. It was Dr. Kevin Ghandi, Amanda's nephrologist, with some shocking news. "John, X-rays show that Amanda's right kidney is toxic and making her sick. It has to be removed." The news literally knocked us to our knees. How could this be?

The night before surgery, with Amanda between us in bed, we explained what would happen tomorrow. Amanda listened quietly and simply smiled, then whispered, "Do I get ice cream when it's all over?" Jackie and I looked at each other, wishing it could be that simple, and held her close.

We watched Amanda ride into the operating room, sitting up, with her trusted friend Teddy at her side. The gifted hands of "Dr. Kevin" removed Amanda's ailing organ and took care of the reimplantation of her ureter into the bladder. Everything looked good, but Amanda's optimistic prognosis came with a warning: Someday, she would need a transplant. "Someday" seemed very far away as Amanda held her own, leaving the doctors scratching their heads about how she was able to do so well with only 20 percent of one kidney functioning. We never told them our secret. Each night before Amanda went to bed and every morning when she woke up, I would ask her a very important question: "Bubs, what are we going to be today?"

She would answer, "Positive, and my kidney is getting better." This became a ritual for us, a powerful bridge between the mind and body. Soon "better" became "perfect" and "awesome" and "incredible." Her strength of spirit displayed itself in her physical condition.

Eight years passed. As Amanda's body changed, the little kidney grew tired and "someday" was fast approaching. Factors of age and relationship made me the best organ donor candidate, and the doctors ordered more tests. I held my breath, and a small voice inside reminded me of my grandfather's death from polycystic kidney disease—the same disease that would eventually lead to my father's death. My sister did not have it, and I had never been tested. I prayed and thought of Amanda's smiling face. Jackie and I sat with the ultrasound tech in the darkness as she slid the wand over my kidneys, searching for any cysts. She said, "I'm not really supposed to tell you guys, but I see two healthy kidneys in there." I knew then that a perfect plan was in place and that everything would be all right. It was the closest thing to a miracle I had ever known.

"Someday" turned out to be July 18, 2002. Amanda and I were wheeled into operating rooms at Children's Hospital at the University of Wisconsin in Madison. My healthy vital organ was removed, and a world-renowned surgeon, Dr. Hans Sollinger, delicately placed it in my daughter's body. It began making urine immediately! For the first time in her young life, Amanda had a healthy kidney!

When I awoke after surgery, the nurse placed her hand on my chest and said, "Amanda is down at the other end of the room and is doing great. Is there anything you want me to tell her?"

My throat raw from the breathing tube, I croaked two words, something she would understand, "Hubba-Bubba," my usual corny greeting to her. With tears in her eyes, the nurse delivered the unusual message, and Amanda, with eyes closed, did what she has always done: She smiled.

As fathers, we always hope to leave a piece of ourselves with our children. For Amanda and me, the bond goes far beyond the physical into a spiritual trust, a feeling for me that some agreement from long ago has been fulfilled. It is a rare thing to give life to your child not once, but twice. Two years have passed since the procedure, and as I watch her head back out onto the court, she glances my way and gives me a big smile and a "thumbs-up." I push back the tears and smile back. I am her father, but she is my hero.

John St. Augustine

Love in a Box

Life is a flower, of which love is the honey.

Victor Hugo

When I was a little girl, I found love in a box all because of a class assignment. On a Friday night I made an announcement at the dinner table. The words bubbled out in a torrent of excitement I could no longer contain. "My teacher said we have to bring a box for our valentines on Monday. But it has to be a special box, all decorated."

Mother said, "We'll see," and she continued eating.

I wilted faster than a flower with no water. What did "We'll see" mean? I had to have that box or there would be no valentines for me. My second grade Valentine's Day would be a disaster. Maybe they didn't love me enough to help me with my project.

All day Saturday I waited, and I worried, but there was no mention of a valentine box. Sunday arrived, and my concern increased, but I knew an inquiry about the box might trigger anger and loud voices. I kept an anxious eye on both my parents all day. In 1947, in my house, children only asked once. More than that invited punitive measures.

Late Sunday afternoon, my father called me into our apartment's tiny kitchen. The table was covered with an assortment of white crepe paper, red construction paper, and bits and pieces of lace and ribbon from my mother's sewing basket. An empty shoebox rested on top of the paper. Relief flooded through me when Daddy said, "Let's get started on your project."

In the next hour my father transformed the empty shoe-box into a valentine box I would never forget. Crepe paper covered the ugly cardboard. My father fashioned a wrinkled piece of the pliable paper and glued it around the middle. He cut a slot in the lid and covered it with more of the white paper. Next came red hearts attached in what I considered all the right places. He hummed a tune while he worked, and I kneeled on my chair witnessing the magical conversion of the shoebox and handing him the glue when he needed it. When he finished, my father's eyes sparkled, and a smile stretched across his thin face. "What do you think of that?"

My answer was a hug and a "Thank you, Daddy."

But inside, joy danced all the way to my heart. It was the first time that my father devoted so much time to me. His world consisted of working hard to support his family, adoring my mother, disciplining my brother and me, and listening to every sports event broadcast on the radio. Suddenly, a new door opened in my life. My father loved me.

Monday morning, my mother found a brown grocery sack to protect the beautiful box while I carried it to school. I barely felt the bitter cold of the February day as I held the precious treasure close to me. I would let no harm come to my beautiful valentine box.

My teacher cleared a space on a long, wide windowsill where the decorated boxes would stay until Valentine's Day. I studied each one as it was placed on the sill, and none compared with mine. Every time I peeked at my valentine box, I felt my father's love. My pride knew no bounds. There were moments when the box actually glowed in a spotlight all its own. No doubt I was the only one who witnessed that glow.

Every day some of my classmates brought valentine cards to school and slipped them into the slots of the special boxes. The holiday party arrived, and we brought our boxes to our desks to open the valentines. Frosted heart cookies, red punch, valentines and giggles filled our classroom. Chaos reigned until dismissal time arrived.

I carried my valentine box home proudly. It wasn't hidden in a grocery sack but held out for the world to admire. I showed it to the policeman who guided us across a busy city street. He patted me on the head and exclaimed about it. I made sure everyone along the way took note of my valentine box. My father had made it for me, and the love that filled it meant more to me than all the valentines nestled inside.

From that time on I never doubted my father's feelings for me. The valentine box became a symbol of his love that lasted through decades of other Valentine's Days. He gave me other gifts through the years, but none ever compared with the tender love I felt within the confines of the old, empty shoebox.

Nancy Julien Kopp

Just Between Us

'Tis in my memory locked, and you yourself shall keep the key of it.

William Shakespeare

I wish that I could have seen his face when he answered the phone. Even though I was married to Marty, I still called home when I needed him.

"Dad, my garage door broke . . . "

"Well, do you need me to pick up a new spring?"

"No. I think I kind of need you to come over. You see, I had places to go and people to see, so while I couldn't pull out like usual, I, um, tried to turn my van around."

"You did what?"

"I tried to turn my van around, you know, like a U-turn. I tried to turn the van and head out the other garage door!" I confessed while stifling my giggles.

For a moment there was silence. I could imagine my father sitting in his favorite chair trying to picture what his youngest daughter had attempted. While he thought, I assessed my situation and concluded there was no way I wanted my husband to come home from work and see my creative attempt to get to the mall.

Within moments my father's thoughts broke into words. "Honey, did you make it out the other door? What exactly do you need for me to do?"

I took a deep breath and tried to find an appropriate way to break the news, yet nothing came to mind. As I had done my entire life, I swallowed hard and then presented my problem to my father.

"Dad, it's like this. My van is stuck in my garage."

"Stuck?"

"Yeah, stuck, sideways."

"Sideways?"

"Dad, I thought that I could turn it around. I simply began backing up and going forward, trying to maneuver my van around so that I could exit out of the second garage door. I had a full tank of gas and I was doing a good job of getting it out myself until now, and well, can you come over and get me out of this mess before Marty gets home from work?"

Within minutes my dad had left his chair and was standing in my garage surveying my dilemma. He scratched his head, placed his hands on his hips and assured me that he had "never seen such a thing." Then without saying a word, yet wearing a grin that hinted, "now I've seen it all," he crawled into the driver's seat and began inching his way, slowly turning the van.

I crawled up on the workbench and watched. My dad caught my eye and gave me a wink. Holding my hand over my mouth, I tried to control my laughter as my father repeatedly drove my van three feet forward then three feet in reverse, while maneuvering the steering wheel. I thought of Marty surprising me, coming home early, finding his father-in-law "driving" in his garage and me cheering him on with passion!

Instantly, I flashed back to the many times my dad had come to my rescue, not questioning me as to the "how or why" of my predicament, but concentrating on the "what now" and the solution. It was no secret—my dad knew that I thought "outside the box." In fact, he'd been one to believe in my dreams, support my attempts and praise my accomplishments. I pondered his patience, wisdom and endless love for me. Today was no different. I knew for certain that, no matter what, I could always call on my dad.

An hour before Marty arrived home, my father beamed as he drove the van out the second garage door and parked it in the driveway. I walked out to meet him, and he rolled down his window.

"Problem solved," he said.

"Just between us?" I asked, securing our secret.

"Between us," he nodded. "Yep, this one is 'just between us,' because no one would ever believe it!"

Janet Lynn Mitchell

I Love You, Pilgrim

Love never reasons but profusely gives.

Hannah More

"Howdy, Pilgrim! You aimin' to sleep the day away?"

I groaned and pulled my pillow over my head. I knew what today was without opening my eyes. It was a day of significance on the level of Christmas in our house. It was John Wayne movie marathon day. Apparently my father had already had a dose or two of the Duke before waking me up.

From my siblings' room next door I could hear him continue, "We got a can o' beans warmin' on the fire and black coffee to warm them bones." I assumed the thud that followed was Naomi's pillow hitting the door behind him while John groaned as I had.

My father had definite opinions about good entertainment. Movies must contain John Wayne or Jimmy Stewart. Music must be that of Handel, Mozart or Creedence Clearwater Revival.

Dad was also a bookworm, and our den showed the

treasure of his collection. John, Naomi and I were an odd combination, inheriting a strong love for books from Dad, and a love of being on stage from Mom. Dad never quite understood this passion, but he always supported us.

During my middle-school years, I joined the band. Dad was at each concert, reading a book until it began and reading again until it was time to give me a congratulatory hug. He always gave me a smile and replied, "Good work. You didn't forget any words."

In high school all of our interests turned to drama. During my senior year I reached the pinnacle—I was cast in our spring musical! I spent countless hours practicing. I'd run tap routines as I combed my hair and rehearse the songs as I set the table for dinner.

Opening night came. Pre-performance rose deliveries were made backstage. When handed my flower, my heart sank. Only Momma, John and Naomi had signed the card.

"What's wrong?" asked Stacie, my best friend and fellow "lady-in-waiting."

"I don't think my dad came."

"Of course he came," she reassured me.

"But he didn't sign the card."

"Maybe he was reading," she laughed.

"Maybe." But I was crushed. Even though he didn't understand my love of it, he had never missed a performance of anything.

The play began and ran beautifully. I danced and sang my heart out. I scanned the audience when I could, but never found my family. During intermission Stacie and I headed to the dressing room. She entered before me and was smiling as I came through the door. There, on top of my costume bag, was a single red rose. The card read, "Break a leg. I'm proud of you. Love, Dad." He had never sent me a rose from just him. He had also remembered the theater superstition of never saying "Good Luck." I was touched. During the second act I not only danced, I flew.

After curtain call I rushed to get back into my street clothes. I grabbed all of my stuff and raced out the door. I hugged Stacie's parents as I searched for Dad. Finally, over in a corner, I saw my family. Flying through the crowd, Mom grabbed me in a bear hug, bubbling over with how great we were.

Then I was face to face with Dad. Book tucked under his arm, he smiled and reached for a hug. "You did a good job," he whispered into my hair.

"I was afraid you didn't come," I said.

"I wouldn't have missed it for the world," he grinned at me.

As we turned to leave, I hooked my arm through his. He laughed and asked, "Tell me again why the boys wore tights. John Wayne would never wear tights."

Aletheia Lee Butler

On the Nose

A happy family is but an earlier heaven.

Sir John Bowring

I will never forget the day I arrived home from kinder-garten to find my dad opening the door for me. At first, I was elated. "Dad! You're home!" As a doctor in training, he was hardly ever home. Often, he had to spend nights at the hospital working thirty-six-hour shifts.

Dad did not waste any time with pleasantries. "Your mother has had an accident."

I dropped my school bag. Horrible visions swam across my eyes. Then my stomach lurched. I was sure I would throw up. Fighting back tears and swallowing hard, I hugged my dad. "What happened?" My need to know outweighed my fear of the answer.

"She was reaching for something in the closet, and her train case fell on her."

My mom had this small, hard suitcase that she always put her makeup in when she traveled. She never went anywhere by train, yet she called it her "train case."

"It broke her nose. I had to rush home to fix it."

"Oh." Good thing he was a doctor. "Where is she?"

Dad hugged me tight. "She's upstairs sleeping. Let her rest."

Was he kidding? For several seconds that felt like an eternity, I had thought that something horrible, something deadly, had happened to my mother. I had to see her.

I tried to get out of his grasp. "Please. I have to see she's okay."

Finally, Dad relented. "Just look. Don't wake her."

We tiptoed up the stairs. Dad opened the door so slowly I thought I'd die of anticipation. There she was, on her back under the covers, her nose and eyes covered with white bandages. Her always-perfect red hair stuck out in every direction. I watched her chest to be sure it was moving. It was.

Dad led me downstairs. "Well, it's just you and me, kiddo. Doesn't Mom give you a snack when you come home from school?"

"Yeah," I mumbled apprehensively, entering the kitchen. The table was set with two placemats complete with silverware, napkins and glasses.

"I've been getting it ready." Dad poured me a glass of milk. "There, nice and cold right out of the fridge like you like it." Then he added a large ice cube. I smiled, forgetting my mother's trauma for the moment. I didn't think Dad noticed these things. He actually knew I put ice in my milk—just one ice cube.

As the fear about my mother subsided, and the awe of my dad increased, my body returned to normal. My senses began working again. I inhaled deeply. *"Mmmm."* Something smelled good. Dad put on oven mitts and opened the oven door. "I hope you like it. Haven't made it since my college days. Don't know how to make anything chocolate."

He did it again. He knew that chocolate was one of my favorite things, especially with milk.

"Baked apples," Dad announced. He put one apple on each of the two plates that sat waiting and then brought them to the table. Dad sliced mine open for me and steam rose out, filling the air with the scent of apples, cinnamon and raisins. And nuts. I hesitated. Dad always told us about apples, raisins and walnuts. I did not like walnuts, only pecans.

"Careful, it's hot," he warned. "And don't worry. I used pecans."

"Pecans? Great."

"Well, let's see if this worked."

Dad scooted his chair close to mine as he moved toward the table. I leaned against him, and he managed to cut the apple with his arm wrapped around me. The warm snack heated my insides, and Dad's love filled me from the outside.

Sure Dad worked really hard and had to be away a lot. But he paid attention more than I knew. He cared. I was sorry that it took Mom breaking her nose for us to share this moment. So, even at age five, I was determined to pay more attention to the things he liked and steal more moments like these without waiting for something bad to happen.

D. B. Zane

"My dad's cooking tonight. I can play
until the smoke detector goes off."

We Are Dragon-Slayers

I cannot think of any need in childhood as strong as the need for a father's protection.

Sigmund Freud

Most knights wear chain mail and carry shields. Not me. My armor consists of boxer shorts and an old T-shirt with a hole under one arm. I am clumsy, not gallant.

I hear the princess scream, as I had dozens of times before—and always when I am sound asleep. Instinctively, I jump out of bed in the dark. It's only 2 A.M. My eyes don't focus. I put my arms in front of me to keep from walking into the door. I stub my toe and curse under my breath. My hand slides along the banister railing, guiding my path. I hear the princess scream again.

I quicken my pace and grope for the doorknob as I enter her room.

"Daddy, the dragon!" she cries.

I rub my eyes as I kneel down next to her bed, trying to focus on her small face.

"Is it the dragon from *Sleeping Beauty*?" I ask.

"Yes," she says with tears in her eyes. I hate this dragon more than the rest of the beasts that torment my daughter at night. While a crocodile or other monster may attack her now and again, the dragon from *Sleeping Beauty* torments her most often. Some of the lesser beasts flee as soon as I enter her room, but not this one. It towers above me and sneers. I smell its hot, stinking breath blowing down on me, but I realize it's my own breath I smell.

Empty-handed, I prepare for battle. No mace. No sword. No lance. I know what dragons fear most. I'd learned the art of dragon-slaying from my parents, both of whom were experts. I use many of their techniques. Dragons and other assorted monsters tormented me as a child. I trembled in bed and watched as my mom and dad quickly dispatched them.

Now I put my hand on the small of my daughter's back and slowly rub in circles that get larger and larger. Dragons hate backrubs. But what terrifies them most are happy thoughts.

"Think about Christmas and going to the beach," I say to her groggily. "Think about Easter and making snowmen. Think about eating ice cream."

I watch the dragon quake at my words. He is severely wounded but flees before I can finish him off. He always runs so that he can come back another night. And he will come back. He always does—sometimes in the same night. But, for the time being, he is gone, and my princess closes her eyes and falls back to sleep.

My personal record is six dragons in four hours. Between dragons four and five, I woke up on my daughter's bedroom floor. Either I'd fallen asleep while rubbing her back, or dragon four had landed a blow and knocked me out. I just remember feeling exhausted.

If you saw me on the street, you wouldn't guess that I am a knight. You'd probably think, *There goes a balding, out-of-shape dad who's pushing forty.* Perhaps you are a knight, too, in our secret society. We disguise our identities by working as accountants and factory workers during the day. We have jobs in offices and construction sites. We don't brag about our exploits. We are humble.

And, if, while dragging yourself out of bed after a night deprived of sleep, you become discouraged, repeat the refrain of the dragon-slayer: *When the sleepless night seems endless, and you are exhausted and irritable, remember that your sacrifice is worth more than sleep. The tender care you give your daughter is not simply to help her rest in slumber. Your actions teach her to raise her own children—with unlimited patience and selfless love. You are raising the next generation of dragon-slayers.*

Remember these words because it is often difficult to feel virtuous when you're standing in the dark in your pajamas.

And, each evening, as you go to bed, prepare for battle. When your princess cries, you will be ready. You are a dragon-slayer.

Timothy P. Bete

Understanding Dad

*Love is the most terrible and the most generous
of the passions; it is the only one that includes in
its dreams the happiness of someone else.*

Jean Baptiste Alphonse Karr

It was August 1970, and at eighteen, I differed with Dad on many things. Over the last few years, my relationship with Mom had become much stronger—we now had a bond that only mothers and daughters shared—womanhood.

I wanted to celebrate my August birthday with friends and was eager to make plans with "the girls." As I rushed home from my part-time job, I found Dad in the living room, sitting on the sofa, staring pensively into space.

"Where's Mom?"

He looked up at me and immediately I could tell he was struggling to tell me something difficult. "Your mom is in the hospital. The doctors want to run some tests. I'm sure it's nothing serious, but she'll have to be there for a few days."

"Are you going to the hospital now?" I questioned.

"Because if you are, I want to come. I need to talk to Mom about my birthday."

"Maybe this isn't the time to bug your mom about your birthday. Can't it wait?"

Sure, I thought, *it's not your birthday. By the time Mom gets home from the hospital, my birthday will have come and gone, and she promised me a set of new golf clubs.*

"Dad, Mom said that I could have a set of golf clubs, and I've been planning to golf with my friends on my birthday—but I can't do that if I don't have clubs!"

"You can rent them; a lot of people do that when they first take up the sport. I have more important things to worry about. Golf clubs are *not* a priority. You can rent them or you may use mine."

Yeah—right! I thought. *I'm four feet, eleven inches tall, and you're five foot eight; your clubs will be too long for little me!*

I pouted in my room, feeling oh-so-sorry for myself, never giving a thought to what Dad must have felt, how frightened he must have been, how he must have missed Mom.

For the next week I was unbearable. I thought only about myself, not about what my mom was going through or what the rest of my family was feeling. The only time I thought about someone else was when I stewed about my father and his stupid golf clubs.

Finally, my birthday arrived. Dad woke me early that morning and said that he and I would visit Mom because she wanted to see me on my birthday. I really didn't want to go; this was my day and I had plans, though obviously I wasn't going golfing.

Dad did not offer me the option of staying home, and I was given no choice. When we arrived at the hospital Dad told me to go ahead, that he would join me in a few minutes. I walked into my mother's room and looked at her in that awful bed. I was overwhelmed with guilt. She looked so pale, so sickly. I could read pain in her face. Yet she looked up at me and opened her arms for me to fall into.

"Happy Birthday, Mar," she whispered. "I can't believe my little girl is nineteen."

"Mom, are you okay?" I knew she wasn't, but I wanted her to tell me differently. I wanted her to be okay—so that what I was feeling about Dad and those golf clubs would make sense. But nothing made sense now, and all I knew was that I needed my mother at home—now!

She held me in her arms and read my mind. "You know," she said, "your Dad loves you so much. He has always expected great things from you, and I think that he's having a difficult time with your independence. He still thinks of you as his little girl, and it's hard for him to let you grow up."

Just then, Dad walked into the hospital room toting a shiny set of new golf clubs, cart and all. "Happy Birthday, Peanut!" Dad shouted. And as he looked into my eyes, he began to cry like a baby. I ran to him and held him in my arms. I wanted so much to tell him that everything would be okay, but I knew in my heart that it wouldn't. Somehow, I knew that things would never be the same again.

Mom came home from the hospital the next day, and at dinner that night Dad told us that she was dying. She had only four months to live.

That night, I looked at Dad in a different light. This man was human. He made mistakes like everyone else, but he was also my best friend, my mentor, my hero. All that I expected from him as a parent was on the line. And he knew it, too.

For the next four months, my dad ran the house like a fine-tuned instrument. He made our lives as bearable as possible. His spirits were always up for us. Life went on as regularly as it possibly could. Even Christmas went off without a hitch, all because of Dad.

Mom left us on December 31. I watched my dad, waiting

for him to fall apart, to scream and yell, to push us away. He never did. He instructed us on our futures. He supported us, as both Mom and Dad.

I only used those golf clubs a few times, mostly with Dad. He taught me to golf. Today, at ninety-one years old, he is still one of the kindest, most intelligent men I have ever known. My children have heard many stories about "Papa," but there is one thing they will never fully know: My dad loved me unconditionally, right or wrong, good or bad. I have tried throughout the years to be half the parent he is, making my children my first priority and sharing the unselfish love he gave me.

Marianne L. Vincent

The Camping Trip

Memory is the diary that we all carry around with us.

Oscar Wilde

I was an Air Force brat. I spent my youth at the U.S. Air Force Academy in Colorado Springs, which practically backs up to the base of Pikes Peak. My backyard was a forest. My parents, two brothers and I loved the outdoors because that's all there was—no malls, just trees and Pikes Peak.

Our home was just a few hours from several national parks and camping spots. We loved backpacking and fishing, and we did it the old-fashioned way. No RVs or fancy trailers for us; all we needed was a tent, a sleeping bag and a hole in the ground.

Our family roadster was a 1968 VW Bus. It was kind of a reddish, orange color. (Okay, it was white with a lot of rust.) Dad had specially modified it for our weekend camping adventures. He would take out the middle bench, leaving the back bench for the three kids to sit on.

Then he bolted the big wooden toy box against the wall, the long way, opposite the sliding door. A portable refrigerator was secured behind Mom's seat.

Somehow, I always managed to get the not-so-prime seat—the one in the middle with no window, wedged between my two brothers—in front of the portable potty in the back. No, a toilet was not a manufacturer's option on the 1968 VW Van; it was one of Dad's add-ons. Basically, it was a plastic trash can with a ring on the top to sit on and a Hefty bag! We'd pray hard whenever Dad took a sharp corner.

These were the days before mandatory seat belts, so Dad rigged his own version. He suspended a large board over our laps and then bolted it to the sides of the van. It was like a combination child restraint/craft desk.

I clearly remember the excitement of taking off on those trips. Mom would be smiling and humming, and Dad would be singing (or trying to sing), "If I Were a Rich Man." And we didn't care that he wasn't.

It was wonderful knowing we had three whole days in the outdoors before we had to return to, well, okay, the outdoors. I can remember smiling up at my daddy and saying, "Daddy, this is the best day of my life," and how he looked back at me with love.

Before each trip, we would get a special toy to play with. One time we got a "Zip and Flip." It kept us quiet and occupied for moments at a time. If you don't remember, Zip and Flip was a plastic paddle that was smooth on one side and had a ridged maze on the other. You'd rip out the wand to set the top spinning, toss it up in the air, flip your paddle over, catch it on the other side and work it through the maze.

So there we were, driving down the highway. I was sitting there, Zippin' and a Flippin.' I flipped my top, and it zipped out the window! To this day my brothers swear that I rivaled the shower scream in *Psycho*!

My daddy stopped that van so fast that you would have thought someone tied a spring to the last guardrail. He threw the VW in reverse and backed up on the interstate to the place where he heard me do my Janet Leigh impression. Cars whizzed by and Mom complained, but that didn't faze my daddy. He jumped out of the van and tore through the jungle of roadside weeds, searching for my toy. My nose was pressed against the glass, watching him as tears streamed down my face.

Twenty minutes later, covered in mud, sweat and burrs, he broke through the weeds—and in his hand was my little red top. He had that same loving look on his face as he said, "Sweetie, let's keep the windows up next time, okay?"

That simple act of heroism may not seem like a big deal—it certainly wasn't a big deal to the rest of my family, who found it downright irritating—but it was a huge deal to me. In his special way, he had just told me that he loved me and would always protect me. He let me know I was the most special little girl in the whole world.

It really *was* one of the best days of my life.

Laura M. Stack

Outstretched Arms

This is my commandment, that you love one another as I have loved you.

John 15:12

The morning started off in the usual way. Our daughter, Annie, pulled away from the curb of our home in her little black Mustang and headed off to school just like she had every other morning of that fall semester. She was a senior at our suburban Dallas high school and would be in the first graduating class of the new century. Annie was really enjoying her senior year and looking forward to going to college where she planned to become a second-grade schoolteacher.

At 9:30 A.M., I was having my second cup of coffee (okay, it was really my third!) and checking my e-mail in my home office. The home phone rang. The school nurse said, "Annie is here in my office, and she has something she needs to tell you." Well, a huge lump jumped up in my throat as my daughter got on the phone. Between her sobs I could barely make out what she was saying, but there was no mistake about what I heard, "Mom, I'm pregnant."

I stifled a sob of my own and said, "Come home, Honey, just come home." I immediately called my husband, Tim, on his cell phone. He was en route to the church where he is the pastor of worship and administration. Through tears I told him the news, and he headed back home.

A few minutes later I heard the garage door open, signaling Tim's arrival. I looked out the living-room window, and that little black Mustang was pulling up to the front curb. Tim rushed in from the garage and opened the front door just in time for Annie to run up the steps and into her father's outstretched arms. I stood there in tearful amazement, watching the two of them in a silent embrace that truly said it all: "I love you. I forgive you. I'm here for you."

Our daughter graduated with her class on May 19, 2000, and gave birth to our first grandchild, an eight-and-a-half-pound boy, on July 12. Within minutes after he was born, she handed him to her daddy, who extended his arms for him. As we caressed him we knew, without a doubt, that sometimes our greatest blessings come through circumstances we never dreamed we'd experience. But it's up to us to love unconditionally and to be there with outstretched arms.

LaDonna Gatlin

"Is this one of those times I'm supposed
to hold your hand or disappear?"

Sour Pickle

'Tis not enough to help the feeble up, but to support him after.

William Shakespeare

"I'm absolutely not going to be caretaker," Jarred* stated adamantly. "She's just going to have to go into a home."

Paula* had agonized over it and talked with her husband, Jarred, for the whole of their fifteen years of marriage, until they'd shelve it. But it was always there, blinking like a Las Vegas neon sign. They tried to figure out solutions, create "what ifs" and make reasonable plans. They worried about what would happen when nature commanded, and responsibility and duty would impel resolution.

Paula felt responsible, even though she was not blood kin, often discussing her distress with her mother and me.

"I just don't know what we're going to do!" she'd lament.

---

*Names have been changed.

Aggie, Jarred's sister, had been born late in his life and grew "strange." For his mother, this daughter was an untouchable, a never-to-be-discussed secret that was crammed into the closet, along with her guilt. She hid the girl from most of society, bending only to go out for weekly groceries, lunch with her son and daughter-in-law, and church. By keeping her away from everybody, the mother was, in some tangled way, cloaking her daughter's existence from the world, her husband and mostly herself. For thirty years Jarred's father, who by everyone's account was as sour as a pickle and equally remote, was not allowed to interact with and clearly showed no interest in this other human being who occupied space in his house. Aggie was terrified of this stranger who was her father. The couple had no friends or family, except Jarred and Paula.

Then the impossible happened. Jarred's mother had a stroke and died. Absolutely certain that their father would completely fail in caring for this strange daughter, Jarred and Paula were fraught with new agonies about Aggie's future.

As the weeks passed, Jarred and Paula spent countless hours up at the little house, but then something amazing began to happen without the counsel or direction of either of them. The father began to take control of a situation he'd never been privy to in three decades. First, he contacted the retarded citizens associations in town to get direction and help for himself and for Aggie. Next, he made an appointment for a complete physical for her, the only one she'd ever had. He was soon told that rather than being a "strange" human, she was a very high-functioning Down's syndrome person, in need of glasses and hearing aids.

"I could never talk to her; I had to shout," Paula declared. "Now, she actually answers questions and converses, instead of saying something completely off the wall. We all thought she was goofy coming up with totally inappropriate sentences. She couldn't hear, for gosh sakes, and she was just trying to be a part of conversations! And she's as nearsighted as a bat!"

We all simply shook our heads, contemplating the years Aggie had spent with that cloistered, well-meaning but frightened mother who was acting out of some misplaced sense of love and duty. In the coming months Aggie bloomed. She began reading simple books and developed a wonderful sense of humor. People heard her laugh for the first time. Paula and Jarred looked forward to being around her and, wonder of wonders, that sour-pickle dad now showed a sense of humor. After a lifetime of non-communication, things were thawing. Often father and daughter were out and about just hanging around with each other, going to the zoo, museums, just about anything. Aggie made such swift strides that, with her father's help, she was placed in a group situation, got a job, held it, and found friends for the first time in her life.

Then another bombshell dropped on the family: The father developed brain cancer. Again, Jarred and Paula agonized about what they would do, how they should take control, banging all the old, tired what-ifs around while they cared for the dying old man. They planned to take Aggie because they were all she had.

Grief-stricken when the father they'd just begun to know and love died, Jarred and Paula moved in to take control of Aggie, but were dumbstruck to be told by their father's lawyer that everything had been set in place months back. With mouths agape, they listened as the attorney conveyed information from the will. The home that had been almost a prison to Aggie, and later the place where father and daughter had at last found each other, had been deeded to the Association of Retarded Citizens. It carried the stipulation that as long as Aggie lived, it would always be her home.

Today, eight special people and their helpers live together happily. They keep house, which Aggie's mother taught her to do brilliantly. They garden. They shop. They live full and meaningful lives for and with each other.

Last year, Aggie began to show a remarkable talent for illustration and painting with watercolor. Some of her landscapes and flowers, delicate and full of subtle color, are displayed and sold at the Association of Retarded Citizens' functions and have been used on the covers of their publications.

Jarred and Paula often take Aggie out to suppers, movies, plays and community events. Jarred is so grateful he had time to get to know his little sister, who is learning a mean game of checkers—and his dad, a "sour pickle" who showed the sweet relish of a dad's love for his daughter.

Isabel Bearman Bucher

Run for Gold

Sports do not build character. They reveal it.

Heywood Hale Broun

I was nine years old in 1967, the year of Canada's centennial celebration. I raced home from school on that bright spring day, bursting with excitement about a Canadian national fitness competition the teacher had told us about. "It's all running and jumping and sit-ups and stuff," I explained, "and I'm going to go for a gold medal just like in the Olympics!"

Around the dinner table that night, my older sister Nancy and I both explained to Mom and Dad about this fitness test. But I knew I wasn't very good at running long distance, so I asked my dad how I could get better at it.

"What about practicing?" Dad suggested. "We could go in the evenings to the track at the high school and do some training there."

"Can we start tonight?" I asked excitedly.

We left the house holding hands and talking. I had to almost run to keep up with my six-foot-two father's long stride. Soon the high school loomed ahead, and it seemed enormous compared to my own school building and playground. When we got there, we entered the gates onto a huge football field surrounded by an outdoor track.

"I have to run the whole way around this track, Dad, and the time it takes determines whether we score a gold, silver, bronze or participant metal. It seems so far!"

"Well, let's give it a try," smiled my dad. "You must be warmed up from the walk, so let's start right here." He chose a spot on the spectator side with a long, straight stretch to run first, and set us up to start running.

"On your mark, get set, GO!" he said, and I took off. Dad ran along beside me, and I was panting hard by the time we made the first turn.

About halfway around I stopped and cried out, "I'll never do it, Dad. We're not even halfway and I'm beat!"

"The problem is your timing. You have to learn to pace yourself if you're going to run the entire race. We'll try again, start off slowly, run more steadily through the middle section, and then sprint to the finish line. Let's see how that works," he explained as we returned to our starting place.

We began to run slowly, and my "coach" murmured encouragement like, "That's good, a bit faster now, keep breathing steadily." This time I got more than halfway around before I began to slow down. "Okay, push yourself now," cried Dad, and so I did. "We're almost there!" and sure enough, we completed the circle.

Every night for two weeks Dad and I walked to the high school and ran the track at least twice. I slowly grew stronger, and my pace began to improve. I loved having him running beside me.

Race day dawned sunny and warm, and since it was a Saturday, my whole family prepared to go to the track meet. My excitement had turned to nervousness, and I bounced around the house as everyone got ready.

"Let's get going, Dad. There will be a huge crowd," I called as I headed out the door.

The walk seemed short that day, and when we arrived at the track there were hundreds of people, loads of cars, and the air was filled with noise and excitement. The voice on the loud speaker called out the race times, and it seemed only a few moments before my event was called.

"Line up behind the 'start' line," the voice instructed. My dad nudged me forward, steering me to an inside position. To me it seemed very strange to have the track lined with spectators and to have other friends lined up along with me. I looked over my left shoulder and saw my dad smiling. He said, "It's just like we've practiced. Start slowly and you'll be fine."

"On your mark, get set, BANG," and the race began. I started to run and watched many of my classmates sprint off ahead. I heard my father's voice in my head saying, *That's it, a nice smooth start. Now just run easy around this first curve and get into a rhythm and keep a steady pace.* I ran steadily and soon began to pass many of the fast starters on the straight backstretch of the track. When I rounded the one curve, once again I heard Dad's voice in my head saying gently, *Now push, and pour it out over the finish line.* I started to pick up speed and used my arms to pump extra energy into the last section of the race. As I ran across the finish line I heard the cheers, and I saw my mom and my sister on the sideline. As I ran a little further to slow down and cool off, once again I glanced over my left shoulder—and saw my dad! Suddenly I realized why he hadn't been on the sidelines with the rest of my family. What I had been hearing hadn't been a voice in my head at all! My dad had run the entire race on the grass along the inside of the track right beside me. When the winners were announced, and the medals were awarded, we both won gold that day.

Ruth Barden

Love's Lance

Clank, clank, clank! Night after night, it kept me awake in the old, ivy-covered, dormitory room. My friends said I was experiencing typical "sophomore slump." But I knew it was more than that. I had an armored antagonist in the form of a radiator, determined to drive me either crazy or off campus.

He won't win this contest, I thought. Finally I could stand it no longer. Armed with a hammer instead of a lance, one night I struck what I hoped was a deathblow and shut off his calcified valves.

"There. That should keep you quiet," I said, snuggling under my duck down comforter on a sub-zero, Providence night. Even with no lifeblood flowing in his veins, that cold obstinate fellow still won the match. *Clank . . . clank, clank!*

Somehow, this story isn't playing out like King Arthur's Knights of the Round Table, I thought.

"I'm sorry," said the janitor. "The system is interconnected, so one radiator cannot be changed."

"Please don't sleep in class," said my professor. Blurry eyes and fuzzy thinking were not helping my reputation or my note-taking ability. And exams were coming.

"We'd like to switch rooms with you, Margie, but . . . ," said my friends.

"No, there are no empty rooms mid-term," said the dean.

"Actually a public park would do just fine," I mumbled, dragging myself across College Hill. I dreaded going back to my cold room with its high ceiling and dark wood floor. The first dorm to be built on campus, it must have been a product of the Dark Ages!

Clank, clank, clank, again my antagonist mocked me. It sounded like, "Get your sleep." That's what Dad had told me seven years earlier, after I got polio. "The reason you got polio is because you didn't get your sleep."

Memories of that dread experience pounded back with each clank of the radiator: high fever, hallucinations and the frightening iron lung beside my bed, which I called "the green submarine." I thought, *Polio left me with this partly crippled leg—all because I didn't get my sleep! Lord, I might get sick. I might flunk out. I might disappoint my parents and myself. Please help me get my sleep!*

The full moon, thankfully, had the good grace to bring Easter early that year, which meant a trip home. The thousand-mile journey only occurred twice a year, Christmas and Easter, and always by train. On board, I immediately converted the small slumber coach seat into a narrow fold-down bed. True to its name, sweet slumber was mine that night!

The next day, I disembarked at Chicago's LaSalle Street Station. Groggy, I collapsed silently into Mom's and Dad's open arms. More typically, I would have heartily embraced them with a steady stream of chatter.

"What's wrong, honey?" asked Dad.

"Oh, nothing much." I downplayed my feelings so as not to alarm them. "I'm just a little tired from a noisy radiator."

"A good night's sleep will do you wonders," Dad said, always the optimist.

I trudged up to the third floor of our brick colonial house. In the days when the home used to bustle with activity, my treetop room had been my favorite getaway place. Now my brother was married and away, our collie was gone, parties seldom given, and absolutely nothing stirred around the big house at night except the wind in the elms. Still, I desired to escape to my dormer getaway. Secure sleep! That was all that mattered now.

Soon my body revived, yet my spirits lagged behind. Lurking larger than life in the recesses of my mind was the image of my ironclad radiator.

My doting dad tried to spark the life back into me with a poke, a hug, a smile, a positive word . . . his love arsenal, which never failed to ignite my heart—until now. I didn't even sidle up to him, a gesture that would invariably cause him to drape his strong arm around my shoulders, pull me toward him and whisper, "Hello, Mugret." Now I had no sidling movement left in me.

Too soon, the dreaded day of my return to school arrived. Mom waved the last good-bye to me at the station as I boarded the New England States train. Just moments before, my busy, corporate dad had been paged away on the loudspeaker for a phone call. Seated in my slumber coach, I opened my books. I thought, *Before exams, this may be my last chance to study with a well-rested mind.*

The train pulled out of Chicago, traveled out of Illinois into Indiana. After a stop at Gary, it continued on its way. Well into the journey, I heard a familiar voice as if in a dream. "Hello."

Eyes lifted from my book, I saw the tall, suited form of a man who looked to be my dad standing by my open compartment door. Stunned, I stared at him like I had seen a ghost. I glanced out the window at the scenery flying by, then back at him. *I left Dad in Chicago. How could he be here on this speeding train?*

His twinkling eyes and playful smile suddenly made him real. "Dad! What are you doing here?" I blurted out.

"Riding with you back to school."

"The whole way?"

"Yes, Honey, the whole way. I even got myself a berth. Your spirits were down, and I just wanted to keep you company a little while longer."

My handsome dad offered his arm and led me to the dining car, where an attentive waiter served us on linen with silver place settings. I felt like a princess.

"Let's sit up in the club car long enough for me to smoke one cigar," Dad said after dinner. He knew how to draw out both conversation and a cigar. So happy in his company, I wished the cigar would last forever.

Back at college, snug in my dorm bed, my sleep was as deep as my heart was full. In my dreams, the *clank, clank, clank* of the radiator became the *click, click, click* of the train wheels. The intimidating radiator lost its final joust to my faithful defender—my dad. Love's lance mortally wounded fear's ploy.

Margaret Lang

2

A MATTER OF PERSPECTIVE

It is the inclination and tendency of the heart which finally determines the opinions of the mind.

Christopher Ernst Luthardt

Safe Harbors and Sailing Ships

When a person is down in the world, an ounce of help is worth a pound of preaching.

Edward George Bulwer-Lytton

I had been a registered nurse for about a year when I decided to move from my home in Milwaukee, Wisconsin, to take a job at a veteran's hospital in Prescott, Arizona. It was a lonely time—my first venture away from home.

I spent many evenings alone in my small apartment worrying about how I would achieve my goals and wondering if the move had been the right decision for me. I often thought it might have been better if I had stayed in Milwaukee.

As I sat on my secondhand sofa, eating my dinner from a burger bag, I thought about home. I pictured myself in the kitchen with my mom, making delicious strawberry jams and grape jellies. Later, I imagined myself sitting at the table with my mom and dad, and my brothers and sister, eating warm apple cobbler topped with dairy-fresh whipped cream. I missed the warmth of home and its love and security.

One day, I was feeling particularly blue. Although I loved my job, my heart ached for my loved ones. *Perhaps it would be better if I moved back home,* I reasoned.

That morning at work I was surprised to receive a package in the mail from my father. He hardly ever shops. What would have inspired him to send me a gift? I tore away the brown wrapper, opened the package and pulled out a poster silhouetting a large ship, sailing into a blushing sunset. The words emblazoned across the gentle reflective waves touched me to the core. "Sailing ships are safe in their harbor, but that's not what sailing ships were built for."

I could see my father's face smiling in approval. For the first time, my decision to leave home and set out on my own felt right. I knew my father, even though he was not a demonstrative, affectionate man, was trying to tell me he missed me but supported my decision to go. He wanted me to be where I felt called to be, and he wanted me to do what I felt called to do.

Mark Twain once said, "Twenty years from now you will be more disappointed by the things that you didn't do than by the things you did do. So throw off the bowlines. Sail away from the safe harbor. Catch the trade winds in your sails. Explore. Dream. Discover."

I knew I would sail farther still, because my quest was championed by my father's love.

Cynthia Fonk with Linda Evans Shepherd

Daddy's Dance

Dancing . . . the body and the mind feel its gladdening influence.

William Ellery Channing

I loaded the last of my retreat supplies in the back of my minivan then kissed my husband and son good-bye. Not only was I excited about the ladies' overnight retreat where I would be speaking, but I had mapped out a driving route that took me right through the town in which my parents lived. I planned to stop and spend a few hours with them, welcoming any opportunity to visit my mother and father, now eighty-three and eight-six years old. But often the visits were difficult.

Daddy was in the throes of Alzheimer's disease, and his comprehension and communication were severely impaired. The progression of the illness was devastating, especially to my mother, his mate of sixty-six years. She was now more a caregiver than a wife, and often Daddy was unable to even recognize her face. I grieved for both of them as well as myself. I wasn't ready to let go of the father I had known forever. He had been so full of life—singing, dancing, joking, laughing. Where had he gone? How did those Alzheimer's tangles in his brain rob him of words, faces and places?

Many times Mama wanted to tell me of personal incidents, thinking I would understand, being the mother and caregiver of an adult son with special needs. But I didn't want to hear humiliating details of Daddy's debilitating disease. This was still my father, the man who held me on his lap and rocked me as a child, put me on my first horse to ride and taught me to drive in an old 1948 Ford pickup truck. This was the daddy who used to show up at my college dormitory to bring me home on weekends when he thought I had stayed away too long. There was no way to divorce myself from those memories, nor did I want to. I held them close to my heart.

Even with the progression of the disease, there were still small windows when Daddy was coherent, like the Christmas he hugged me and looked into my eyes and said, "You don't come home enough." I blinked back tears and said, "No, Daddy, I don't." He didn't remember the responsibilities I had at my own home.

And just a few months earlier, when I called to tell him "Happy Birthday," he gave me a delightful recap of his day before regressing into unintelligible words and phrases. Once when I presented him with a framed picture of myself as a gift, Mama asked, "Do you know who's in that picture?"

He smiled and pointed directly at my face and said, "That's my baby."

Indeed, I would always be his baby girl.

But today, after arriving at my parents' home, Daddy gave me a quick hug then went to the bedroom to take a nap while I sat at the kitchen table with Mama. She spilled out her fears, resentment and pain. She had no idea how to cope with Daddy's anger when she didn't fulfill his requests. But how could she possibly know what he wanted when she couldn't understand his words or gestures?

Because of my own son's lack of communication, I could identify with her frustration, but it seemed harder for my mother. This was her husband, and it wasn't supposed to be this way. This was the time she had dreamed of traveling and relaxing after many years of hard work. Daddy got up from his nap several times to make trips to the bathroom, always requiring Mama's help with snaps and zippers on his clothing. Neither of them liked this situation, and both were argumentative and irritated with each other.

Finally, I left for the retreat, but my heart was heavy. As I drove, I thought of the anger, fatigue and emotional pain that my parents were experiencing and wondered if they ever had a happy moment. I loved them and wanted to help, but had no idea what to do. As I guided the car along the highway, I prayed for peace, harmony, love, health and even joy in their lives.

The retreat provided a refreshing respite for my body and soul, and I was in great spirits as I headed back home. Again, I stopped for a visit with my parents, hoping things had improved.

I pulled into the driveway just ahead of my brother, and we congregated in the living room with his guitar. Monte played and sang several songs, then Mama and Daddy joined in. By the time they hit the old hymn, "I Saw the Light," Daddy was singing every word from memory and smiling from ear to ear. I sat in awe as I watched his whole countenance change.

Suddenly, Daddy, who normally shuffled and slumped when he walked, jumped up from the couch and began to dance a jig to the music, his face alive with pure joy and fun. Then he put his hands out toward Mother. She stood up beside him, and together they two-stepped across the living-room floor, both of them laughing and gliding as I remembered them doing when I was a child.

I sat in a chair, clapping my hands in time to the music and wiping away tears. I had forgotten how much music had been a part of our family while growing up. I couldn't count how many times Mama and Daddy had stood beside our old upright piano and sang while I barely plunked out a melody. Daddy also led the singing at our little country church and even sang while he worked in the fields, often letting me ride on the horse's broad back while he guided the plow behind. My mind flooded with wonderful memories. Good times and hard times, but happy times. Soon Daddy plopped down on the couch, a smile still lighting up his face.

I left for home with a new peace and joy in my heart and again prayed for my parents while I drove, this time thanking God for the love and happy times they still enjoyed.

I know there will still be hard times in the future, but I'm thankful for this beautiful memory and reminder to celebrate every moment in life—perhaps, even dance in it!

Louise Tucker Jones

The Adventure

True fortitude of understanding consists in not suffering what we do know, to be disturbed by what we do not know.

William Paley

"What's his location?"

My father's face was a mask of concentration as he pressed the cordless phone to his good ear. He jumped up from the couch and ran to the window, ripping aside the curtains. "I see him!"

What in the world? I had arrived moments earlier only to step into what seemed to be a crisis.

"Dick, don't let him out of your sight." Dad put down the phone. I heard him mutter, "I'm getting the gun."

A gun? I followed him down the hall. He stood in front of the midnight blue Fort Knox safe and pulled out a shiny pellet gun. He aimed it at the wall, staring down the barrel.

"Dad?"

He put his finger to his lips. "Stay in here."

I raced to the kitchen. Mom stood in front of the sink casually peeling potatoes.

"Mom?"

She smiled and put her fingers to her lips.

"Mom, Dad has a gun!"

"I know, Honey," she said, stripping a long, curling peel into the sink.

Dad had just recovered from a heart attack. He was in good health again, but he lived life as if he has nine to spare—and he was on about number seven at this point.

When he was a boy, he leaped from bridges into lumbering trucks carrying sweet watermelons. As a teen, he threw bullets into the fire and dove for cover when they exploded and ricocheted through the night air. He left home at sixteen and fought in the Korean War. He didn't stop then. Just last spring we rushed him to the hospital after he fell twelve feet with a chainsaw in his hands. A branch broke and crashed into the ladder, and Dad landed on his back. His arms were stiff to keep the chainsaw from splitting him in two. His back fractured in four places.

Now he was chasing a prowler with a pellet gun, still angry at the thieves who had recently tiptoed through the night and stole forty years' worth of tools.

Phhhhht. One shot.

I rushed to the garage door, pulling it open with a *whoosh*.

My father knelt on the cold, concrete floor, the gun aimed to the sky. "I got him." He grabbed the phone out of his hip pocket and punched the numbers. "Dick, it's over. Why don't you come over? We'll hang him in the garage."

Oh, no! The pellet gun would have only injured him. I ran into the house. "Mom, you need to call someone!"

"Did he get him?" she asked.

"Yes. Now he's going to hang him in the garage!"

"Good. He's done a lot of damage in the neighborhood."

I struggled to find the right words, wondering when my parents had lost their minds. Dad walked in. His face was somber. "Do you want to see him, Suz?"

"No!"

"Shame I had to shoot him."

I was speechless.

"Karen, put on some coffee. Dick's coming over. Jo might be coming, too. I'm going to call the neighbors down the street."

A hanging party? I felt sick. I sat down across from my father. "Dad, I know retirement has been an adjustment, but this is taking things too far."

Dad looked up, a confused look on his face.

"You can't take the law into your own hands. This is really over the edge."

My mother stuck the mixer in a bowl. A small smudge of icing flew out of the bowl and landed on her lip, where she promptly licked it off. "What are you talking about?"

"Dad is stalking someone with a pellet gun and now he's hanging him? Dad, it's only tools. It's not worth your life." I stopped in mid-sentence as my dad chuckled, then broke out into outright hee-haws.

Mom bit her lip, unable to keep the grin from her face.

By now Dad was laughing so hard he could hardly stand. He weakly waved me into the garage. I cringed at the sight I was about to see.

He flipped on the light and pointed to the corner of the garage. "Lookee there."

I strained to look but saw only shadows.

"He's kind of small. You have to get closer."

I peered into the corner. Nothing. My father put his arm around my shoulder and pulled me closer. A tiny bird with black and yellow markings on his belly hung limp, his tiny beak stuck into a crack in the wood.

"The yellow-bellied sapsucker," my father said, gently

picking up the small creature. "He's beautiful, isn't he? We tried to entice him with birdseed. We tried to trap him so we could set him free elsewhere. But this was our last resort. The little guy has destroyed half the trees on the block." He pointed outside the garage door. "See there?" I stepped into the fading sunlight. Dad pointed to the deep holes burrowed down the ailing tree.

"So this is your prowler?" I asked sheepishly.

"That bird has been driving Dick crazy. That little bird wasn't going to be satisfied until he ruined every pine tree on the street. Dick's seventy-five, you know. He can't be chasing birds all day."

I didn't think it was a good time to remind Dad that he was seventy.

As we walked inside, Dad started laughing again. "Mom, she thought I was stalking a prowler with a pellet gun." His laughter, complete with a snort, filled the kitchen.

I blushed at my foolishness. I was fully prepared to ask my father's forgiveness for misjudging him, so I followed him down the hall. I stood by as he put his pellet gun in the safe and shut it with a click.

"Hey, Mom," he called out, "hold dinner for me. I'm going on the roof with the chainsaw. I saw some limbs that needed a bit of a trim."

I sank onto the bed and put my head in my hands. The adventure of the yellow-bellied sapsucker was over, but I had a feeling another was just about to begin.

Suzanne Eller

Fired from the Peanut Patch

The sweet remembrance of the just shall flourish when he sleeps in dust.

Nahum Tate

I had no idea how to "shake" peanuts, nor did I care. At ten years old I was just happy to get away from the house and not have to scrub dirty, bug-infested fruit jars for Mama's canning.

After a half-mile walk, my brother, Jimmy, a year and half my senior, and I arrived at the peanut patch. I don't know what I expected, but whatever it was it didn't match what I saw. There were vines crawling all over the ground. The attached peanuts were covered with clods of dirt and provided homes to numerous insects and spiders.

Jimmy had worked in the field with my father and older brothers before, so he came prepared with a pair of heavy work gloves. I, on the other hand, brought nothing except my lunch—a cold, scrambled-egg sandwich and a fruit jar filled with ice water. After the owner guided us to a patch of the field, Jimmy dug his hands into the dirt and shook the daylights out of the peanut vines. I watched and frowned then shook a vine gingerly, getting a face full of dirt.

By noon, it was obvious to Mr. McElhannon that I was not an asset to his peanut patch so he sent me to his cotton field another half-mile down the road where I was handed a tow sack with an attached strap. I looped the strap over my small body and began plucking the soft, white cotton from the hulls. The sun was scorching hot, and the thought of washing fruit jars at home didn't seem all that bad anymore. The rough bag still held a strong aroma of seed or feed, which, I was not sure.

Finally, it was quitting time, and I weighed in my little bag of "fluff." The woman placed two coins in my hand. I stared in disbelief. I had worked all day and earned only two cents. I left the cotton field and trudged up the dusty road to the little country store where I was to meet my brother and my father. I was tired, thirsty and humiliated.

Jimmy met me at the door while swigging down an ice-cold bottle of Royal Crown Cola, which he paid for with his earnings. I didn't even have a nickel for a bottle of pop. Jimmy bought one for me. Suddenly, I saw Daddy's pickup and watched as he got out, walked up to the store and pulled open the squeaky screen door. Jimmy ran to show him how much money he had made. I held back. Finally, the inevitable question came.

"How much money did you make, Sis?" Daddy asked.

I stared down at my dirty shoes, then brought my hand from behind my back and opened it to show him my two pennies. Tears pricked the backs of my eyes when I told Daddy about my day. I was certain he would be mad, but instead he roared with laughter and pulled me to his side. Then he turned to the other men in the store.

"Hey, listen to this. Louise worked all morning at McElhannon's peanut patch. He fired her without pay then sent her to the cotton field where she worked all afternoon and was paid only two cents." Everyone agreed that was a lot of work for such a meager amount of money. Daddy hugged me even closer. He was actually proud of me. Proud of my efforts and tenacity.

I learned a lot about my father that day and in the following years. As I grew up, Daddy demonstrated his love in a multitude of ways. He cheered me as I played basketball, watched with pride when I graduated as valedictorian of my senior class, and even appeared unannounced at my college dormitory to take me home when he missed me.

He delighted in lavishing love on my children with rocking horses, silver dollars and precious lullabies. He cried with me when my husband was overseas and stood by my side at the grave of my young son.

Throughout his life, Daddy remained my hero, blessing me with love, laughter and song. He gave me a heritage of hard work along with a strong faith in God. And though he never once told me his philosophy of life, I began to understand it at that little country store, over forty years ago, when I was fired from the peanut patch.

Louise Tucker Jones

Man of Few Words

*A talkative fellow may be compared to an
unbraced drum, which beats a wise man out of
his wits!*

Owen Feltham

I was an extremely verbal child, and growing up with
my dad was an experiment in linguistics. My father was a
man of few words. Whenever I wanted his permission for
a certain activity, I planned a speech that included who
would be there, where it would take place, how long it
would last, and why it was an incredibly wonderful
opportunity for me. He would listen and then say either
"Yes" or "No." There were never any qualifiers; not "Yes,
but be home by dinner" or "No, unless you can convince
me otherwise." It was yes or no, plain and simple.

I remember being particularly frustrated with "No"
answers. I'd present my best argument, supporting my position with facts and logic. But my father didn't debate with
me. He'd say, "Didn't I already tell you no?" If I persisted, he
would sigh, "No, Elaine, end of report." And that was that.

My father's phone messages were also lessons in patience and long-suffering to a teenage girl. I was quite active in high school. Not only did I enjoy being involved in many areas, but I came into contact with many a gorgeous teenage hunk. I can recall one bountiful day when I had met two great guys and had given each of them my phone number. The first words out of my mouth when I walked through the front door were, "Dad! Did anyone call?" His answer, of course, was simply, "Yes." I queried for a more accurate description of the caller. His answer? "A boy." Since I had met two guys that day, this did not help me. I ran to my room in tears.

Knowing my dad's aversion to language in general and his propensity for terseness, it surprised me to hear that he was going to teach the eleven-year-old boys' Sunday school class. He did so for not one, but many years. I always wondered if he actually said anything, or if they all just sat in their chairs and stared at each other. I was sure that if people were waiting on my father to break the ice with sparkling conversation or a springboard comment, they'd be sorely disappointed. Still, September after September, my father hung his sign outside the Sunday school room: Mr. Ernst—Eleven-Year-Old Boys.

When I was a junior in high school, I met another one of those hunks. Larry was a big ol' boy, as my daddy called him, the halfback for his high-school football team. We dated all of my junior year and were still "going together" when Larry was drafted to play football for the University of Texas in Austin. By this time, I was a high-school senior. The University of Texas was having a great football season, and Larry invited me to come to Austin for a big celebration. It was arranged—my dad would drive me and attend the game with me, and then I would be Larry's date for all the after-game activities.

Dad and I made the quiet drive and arrived on campus

just as the football team was entering the athletes' dining hall. As a mere high-school student, I cringed entering a college dining hall and having the entire University of Texas football team staring at me, no doubt thinking, *What is that high-school girl doing in here?* But my dad was undaunted. He marched right in, and I followed sheepishly.

Larry was busy eating and didn't even notice us. I stood frozen, paralyzed by my insecurity. Then from across the room, I heard a shout and watched as the quarterback ran across the room and threw his arms around my father. "Mr. Ernst!" he yelled. "Is that you?"

"Hi, Allen," Dad answered. "Have you found a church down here yet?" The man of few words had spoken.

By then, the football players were gathering around my father as Allen introduced them to the Sunday school teacher he had as an eleven-year-old boy. Larry finally made his way to me and cautiously whispered that I should pull up my bottom lip from the floor, as indeed I was standing in disbelief, my tonsils gleaming.

Years later, as an adult surrendered to special service, I worked full-time on a church staff as a children's minister. The hardest task before me each summer was to recruit the Sunday school teachers for the following autumn. I honestly had to *beg* for teachers. No one wanted to teach the young ones. After all, they were just children—does it matter a lot at that age?

It matters. Eleven-year-old boys grow up to be young men. My father may not have been the most verbal man on the planet, but he communicated a sense of decency, fine character and good will. He lived a life that was a role model to young boys like Allen. Perhaps the sign outside his Sunday school room should have read: Mr. Ernst— Man of Few Words—The Right Ones.

Elaine Ernst Schneider

Retirement Plan

Don't think of retiring from the world until the world will be sorry that you retire.

Samuel Johnson

My contentment as a full-time homemaker was shattered in 1974 when my husband left me with three children to raise alone.

Three weeks later, the Lord snatched me from the brink of death from a ruptured aorta. I faced long recuperation, then years of struggle to find my niche in the job market. By 1978, I held a corporate position with benefits, which would enable me to support my children and then enjoy retirement by age sixty-five.

Then my daughter became pregnant and incapable of caring for a baby. However reluctant I was to take full responsibility for a toddler, I saw no alternative but to gain custody of April,* my frail grandchild.

The magnitude of my responsibilities overwhelmed me.

---

*Names have been changed.

At forty-five, I was weary, and with yet another mouth to feed at the same time I had to plan my retirement, I had to hang onto my job. I could not afford nursery school for my precocious granddaughter, so I bartered the use of our large game room to a small Montessori school in exchange for her schooling and daycare. My beloved daughter's child calling me "Mother" broke my heart, yet once I embraced the role, the tension relaxed.

But our household calm would be short-lived.

During a family trip to my hometown 200 miles away, I planned to visit Daddy at the family stock-farm. Though aging and partially paralyzed from a years-ago tussle with a brain surgeon's scalpel, the tough old cowboy-farmer still enjoyed keeping a few head of cattle and horses.

When I called ahead, Dad's weak "H'lo" filled me with dread. "I'm in bad shape," he admitted. We arrived to find the old rock farmhouse filthy and heavy with the stench of diarrhea. Dad hadn't eaten in days, maybe weeks, from the looks of him. When I offered him water, he refused, exclaiming, "It gives me the runs!" I could see I was dealing with the late stages of severe malnutrition.

With Dad's aversion to anyone telling him what to do—particularly doctors—I knew I had a tough battle on my hands . . . a battle I had to win.

Careful not to spook my irascible sire, already skittish as a colt on first ropes, I cajoled and wheedled until he took a few sips. He soundly rejected my offers to take him home with me or to a hospital. "Jest leave me be out here on this hill so I can die in peace!" I'd had a good teacher in handling headstrong broncs, and I resolutely offered option after option. He studied me like a calf eyeing a new gate, then called a truce. "I reckon I'll jest go home with you."

It was a long 200 miles (with windows wide open) turning in at every Dairy Queen between the farm and home. I'd badger him until he drank a few sips, feebly managing a straw with his good left hand. He fumbled a hamburger until he wore most of it, adamantly refusing help. "If'n I cain't feed muself, I jest won't eat!" Once home, I could pulverize his food, add juice and liquid supplements, and he'd drink his sustenance through a straw.

I called my doctor friend. "I've got a broken down ol' cowboy here who refuses doctors but needs feedin' and waterin'."

He said, "If you don't put a stop to the diarrhea, it sounds like he's got maybe two days to live. I'll send out a prescription. Call if he decides to let me check him over."

Though divorced many years before, Mama and Daddy were still devoted to each other, so she rushed to his aid, and mine, promptly herding him into the bathtub. Over her shrill "Hold still!" came his gruff protest, "I ain't been plowin'. Muh ears ain't dirty!" She finally got him cleaned up and into bed—where he stayed for twenty-one days with Mama patiently attending his every need.

Normally, at five-feet-seven, Daddy weighed one hundred sixty pounds of hardy muscle. When he regained enough strength to stand, he weighed in at only ninety-three pounds.

Mama returned to her home, leaving the crotchety ol' cowpoke to me. April became a fixture at her great-grandpa's knee, and they both thrived, often entertaining each other.

My hard-won career long since abandoned, I took in sewing to support us all, leaving my need for a retirement plan to the Lord. One by one, the older children graduated and moved out.

While Daddy's physical strength gradually deteriorated over the coming years, his mind remained sharp as a razor. I found myself captive to his incessant storytelling, which I had scorned as a youngster, and was soon writing a weekly newspaper column recounting my childhood with a funny, braggadocio show-off daddy, and a no-nonsense mama who served as his straight man. National magazines published articles of my joys and heartbreak as a mother.

Eleven years after I had taken them in, April, Daddy and I moved back to the farm, where Daddy, by then bedridden, could gaze dreamily out the window over his beloved homestead. April, a beautiful, healthy, popular honors student and cheerleader, enjoyed riding horseback . . . a sport that brought plate-size belt-buckle awards to her, and contentment to the old horseman.

Not long after returning to the farm, Daddy died peacefully in his sleep, his pine casket majestically borne to the Last Roundup in a mule-drawn buckboard.

April moved away, married and had a child of her own.

Now pushing three-score years and ten, I drive a pair of dun mules hitched to a covered wagon, keep a few chickens and cut my own firewood. Social Security checks make for a modest retirement, supplemented by some bartering and publishing articles in which I encourage folks, young and old, along life's rugged trails. And I sell a few books of cartoon-filled true tales of how my daddy once rode his broncs into the house to prove they were ". . . as polished as ye Mama's hardwood floors."

A single mom taking on the responsibility for four generations under one roof was surely orchestrated by a God with infinite wisdom. Only through the filter of such unbidden adversity can I look back on my own rugged trail with the satisfaction that I am exactly who God called me to be: mother, daughter, writer, caregiver.

I cared for His own, and He cared for me . . . a great retirement plan.

Bettye Martin-McRae

Father Meets Cat

There are two means of refuge from the miseries of life: music and cats.

Albert Schweitzer

My father hated cats. Or so he told us when my sister and I begged for one when we were kids. If we persisted, he catalogued all their bad traits. Cats were lazy. Cats ripped furniture. Cats required too much care. The list went on and on.

After I graduated from the university, I moved to another city. As soon as I unpacked, I headed to the local humane society and adopted a black and brown striped tabby named Tiger. My father harrumphed at the news and predicted a dire end for all my furniture. Tiger must have overheard the conversation because she set out to prove him right.

My father harrumphed even louder the first time he encountered Tiger. The meeting did not go well. As I pointed out to him while I bandaged his hand, drumming one's fingers on the edge of a chair could be seen as a game if you're a cat.

"Only if you're an attack cat," he muttered under his breath. He glared at Tiger who turned her back on him and proceeded to wash her paws.

From that day on, my father and Tiger gave each other a wide berth. My mother, on the other hand, sent Tiger birthday cards and posted pictures of her on their fridge, much to my father's disgust.

I replaced my sofa and got a second cat. A lovely gray and salmon color, she came complete with parasites. Although I officially named her Salmonella, I called her Sammy for short. I waited a month before breaking the news to my father. This time, he snorted in addition to harrumphing.

On his next visit, when he thought I was downstairs, I overheard him talking to Sammy outside my bedroom. "Aren't you a pretty cat. What nice soft fur you have." From the sounds of her purring, I'm fairly sure their encounter involved some serious tummy-rubbing, too.

Over dinner, I asked him what he thought of the newest addition to the family. "She's okay," he said, "for a cat." Then he quickly changed the subject.

A week later, my mother told me my father, whose name was Sam, proudly informed all his friends and relatives I named the "good" cat after him. I didn't have the heart to tell him differently.

During his visits over the next couple of years, Sam and Sammy forged a bond.

Once I thought he was sufficiently softened up, I began a campaign to get my parents their own cat. I mentioned how nice it felt to come home to a warm, furry body that licked your hand in appreciation. I also quoted studies that proved having an animal provided health benefits.

No matter what I said, my father countered with a reason not to get a cat. When my mother weighed in on my side, he gave her a choice: get a cat or continue to travel.

With both her daughters and granddaughters living out of town, she conceded defeat. She would have to get her dose of cat-cuddling during her visits to me.

Although my father thought he'd won the war, I knew the battle had just begun.

Five years later, my father was diagnosed with kidney disease and began dialysis. I decided that would be the perfect time to get my parents a cat so they would have something to focus on besides his illness. Since their traveling days were over, he couldn't use that argument anymore. As far as I was concerned, it was a win-win situation. I would win the war, and they would win—a cat.

I visited on Mother's Day and informed them that my mother's gift would be a cat. My mother beamed. My father snorted. I pointed out that the cat was for her, not him, and he could ignore the animal all he wanted. He snorted a second time and marched out of the room.

Two hours and one hundred and ninety dollars later, Puss Puss came home, accompanied by a red nylon carrying case, a litter box, forty pounds of kitty litter, a brush, four different kinds of cat food, three toys and a scratching post. My mother and I set up the litter box, showed Puss Puss where it was, and watched as she explored the basement.

Loud footsteps announced my father's arrival. He stared at the cat for a minute and proclaimed, "The first time she scratches the couch or me, she's out the door." Satisfied he had made his point, he glared at me, turned around and went back upstairs.

Puss Puss, unaware of how tenuous her welcome was, purred her approval of her new home. After playing with her for a while, my mother and I decided to let her investigate by herself, and we went upstairs for coffee. Half an hour later, I headed down to check on her. No cat.

I called her name. I got on my hands and knees and

peered under furniture. I rattled a box of food. Still no cat.

I raced upstairs, thinking she might have sneaked up unnoticed. I checked the living room and dining room. Nothing. I went to the second floor and checked my old bedroom and my sister's. Empty.

That only left one room. As I neared my parents' bedroom, I saw my father stretched out in his La-Z-Boy chair—with the cat curled up in his lap. He was so engrossed in petting her that he didn't hear me. I tiptoed away and told my mother that everything was all right. In fact, it was perfect.

For the next three years, Puss Puss was my father's constant companion. Every time I visited, he told me the same thing: "That cat is great company—for your mother."

Like I said, a win-win situation.

Harriet Cooper

The Artist

Art washes away from the soul the dust of everyday life.

Pablo Picasso

The people in the small town in which our family lived called my dad the miracle man. Martial artist, photographer, worker in wood, skilled fly fisherman, the big laughing Swede excelled in everything he put his mind to. My hero, my inspiration, there was nothing he couldn't tackle and win. And he taught me to do the same—or die trying.

But his attitude was severely tested when, in his late fifties, Dad's fishing-buddy doctor sadly shook his head and turned away. The news of his mysterious illness scared my dad. It scared me, too. I didn't know he wasn't invincible. But I should've known his Viking spirit would defy the odds of his six-month sentence the way he always defied the odds—every time.

He became housebound, having to give up the pleasures of his trades, the pleasures of his hobbies. To assuage his growing frustration, Dad took up painting. But as his hands became crippled, his fingers bent and gnarled, he used too much color; bold colors I helped him mix, colors flaunting the ashy sickness creeping over him like a choking weed. Determined and unwavering, Dad painted hour after hour. He slashed his brush on the canvas in wild controlled strokes, the painted rivers becoming pits of fear brooded over by great swirling fogs, gray and damp with thunderclouds, heavy and swollen, raining grief on his favorite fishing spot till, finally, he obliterated the sun and denied it light. There were no dreams on his canvas, no hope, no miracles.

It was awful watching him, and I quaked in fear wondering how I'd cope when the proud warrior crumbled, dreading with an inner chill the thing I could not speak of.

As the days and months and years passed, he painted on in wooden resolution, precisely focusing his images in exact compositions, as if he could find through the rivers of loss tidy answers to the suffocation of a life.

I cried the day he laid his brush down in exhaustion, the day he retreated to an interior place in his soul I couldn't reach. He turned his face to the wall, his six-foot frame broken, his black hair long turned white, his warrior fingers in clenched-like claws. I stared at the thin, bent back and cried, listening to every wheezing breath.

Every day I visited the once proud and handsome man and it was the same. He would not turn to me. He would not respond. I went away. I grieved.

One day, perched on the edge of his cot and looking at his silent face, I wondered how long it had been since talk of the glory days, the days of his superb strength, his raucous laughter. His bigger-than-life dreams scattered now like dust on the burial cloth of many canvases. But it didn't matter, as suddenly I perceived the cramped and embittered spirit of Dad had, in a wink of time, transformed. Perhaps it had been transforming over long, lonely years, or days, or hours, and I just hadn't noticed it. Ashamed at my lack of perception, I realized that somewhere, somehow, his soul had sweetened, grown; a winter thawed in a river of refreshment in the forgotten arms of God.

I understood with growing excitement that a new art had been painted in the secret places of his being, an art that was still drying in pristine shades, conceived in the sphere of awesome courage, tenacious will and stark imaging.

A few days later I found Dad with a paintbrush in his hand, marveling at the careless, brilliant light that spilled from the uppermost corner of his canvas like laughter washing the mountains gold, the shining river crystal blue. The light sparkled on leaping salmon, on gleaming pines that lined the riverbank, and on the fisherman radiating robust health as he cast his line far downstream. I looked closely. It was my father. He'd found his way to a place free from pain, where he was gloriously whole once again.

"What's the answer, Dad?" I questioned, quietly wondering at his peace. But I knew the answer. He'd learned to embrace life the way it was, not the way he wished it to be. I looked at his smile and knew him to be a happy man. He'd wrestled his demons, crushed them under wobbling feet, a conqueror rising from the pit of destruction to conquer one last and glorious time. How I loved this man with eternity beckoning him closer and closer, one foot on Earth, the other in heaven. How he loved me, his princess, forlorn at the thought of losing him.

He paused in his work. "I have so little to leave you with, Janet," he said sorrowfully, shaking his head.

I swallowed the lump in my throat as I touched his bent and bony shoulder. "Dad, that's not true," I gasped, appalled. "This long, weary illness of yours has given me something no one else will ever be able to give!"

He looked surprised as he smiled with the humblest smile I'd ever seen and, putting down his brush he waited, looking quizzical. "What's that?" he asked in a burst of gentle humor.

The lump in my throat grew as he teetered slightly, holding onto my arm for strength. "You've taught me the art of living, Dad. And it's a masterpiece. It's something to be proud of, a legacy I prize beyond measure. You've run the race; you've fought the fight. You've won."

My father cleared his throat in embarrassment as tears poured down my cheek. I gently hugged him, and he wiped my eyes, my hero, my giant. I knew he would go soon, that this would be his last work. Together we turned to the canvas. "I need to be painted into that picture, Dad," I said, nodding at the golden stream. "I want to stand beside you."

Janet Hall Wigler

Finding Lost Love

In life there are meetings which seem like fate.

Owen Meredith

"I want to try to find Sarah,"* my eighty-one-year-old father announced to me one day.

"Why now?" I asked.

I knew that Sarah had been his first true love in college, at Rutgers University in New Jersey, where he studied pre-med. In 1934, at twenty, he contracted a life-threatening case of tuberculosis and had to travel to Colorado for treatment. At their tearful good-bye at the train station, Sarah had said she felt she would never see him again. My father had reassured her they would be together. She had written to him faithfully, even though his recovery was doubtful. Then her father's death changed her family's financial stability. They wanted the security of marriage for her and had pressured her to start dating. When my father had recovered after several years and

---

*Names have been changed.

returned to New Jersey, Sarah was engaged to a doctor.

My father had been advised not to pursue his medical career because it would be stressful and expose his weakened immune system to other contagious illnesses. He had not yet found another career. He knew he wanted to live in Colorado, where the slower pace of life had helped him regain his health. He felt he had no future to offer Sarah compared to the doctor, so he had never contacted her. After returning to Colorado, he met my mother, and they were happily married for forty-four years.

"Well," my father answered, "your mother's been gone for a few years now. I would like to see Sarah and thank her. If she hadn't kept writing to me while I was in the tuberculosis sanatorium, I know I would have died. She gave me the inspiration to get well."

I knew this was important to him so I said, "Dad, I'll help you as much as I can."

"Great," he replied. "It will be a fun adventure for the two of us."

So, the search began. My father only knew Sarah's maiden name, and we assumed she married in New Jersey. At the time, we did not have access to the Internet so he just started telling people about his search. He spoke to a friend who worked in his office building, and through her contact with the head of the vital statistics department in New Jersey, we found out that Sarah's married name was Hostad.* My father called this "beneficial coincidence" a "co-inky-dinky." This was one of Dad's special "words to live by" that he developed because of his brush with death as a young man.

My dad's cousin, a doctor, suggested that we contact the medical society for any records on Dr. Hostad. We found out he had been a gynecologist in New Jersey. We decided to call numbers in New Jersey for anyone with the last name of Hostad. It was a tedious job, but Dad said we had to "practice patience."

One day he called me and said, "I just finished talking with Dr. Hostad's brother, and I have good news and bad news."

"What's the bad news?" I asked.

There was a long pause, and then my dad said, "Sarah died a few years ago."

"Oh, Daddy, I'm so sorry that you aren't going to be able to talk to her," I responded.

"I'm sad, but you know I always tell you, 'Don't be sorry.' I wish things were different, but the good news is that Sarah's brother-in-law and his wife are coming to Denver next week, and they said they would love to meet us for lunch. Isn't that another co-inky-dinky? They also told me Sarah has a daughter."

My dad sounded happy and excited, but I was not sure how I felt about Sarah's daughter. I wondered what she was like. Did she know about her mother and my father? I kept these thoughts to myself, however, and said, "Great, hopefully we can get more information."

At the luncheon date, my father told the Hostads how wonderful Sarah had been to him, and how he felt she had saved his life with her letters of encouragement. After he spoke, there was a long silence. They looked somewhat shocked and told us that Sarah had not been very happy, that she had struggled emotionally. The lighthearted, warm and giving person my father described was not the Sarah they had known. They did say she had been a very beautiful woman, and they were glad to know she had been such a positive influence in my father's life.

At this point I said, "What about her daughter?"

"Her name is Lynn.* She's a little older than you are. She lives in Boston, is divorced and has a grown daughter. She works as a psychologist with prison inmates. Here's her phone number," they answered. As our lunch ended, we thanked them for sharing their information.

That night my father called Lynn. Then he called me and said, "Lynn told me that her mother had often talked about me, and she knew the whole story about her mother and me. She wants to meet us in Denver for a few days in the fall. I told her she could stay with me."

"Dad, that's great, but I don't really know if she should stay with you." I was suddenly very concerned. In my mind, Lynn was a stranger. I felt very protective of my father. As an only child, I had fantasized that she could be like a sister, but could she be trusted? What if she was angry or resented him?

"No, I insist she stay here. We won't have enough time otherwise. Don't worry, you know what I always say, 'Worry is like paying interest on money you haven't borrowed yet.'"

"Okay," I agreed, but privately I decided to intervene if I had any doubts when I met her.

A few months later, we found ourselves waiting inside the airport terminal to pick up Lynn. I had butterflies in my stomach and clutched my dad's hand tightly. I knew he was excited, but his face looked calm and relaxed. Suddenly, she was standing in front of us, greeting us warmly.

As my dad hugged her, I noticed that she looked a lot like me, but with redder hair. Once we arrived at my father's house, we settled at the kitchen table to talk as my dad prepared dinner. My dad said, "Lynn, your mother saved my life with her love and encouraging letters. I want you to know how thankful I am."

"You meant a lot to her, too," Lynn replied. "She told me how sweet and loving you were to her. She loved you until she died, and when she was unhappy, she used to say she was going to go find you!"

As we continued discussing Sarah and my dad's history, my previous concerns vanished. I realized that I felt totally comfortable with Lynn. The relationship among the three of us blossomed through the years until my father's death, and Lynn and I have continued as "sisters in spirit." My search with Dad for his lost love strengthened our closeness and confirmed his guiding life principle. Indeed, "love conquers all."

Marna Malag Jones

A Father's Gift from a Daughter

The heart of the giver makes the gift dear and precious.

Martin Luther

To successfully raise any child these days is hard work, to say the least, and it is often both physically and mentally taxing for a mother and father. The fruit of this labor of love may not be seen for years after the child has left home and becomes a parent. There is no instruction manual or book of "what-ifs" that comes with each child when they are born, nor a timetable of what to do and when. Each day is a new challenge unto its own, where success is often marked in fractions of an inch rather than yards and miles. So how and when do we as parents know when we have had success?

My answer came one Father's Day. To coin an old saying, "It's not the gift but the thought that counts." So it was on this day when I was given two craft boxes as gifts from my grown daughter, one the size of a cigar box and the other the size of a large ring box. "Daddy," she said, "please sit with me on the floor like you did years before."

So we sat down upon the floor together and she handed me the first box. "Open it." Inside was a letter and what appeared to be a child's collection of odds and ends. "Daddy," she said, "read the letter first."

Dear Dad,

The older I get the more I realize what an important influence you've been in my life. So for Father's Day I decided to give you two memento boxes, both filled with special memories and things I keep close to my heart, things that you once gave me. In the first and larger box you will find just a few of my special reminders of you and times we shared together, just we two.

1. *A pair of shoestrings tied with a bow. These are reminders of the hours you spent teaching me to tie my own shoes so long ago.*
2. *A Band-Aid, to remind me of all the scrapes and cuts you fixed on my elbows and knees teaching me to ride my first bike.*
3. *A wee storybook, for all the special made-up bedtime stories you read to us all at night.*
4. *A pack of a child's learning flash cards, a symbol of your teaching me and helping me through my years of school even when I thought I knew it all.*
5. *A marble. I wish it was one of the ones you gave to me and I lost, from your special ones you played with when you were in school.*
6. *A sewing kit and a wee sewing machine reminds me of the real ones you gave me and on which you taught me how to sew.*
7. *A piece from my childhood blanket that you would always cover me up with each and every night.*
8. *A broken heart, symbol of all the broken hearts and heartaches you helped me through.*
9. *A silver dollar reminds me of all the times you gave me*

your last dollar when you least could afford to but knew in your heart when I really needed it the most.

10. *A tissue. This is for all the times I cried on your shoulder and you dried up all the tears because you cared.*

11. *A leaf; a symbol of nature that you taught me to understand, enjoy and respect.*

12. *One aspirin reminds me of all the headaches I must have given you and Mom over the years, yet you seldom complained. I know it should be a truckload if the truth be told.*

13. *A piece of candy, to let you know how sweet these memories are still to me.*

14. *Last but not least, a photo of my children and me, to remind me to teach my children all that you and Mom have taught me, and to share with them the love that only parents like you both have given to me.*

I had tears in my eyes and an ache in my heart as she gave the second, smallest box to me. "Open it now, please," she said.

Inside I found another note and in this one she wrote:

Daddy,

In this box I was going to put all of what really made a difference to me. All of what it was that you gave me to make me what I am today. But if I gave it back to you then I would have the best part of me missing, which is all the love, hugs and kisses you gave me from the time I was born till now, and for which there is no box large enough. So I think I will hold on to these and share them with my children who I hope one day will understand what a wonderful gift they are to give and receive. I love you, Daddy, and Happy Father's Day!

Yards and miles of success.

Raymond L. Morehead

Dirt Cheap

Frugality may be termed the daughter of prudence, the sister of temperance, and the parent of liberty.

Samuel Johnson

"When I die, just put me in a trash bag and set me out at the curb," my father would often say only half joking.

"I can't do that," I'd laughingly reply. "It's against code!"

"Well, don't waste a lot of money to plant me," he'd say.

A child of the Great Depression, my father lived simply, by choice. He wanted to die simply, too. Although he had a small nest egg put away, he loathed spending money on things he thought were unnecessary—and that included fancy caskets and expensive funerals.

This point was brought home to me when my mother died. The funeral director tried to convince Dad that Mom deserved only the best. Dad thought the best was wasteful.

"Why do you think I would pay for a box made of solid cherry when you're just going to plant it in the ground?"

he asked the director pointedly. "Don't you have a cardboard box?"

Clearly shaken by my dad's bluntness, the director sold us the bottom-of-the-line model.

When Dad died of lung cancer fifteen years later, I knew just what I had to do. At the funeral home, I turned to the director and said, "He wanted to be buried in a trash bag and set out by the curb. What's the closest you've got to that?"

"Ah, a man like my father-in-law," the director replied. "I know just what you want." He then detailed plans for cremation and a simple church funeral. "And since your dad was a veteran, we can bury him in Denver at Logan National Cemetery."

"How much will that cost?" I asked.

"Nothing," he said.

The price was right! "Sold."

After the funeral, we were handed a plain, white cardboard box that held Dad's ashes. On the way to the cemetery each of us wrote a parting message to Dad on the outside of the box.

"Your spot's over here," the cemetery guide said when we arrived. "They've just finished digging." He led us to a small hole less than one foot in diameter and several feet deep. "Do you have the ashes?" he asked.

I handed him the cardboard box that encased Dad's remains. As we watched, the cemetery worker took the box from the guide and began to wrap it in black plastic.

"What is he doing?" I asked, bewildered.

"I'm sorry," the guide lamented, "but we put the remains in this sack so that we can respectfully lower the box into the grave site."

"No, it's okay," I assured him. "Dad always wanted to be buried in a trash bag! I guess he got his wish, after all. It's not the curb, but it will have to do."

Lynn Dean

My Father's Hands

The hand is the mind's only perfect vassal.

Henry Theodore Tuckerman

My first memory of anything is of my father's hands placing my new baby brother in my mother's arms. It is a snippet of a memory. I can see Daddy's hands, my mother's smile and my brother's red, screaming face.

My father was a man small in stature, never weighing more than 150 pounds, but to me, a child, he was a giant who could accomplish anything. He made things grow, fixed everything from a car to a skinned knee, kept the forest fires away from our house, brought home venison and wild mushrooms, and made the thunder and lightning stay up in the sky. I knew he could rescue me from the highest tree, the darkest night, the swiftest river or any situation my curiosity got me into.

He taught me the basic rules of life: don't lie, work hard, keep your promises, love your family whether they are right or wrong, protect them when they need it and let them fall once in a while. My father's wrath was towering and his justice swift.

My childhood was spent in a small town in the mountains. Infrequent days off were spent tramping the mountains and canyons near our home. I learned early to walk quietly through the woods, to watch to see how and why things grew as they did, how to get home if I was lost and how to tell a rattlesnake from a bull snake. My father's hands taught me to put a worm on a hook, ride a horse, shoot a rifle, plant a seed, make biscuits and give comfort.

My father's hands taught me about hard work. I can see his hands building a rock wall stone by stone, making that old Chevy run a little while longer, or creating things with wood. He taught me that you worked until the job was done. I can remember taking clothes to him at the office because the forest was on fire, and he wouldn't leave his job as dispatcher until the job was done. Later, when he owned his own business, those same hands were busy for sixteen hours out of every twenty-four.

My father taught me about handshakes and being polite and to call everyone older than you—and that was everybody—Sir or Ma'am, and to shake his or her hand firmly. And once you shook someone's hand after reaching an agreement, you did what you promised to do.

My father's hands taught me the value of learning on all levels. He taught me to love books and value those rare and wonderful teachers who came into my life. He had been forced to leave school at the age of twelve, but he believed in education, and we spoke often about how important it was in life. He always believed in leading by example, and in my senior year of high-school, we did homework together and received our high-school diplomas the same year. I was so proud of him for going back to school after delaying his dream for twenty-nine years.

The time came when my father's hands seemed always

to be holding me back, not letting me go and do and explore. I know now that he was trying to keep me safe. He couldn't, of course, and I think that hurt him greatly. When death touched my life and broke my heart for the first time, he told me everything would be all right, but he knew the thunder and lightning had come down from the sky, and he couldn't put them back.

We fought, and I grew to resent his structure, his rules and his inflexibility about right and wrong. He didn't change, and I saw him as a relic lost in the modern world. His rules didn't seem to fit the world in which I lived. My life seemed too complex for the simplicity he had taught.

Then I married, and my daughter was born.

Suddenly my world became simple again. There was only one important thing—my child. I began to understand the basic rules that he had spent twenty-five years trying to teach me. They would keep my child safe in the midst of the world's chaos. I tried to teach my daughter all the things my father had taught me, but I found I didn't have the talent for teaching he had, so he taught her as he had taught me. When my husband no longer believed in living by the rules, my father's hands once again reached out to protect us. He made me believe I was strong enough to make my own decisions and take care of my child and myself. Because he had never lied to me, I believed all that he told me, and I did survive and finally became fully adult.

Shortly after my dad held his great-grandchild for the first time, we got the diagnosis that he had a 50 percent chance of surviving the next few years. He put every ounce of his strength and will into fighting the disease. He never ceased to be positive, and he was always trying to make sure all of us were okay, even while his body was slowly wasting away. The man who used to run up a mountain-side and hike all day in the river canyons couldn't take a walk or go fishing. His family rallied around him.

Daddy's hands began to shake and grow weaker; the skin began to bruise and tear like parchment paper. His hands more often held a cane now than a tool. I told him he couldn't go yet because he hadn't taught me all I needed to know. He smiled and said that I knew enough.

My father's hands came to symbolize for me his love for his family, his integrity, his work ethic, and his plan to go on ahead to make the next world an even better place for us.

Dena Smallwood

The Obituary

Of all that is written, I love only what a person hath written with his blood.

Friedrich Nietzsche

Our family knew when dad was dying. He had a brain tumor. Since I was the oldest of the four children and a novice writer, I was going to do an obituary that would be a true masterpiece. A tribute to a simple man whom I wanted to have more than a one- or two-paragraph passing. Not the typical "he was born here, lived there and will be buried somewhere else" kind of obituary. I wanted people who read obituaries to know who my father was when he passed away. He was extraordinary to us. I wanted people to know that.

But when I sat down, the words did not come easily. How would I describe this gentle man whose Austrian-Hungarian parents had come to America, like so many others, to seek peace and prosperity? How would I write, in such a short space, of how my dad never finished grade school because he became the sole supporter of the family in his early life? How he awoke in the wee hours of the morning to work on a milk truck or in a bakery before he could even consider going to school. The Depression was his classroom. He made the most of it.

And then, when he did become a young man, there was another "war to end all wars" in progress. His country said he could not fight overseas because his family needed him. His brothers went instead, one becoming a decorated soldier. Dad happily signed on as a cook on troop trains. He wanted to do his part. On one of those many trips he took during the 1940s, he stepped off a train on a cold, snowy night in the small town of Oswego, New York. He lost his heart there and married my mother soon thereafter.

How would I describe in one short column of cold type how he worked two, sometimes three, jobs to maintain a growing family, always finding his way back to being a cook, a chef, something he enjoyed immensely? Should I tell how he passed up an offer to work in an elegant restaurant in New York City because his family was rooted in a small upstate town? Did he ever regret not going? No one knew because he was not a complainer. He didn't dwell on what might have been.

Though we probably hadn't told him very often, I wanted to tell the world how he was a great father. How he could discipline without striking a blow. He had hit me only once when I was very young and ran in front of a car. He left a mark. He never touched any of his children again. He didn't need to. When Dad did get angry, his message was quite evident.

Where do I mention about how he always stood by us? How he was proud of whatever small achievement we accomplished growing up. How, although his life had its miseries, his smile and dry sense of humor filled a room as his eyes sparkled with life.

How do I tell those people reading about his death that his life was not one of fame or great wealth, but a simple one that came to an end too soon for all of us? How he showed us by example. How he did whatever job he had with pride and dedication. Do I put in the story about him trudging through a "lake-effect" blizzard from our home to the state college several miles from our house so he could make sure the students were fed in the dining hall he managed? Where do I tell about his friendships with people of any race or religion, as long as they were honest? He accepted anyone, even though it wasn't the most popular ideology of the day.

And when a spinal tumor shut down his legs after twenty-seven years of employment, he quietly took up residence in a wheelchair, which was not a burden to him, just another part of his life. He wheeled proudly to my college graduation and alongside me later when I married. And when that marriage fell apart, he was there, too, for quiet comfort. There was no criticism.

How would I tell the reader that he raised my only daughter so lovingly from that wheelchair while I went back to work three weeks after she was born? He was a magnificent babysitter. There wasn't a fussy baby who didn't become quiet when she sat on Dad's lap. He'd leave a legacy of calm and content.

When an alert physician finally diagnosed his first debilitating ailment as a small spinal tumor, he readily agreed to the six-hour-plus operation if it meant standing and walking again. I wanted to write about our joy when the doctor tapped the bottom of his feet in that hospital bed and there was feeling again. And, although he never walked totally unassisted again, he was extremely grateful for the new mobility. And he used every minute of his extended life.

Should I write, too, that cancer, probably from those

early years of many unfiltered cigarettes, would finally be the unbeatable foe? How he gradually lost the ability to eat, to speak and how he'd write us notes on the same pad on which he kept his crossword puzzle words? (Despite his lack of education, he did difficult crossword puzzles, writing down the words he didn't know and looking up their meaning in the dictionary.) Should I mention that my father would never have considered, had he lived today, a lawsuit against a tobacco company? He accepted the responsibility of his actions throughout his life. It would never have occurred to him to do otherwise or to blame someone else for something he had done.

He was taken to the veterans hospital in Syracuse, New York, just a few days before my birthday in December 1985. He asked to come home to die in early January, and on the twenty-first of that month, he did so, in the old house where he had lived happily for over thirty-five years.

I had finished my obituary by then. My brothers and sister had already picked out the "pine box" he always laughed about being buried in. The state of New York wouldn't let us put it under the spreading maple tree out in the backyard, but he didn't know that. What I had written appeared in the local newspapers. I never was satisfied with it. It didn't come anywhere near what I had envisioned. I never felt it conveyed what my dad's life had been like and what his passing meant. It just couldn't be put in that one article.

I have a copy of a memento the newspapers provided with his obituary and photo on one side, and a prayer on the other. I have it tucked alongside a mirror. I look at it often, that feeble attempt at what I wanted to be my best piece of writing.

Several years after his passing, my daughter brought home an essay done in elementary school about how her grandpa's passing had affected her. It was much better than my meager words, I thought. And then, a few months ago, I met a man who had worked with my dad many years ago. He said, "You know, I still miss your father. He was like a dad to many of us growing up. He was a great guy. His sense of humor . . . " His voice trailed away as we both choked back tears.

Suddenly, it hit me after all these years. I didn't need to create a masterpiece to tell the world about my dad when he died. He had created his own wonderful masterpiece while he lived. I could never put it into words. I didn't have to. He had said it all quite eloquently.

Carol Haynes

3

LIFE LESSONS

He didn't tell me how to live; he lived and let me watch him do it.

Clarence Budington Kelland

The Great Candy Bar Debate

All sects are different because they come from men; morality is everywhere the same, because it comes from God.

Voltaire

Evening meals were sacrosanct at our little house in Burbank, California. Only genuine illness or events of compelling academic or spiritual importance excused us. Mother provided the food, Dad the entertainment. I was almost of age before I realized that not everyone's evening meal involved vigorous, fun, intellectual debate.

At Friday dinners, Dad took a little tablet out of his left breast pocket. Every time he encountered a word he did not know, he wrote it down there. By Friday, he'd looked it up and the games began.

"What is a *fillip*?" he asked.

When neither my brother nor sister knew, I was relieved. As the youngest child, if I occasionally knew an answer, I felt really smart. That evening we all fell short, not knowing that a *fillip* was the quick, striking motion made by flipping a long finger away from the thumb. In our vernacular, it was a "thump on the head," Mother's discipline technique of last resort.

When spelling, vocabulary and current events played themselves out, Dad delighted in moving us on to his next favorite arena: ethics.

"What would you do if you were walking into a store and noticed that someone had left his car lights on?"

Of course we asked some clarifying questions like, "Was the car locked?" "Was it a nice car?" and so on.

My brother Jim came up with a plausible answer. "If the car's unlocked, you reach in and turn the lights off."

This response pleased Dad. "Yes. Would you tell anyone about it?"

"No."

"Right again. Just do the good deed and let it go at that."

The morals of these ethics discussions were consistent: do well, don't brag, be honest and throw yourself across the tracks to stop an oncoming injustice. We usually aced Dad's ethics quizzes.

The mock situation that stopped us in our tracks came to be known as the Great Candy Bar Debate. Dad brought it up periodically, and it became a chronic family controversy.

Here's the situation: You approach a candy machine, coins in hand. You can't wait for that Snickers bar to drop into the tray. But before your coin drops, you notice that there's already a candy bar in the tray. What do you do?

The only clarifying question three kids needed was, "What kind of candy bar?" Unless it was something vile like marshmallow, that candy bar was history.

"I'd take that candy bar and put my money back in my pocket," Jim said. Surely he knew this was not the right answer, although it made such sense.

"That's tempting, but that candy bar does not belong to

you. You haven't paid for it," Dad instructed.

"I'd still take it," said my sister, Andrea. "The candy bar company knows they'll lose a few that way."

"That's a rationalization. Their business is not your concern. You shouldn't take something you haven't paid for."

"Well if I don't take it, the next person will," Jim said.

"Another rationalization. That next person will have to answer for stealing that candy bar on Judgment Day. You'll have done right, leaving the candy bar in the tray."

About now, Mother tried to arbitrate, asking Dad if the question about candy wasn't too tempting for three kids.

Dad became spirited. "I cannot imagine a justification for taking a candy bar you hadn't paid for! How would you explain that to God?"

I could see Dad's point, but I wondered if I couldn't find justification somewhere. I knew that in the real world, every one of us except Dad would take that candy bar and eat it.

Dad's honesty plagued him to the end of his life. As a retiree, he and Mother occasionally worked as movie extras in Hollywood. The pay was minimal, twenty bucks apiece. Sometimes it was given in cash, "under the table." Most of the folks probably had a quiet dinner out on the earnings. Dad kept books, noted every dime of income, claimed it on his IRS Form 1040, and paid the tax he owed.

When Dad's memory began to fail, things got complicated. Mother took him to the attorney to see how to get him the medical care he needed without bankrupting the family. Dad didn't comprehend much, but he wanted no legal shenanigans that might ensure his medical care but jeopardize his soul.

Fortunately, as a combat veteran of World War II, he was eligible for treatment through the VA. To qualify for the Dementia Program, Dad took a battery of memory tests, which included vocabulary.

The psychiatrist told Mother, "I can't find a word he doesn't know. When we got to 'frangible,' he gave me synonyms and antonyms."

Dad was their favorite patient after that, a kind of "dementia savant." He told the best stories and remained his charming self. He just didn't know what day it was.

The time came when the doctors could do no more. They called Mother one morning. Dad was fading fast.

By the time we got there, Dad lay still and gray against the white sheets, his pulse faint. We wept. Then we dried our tears and started telling him stories. With the family reunited there, things felt strangely festive. When we started to get hungry, I went downstairs for snacks.

The lounge was filled with patient-veterans in various states of illness and decrepitude. I bought sodas from the machine, and then decided to get a Snickers bar. Approaching the candy machine, quarters in hand, I noticed a Three Musketeers lying in the tray. I looked up toward Dad's room, toward heaven. Was this a test? Was this a joke?

Across the room, a Vietnam-aged veteran, an amputee on crutches, said, "Aw, geez! I forgot my money, and I'm starving! Can I borrow change from somebody?"

"How about a Three Musketeers instead?" I asked.

"That'd be great."

I handed him the misbegotten bar.

With drinks and candy I'd paid for, and the solution to the Great Candy Bar Debate, I returned to Dad's room. Everyone agreed that giving it to a hungry veteran was the brilliant justification that had eluded us all those years.

Later that evening Dad slipped away. I know he heard everything we said. I'm pretty sure I can explain every nuance of the Great Candy Bar Debate to the Almighty when the time comes. I just hope my explanation will satisfy Dad.

Naida Grunden

"Yes, Daddy, I Promise"

*Retribution is one of the grand principles in the
divine administration of human affairs.*

John Foster

The security guard grabbed my arm. "Come with me,"
he barked, leading me back inside the discount store and
into the office. Then he pointed to a lime-green chair. "Sit
down!"

I sat. He glared at me. "You can give it to me or I can take
it, your choice. What'll it be?"

As I pulled the package of hair ribbons out of the waist-
band of my jeans, I could feel the sharp corner of the cardboard cutting into my skin. I handed it to him and
pleaded, "You're not going to call my dad, are you?"

"I'm calling the police. They will call your father."

My head dropped onto my hands and I sobbed, "No,
please! Can't you just let me go? I can pay you. I have
money in my pocket. I'm only fourteen years old. Please, I
won't ever shoplift again!"

"Save your tears, they won't work on me. I'm sick of you

bratty kids stealing, just for the thrill of it."

I sat, trembling with fear and shame.

The police arrived, and they exchanged muffled words with the guard and the office manager. I overheard one of the policemen say, "I know her father." I also heard, "Teach her a lesson."

The policemen walked me to their black-and-white car and opened the back door. I got in, and they drove me through the middle of our small town. I slouched down into the seat so no one could see me as I looked out the window at the evening sky. Then I saw the steeple of my family's church, and the guilt pierced me like a dagger. I thought, *How could I have been so stupid? I've broken my father's heart . . . and God's.*

We arrived at the station, and a round woman with a square face asked me questions until I ran out of answers. She pointed to the door of a large open cell and said, "Sit. Wait."

I walked in, and my footsteps made an echo that bounced off the bars. The tears started again as I sat down on a hard bench and heard her dial the telephone and say, "I have your daughter in a cell at the police station. No, she's not hurt. She was caught shoplifting. Can you come and get her? Okay. You're welcome, good-bye." She yelled, "Hey kid, your father's on his way."

About one hundred years later, I heard his voice say my name. The woman called me up to the desk at three times the necessary volume. I kept my eyes on the floor as I walked toward them. I saw my dad's shoes, but I didn't speak to him or look at him. And, thankfully, he didn't ask me to. He signed some papers and my jailer told us, "You're free to go."

The air was dark and cold as we walked to the car in heavy silence. I got in and closed the door. Dad started the engine and drove out of the parking lot as he looked straight ahead. Then he whispered in a sad and faraway voice, "My daughter . . . a thief."

I melted into repentant tears. The five-mile drive felt like forever. As we drove`into our driveway, I saw my mom's silhouette at the back door.

More shame came in a tidal wave.

After we entered the house, Dad finally spoke to me. "Let's go into the living room." Mom and Dad sat together on the couch, and I sat, alone, in the stiff wingback chair.

Dad ran his fingers through his hair, linked our eyes and asked me, "Why?"

I told him about the first time I stole a tube of lipstick and how I felt equal amounts of thrill and guilt. Then the second time, when I took a teen magazine, the guilt faded as the thrill grew. I told them about the third time, and the fourth and the tenth. Part of me wanted to stop the confession, but it gushed out like an open fire hydrant. I said, "Each time I stole, it got easier—until now. I can see how wrong it was." Hot tears bit my face as I said, "Please forgive me. I'll never do it again. Stealing was easy; getting caught is hard."

Dad said, "Yes, and it's going to get even harder." He asked Mom to hand me the notepad and pen that were sitting by the telephone. She walked over and patted my hand as she placed them in my lap. Dad continued, "I want you to make a list of all the places you stole from. Write down what you took and how much it cost. This is your one chance for a full confession and our forgiveness. If you ever steal anything again, I will not defend you or bail you out. We will always love you, but this behavior will stop. Here. Tonight. Correct?"

I looked at his face, which had suddenly aged, and said, "Yes, Daddy, I promise." As I wrote my list of offenses, Mom warned, "Make sure you haven't forgotten any; this is your only chance."

I finished writing. "Here's the list." I went to the couch and handed it to him, and I asked, "What are you going to do with it?"

Dad looked at the paper and sighed. He patted the cushion, and I sat down between my parents. "Tomorrow morning, we will go to all the places on your list, and you will ask to speak to the manager. You will tell him that you are a shoplifter. You will tell him what items you stole from his store, apologize, and then repay him. I'll loan you the money, and you will work all summer to pay me back. Do you understand?"

With my heart slamming and my palms sweating, I nodded.

The next morning, I did exactly as he asked. It was impossibly hard, but I did it. That summer, I repaid my father the money, but I will never be able to repay him for the valuable lesson he taught me. Thanks to his courage, I never stole again.

Nancy C. Anderson

The Lesson

Screech! Crash! The old black pickup truck in front of me stopped. I didn't. I slammed into its rear, crushing the fender and bending the driver's door of my car. Except it wasn't my car. It was my father's. I shouldn't have been driving it, and now I had destroyed it.

The farmer climbed out of his truck, slowly and deliberately, and looked at the damage. I sat sobbing, my lip bleeding where I'd bitten it. He was quite concerned, but we managed to exchange names and phone numbers before he pulled out onto the highway again. I cautiously followed, knowing I dared not go home. I'd be in big trouble.

It was my high-school graduation day. I drove to school and crawled out through the passenger door. Surveying the mangled fender, contorted door, scrapes and dents, tears flowed down my face, which was rapidly becoming more swollen by the minute—I didn't cry "pretty." I climbed up a ladder in the gym and began draping crepe paper for the dance that was to follow the ceremony. Word traveled fast, and soon a teacher stood at my feet.

"You'll have to go home to get dressed for graduation

sooner or later," she reasoned. "Sooner would be much better; you have to tell your parents."

I finally agreed and slowly drove home. The "Death March" sounded in my ears.

My mother took one look at my face when I walked in the door and screamed, "What on Earth happened?"

I hung my head and tears spilled from my eyes again. "I crashed Daddy's car."

She threw up her hands in dismay and rushed to the backyard where Dad was grilling burgers.

"Stop cooking, Ted. We're not going to eat. Jean has wrecked your car."

He looked at her and quietly said, "Is she hurt?"

"No, except for biting her lip."

"Well, then, what does that have to do with eating dinner?" He flipped a burger, piled it on a plate with the others, then walked across the yard and put his arm around me. "Let's go in and hear all about this—if you're sure you're all right."

I sniffled and nodded.

The phone was ringing when we got to the back door. The farmer wanted to make sure I was safe and had no other injuries. He refused to let Daddy pay for the scrapes on his truck.

I pressed ice to my lip while Mother brought cold washcloths for my swollen eyes. My father smiled at me and whispered, "Cars can be repaired . . . "

I graduated that evening with my family in attendance, joyful I had earned my diploma, yet knowing my greatest lesson had come from my father. High school taught me what is important in books. Daddy taught me to value what is really important in life.

Jean Stewart

"Tell me again, Melissa, how slowly and carefully you drove Brownie to the vet."

How to Trust, Dad-Style

I think we may safely trust a good deal more than we do.

Henry David Thoreau

My dad had traveled many miles to visit me in St. Louis from his small town of Braintree, in Essex, England, the town where I was born and raised. It was a backwater market town where the crime of stealing an egg from the supermarket was reported in the local paper.

Dad, recently widowed, stayed a month. I was at work for a couple of those weeks, and he liked to walk my huge golden retriever, Dustin. He had his routine, and I always reminded him to lock all the doors before he left. It was unseasonably hot for October. Dad marveled at the high temperatures and enjoyed the nearby park.

I purposely did not tell him that the two young men next door were troublemakers. They had been known to throw their mother out of the front door, steal her groceries and, after she had forgiven them, come back to borrow money for drugs. I knew a story like that would terrify my gentle dad. Besides, things had been quiet over there lately. If the boys made a ruckus, then I would explain the situation. Dad was already alarmed at the number of sirens screeching by on my street. He was not used to the fast pace of city life.

Usually, upon my return home from my job at the library, Dad made a light supper or "tea" as he called it.

I got home one hot Tuesday, worried that my dad might have gotten overheated on his walk, but, no, he was more cheerful than usual. His eighty-year-old face shone with excitement.

"You'll never guess what happened to me today," he said. "It could have been unfortunate, but it worked out well." I sipped my tea, slipped off my shoes and waited.

"I locked myself out," he began. "When I got Dustin's leash, I put the back-door key down on the table and left it."

"Oh, Dad, you should have called me at the library," I said.

"Didn't have a penny with me," he went on. "I was worried because by the time we got home, Dustin was really thirsty and I was pretty warm myself."

"Did you pick the lock?" I asked, trying to remain calm. I would have been amazed if he had because it was quite a complicated sort of lock.

"No," he went on, "those nice young men from next door helped me get in."

My shock must have been evident on my face. I almost got up from my chair to check the silver and my jewelry box. Dad always left a pile of dollars and coins on the bedroom dresser and that door was wide open. I noticed that the money was still there.

"After we got in, I gave the dog a drink, then I made a pot of tea. Those chaps and I sat and talked for a bit here in the kitchen."

My dad's "guests" had never even spoken to me.

"Those boys have had some troubles," Dad shook his head sadly and sighed. "They sure did help me out with that lock, though."

I gulped my tea and later found nothing missing from my house. Dad was pleased that he had solved the problem.

The remaining time of Dad's vacation went quickly. Many times I went out in the yard to watch him chatting with his new friends. His trusting nature had been rewarded. Maybe the boys had reformed.

The locked door wasn't the only thing opened that day.

Sylvia Duncan

Of Wings and Strings

The voice of parents is the voice of gods, for to their children they are heaven's lieutenants.

William Shakespeare

How long had it hibernated, I wondered, *in the corner of Daddy's garage?*

There it slumbered—an ancient ball of string—afloat in the puddled lines of cobwebby cane poles, shoehorned between tins of crackled boot polish and rusted coffee cans full of assorted nails—both straight and bent.

Rousing it from its sleep, I plucked linty wisps from the knotted wad. We children—grown now and scattered to the four winds—had been reeled home to cull and pick through the hoarded relics of our beloved father's life and, as familiar as a favorite cousin, the ball of string was the treasure I snagged. It tied me to family, to home, to Daddy.

I claimed it; I pocketed it; it was mine. And so were the memories it evoked. Way back when, in an era before America was prepackaged and disposable, our family valued the virtue of thrift: holding fast to our possessions to lengthen their lifespan. Daddy glued broken dinner plates, replaced chair legs, patched flat tires; Mother let down hems, salvaged odd buttons, and washed and reused tin foil; Grandma split worn sheets down the middle and stitched them together, outer edge to outer edge, good for another six or seven years of service.

And we kids saved string.

Twine from packages, leftover ends of crochet thread, whatever we could salvage and add to our burgeoning balls. After all, string had its uses. It was good for fashioning macaroni into necklaces, pulling a loose tooth, tying around a pinky as a homework reminder and finger-weaving Cat's Cradle, Jacob's Ladder or Crow's Feet.

But string also had a darker side.

Calling her "bear bait," Jimmy Winslow, our neighbor two houses down, once tied his sister Marla to a telephone pole until her mother rescued her and told Jimmy she'd show *him* bear bait! Not to be outdone in our own grisly play, Connie and Donna and I built miniature gallows and attempted to lynch condemned—but top-heavy—horny toads.

Mostly, though, we saved string for flying homemade kites.

Mother flattened and ironed crinkled gift-wrapping paper she'd hoarded since last Christmas—faintly scorched gold foil with jolly faced Santas and candy-cane stripes that we pasted and spliced crazy-quilt style onto paint stir-sticks scrounged from the corners of the garage. Finally, we pawed through a mildewed cache of rags (bed sheets even Grandma couldn't salvage) on the back porch to rip and tie on as wispy tails.

Knotting our string to the diamond-frame contraptions, we answered the siren call of "the hill," a gemstone of undeveloped and overgrown property ringed by our rural neighborhood. The hill: where ghosts roamed, imaginations soared and victories triumphed. I trailed the others as they scurried ahead, slowed by the firm knowledge that mine would be the kite that couldn't fly.

No matter how brisk the breeze or how diligent my efforts, my kite dogged my feet like a temperamental toddler. It waddled across the grass then actually rose a bit, right along with my hopes, before it flapped and fluttered and flopped to its back like a wounded goose.

Oh, how I wanted it to take flight. Marla could fly a kite. Connie and Donna could fly kites. Even wicked Jimmy Winslow could fly a kite. Mine was always doomed.

On this particular day, Daddy must've been watching from the front porch. He appeared beside me and laid his large workman's hand on my shoulder. "You need to give it more line," he explained.

"It still won't work. It never does."

"Just let it find its way." He turned his tanned face into the quickening breeze. "Run!" he shouted, grabbing the string above my clinched fist and racing with me into the wind as my cotton play dress slapped, then flattened against my thighs. "Okay, give it some slack . . . *now!*"

In spite of the kite's insistent tug, I held back. "But what if it breaks away? I don't want to lose it."

"Now!" he repeated.

Reluctantly, I reeled out the string with Daddy urging for more. And even more. The kite caught an air current, staggered, then nosed its way upward like an uncaged bird winging toward freedom.

"It's flying!" I flashed a wide grin at the sky.

"Hold on firmly, but loosen the line some," Daddy ordered.

As I eased out the string, I felt the kite's heart thrum an erratic beat down the taut length of it. My own heart echoed the rhythm. Farther and farther the kite flew, gliding yet hesitating to glance over its shoulder as if asking permission to continue on. Sipping a first taste of liberty, it dipped and bobbed and whirled, dancing to the strains of music I felt but couldn't hear.

I turned to Daddy. "What holds it up in the sky?"

"Why, you," he shrugged, ". . . and, of course, the string."

"Oh, Daddy, that's silly. The string holds it down, not up."

"Look over there," he pointed at a tree whose branches impaled the bleached bones of a kite. "That's what happens when you let go of the string. The kite flies away but eventually it falls, see? The thing that anchors it lets it soar."

So, the string—those odds-and-ends pieces we had virtuously conserved and diligently collected—really did keep the kite up even while holding it down. And that oddity made sense to me, the young child.

The very things that anchor us actually let us soar. Things like values and family and love—virtuously saved and diligently strung together—create the lifeline that offers us freedom even while it connects us to home.

Yes, I caressed the raggedy ball of string nestled deep in my pocket. *This is the heirloom—and the lesson from Daddy— I'll treasure.* And I looped the loose end around my pinky, just as a reminder.

Carol McAdoo Rehme

Just a Walk in the Park

The events of childhood do not pass but repeat themselves like seasons of the year.

Eleanor Farjoen

She was the wisest person I'd ever met. With messy hair and tattered clothes, she never cared one bit about success or wealth. It seemed that her only job was to laugh all day, which kept her healthy. She listened well and, in her own innocent way, sought out the truth in everything. Her mind was a sponge in search of right. Her heart was pure, and she had no qualms about sharing it. In her eyes there was peace, while her mouth spouted the kindest words I'd ever heard. She was polite and good, trying desperately to choose right over wrong. In her smile there was forgiveness and healing, and she was an open book when it came to her feelings. The word "shame" was never affiliated with her true emotions. She worried so much less than most, and her sleep was sound. I often wondered if she'd found the secret to true joy. Her only possessions in the world were hope and love, and for that she thanked the Lord daily. I felt blessed she was my daughter; Aubrey was four years old, and I couldn't have loved her any more.

I remember that day when the trees were still bare, and we had to wear bulky winter jackets. As soon as we rounded the corner and saw the park, somehow, at that very moment, spring arrived. With shoes unlaced, only our noses could run faster than our feet. My best friend, Aubrey, beat me to the bottom of the hill. She was small, but she was quick.

First, we tackled the slides, but that was only a warm-up. From there, it was on to the real games. Like two wild gorillas we hit the jungle gym hard. Before long, our coats were unbuttoned, and the brisk air seemed hot. While playing hide-and-go-seek, either my big butt or her giggles gave us both away, so we decided on tag. That was the most fun. We laughed, really laughed, and meant every second of it. There were no adults there to tell us what we couldn't do. We were king and queen, and, knowing this, we quickly claimed our territory.

We built a fort under the jungle gym. Resting on a floor of dirt and wood chips, Aubrey made me a birthday cake out of mud. She sang out of tune as I blew out the candles. Then, to my surprise, she found it—a treasure, the most valuable thing on Earth—a bottle cap. Quietly digging a hole, we buried our treasure where nobody would ever find it. I marked the spot with a stick, and we promised each other that we would tell no one. It was our secret; something we could rediscover at our next visit to the park.

Covered in sweat and dirt, we shared a swing for the last time that day. Aubrey talked about her life, and I listened because that's what real dads do. Racing to the top of the hill I beat her home but, looking back one last time, I realized something: I had just enjoyed one of the best days of my entire life. There had been nothing but laughter, yet somewhere through it all, something very serious happened: I'd been reminded that I was still alive, alive to run and play and laugh. The simple experience was so profound, I was inspired to run home and pen several poems.

The truth is, although she was only four years old back then and twenty-five years younger than me, Aubrey taught me that I still had much to learn. In those days, I honestly think she knew more than me. And whenever I recall days like these, I'm sure of it.

Aubrey is an adolescent now, and I move a little slower, think more before speaking and take a little longer to do the same things I could when she was four.

Last week, she was asked to baby-sit our neighbor's five-year-old son, Ricky. When I heard she was planning to take him to the park, I asked if I could tag along and watch. Somewhere along life's way, I'd become so busy with imaginary deadlines that I'd forgotten the blessings of innocent fun. It had been years since I'd gone to the park. Aubrey was thrilled to have me along.

Upon arrival, while Aubrey and Ricky headed for the swings, I said hello to the other adults on supervision patrol. Most offered a grin, a nod or heavy sigh, and then quickly returned to the army of small children on the jungle gym. I took a seat and tried to get comfortable on the hard, green bench, opting to do some people-watching. In truth, I've made few choices in my life that turned out better. You see, as I sat on that bench and watched my daughter play with our neighbor's little boy, I realized something priceless: Through the years, all the times I thought my little girl wasn't looking, she had been. My examples had clearly paid off. Aubrey was a genuinely good person, the only perfect measurement of success for a father. I quietly wept tears of pure joy.

In time, Ricky approached. With his muddy face, he

asked, "Will you play with me, too?"

"Geez, I don't know, Ricky. I'm getting a little old to be running around this park."

Little Ricky wouldn't hear it. As my daughter watched on in amusement, he begged for me to play with him. I shook my head in disbelief. With all the kids running around, he actually wanted me to play with him. For the sake of not disappointing anyone, slowly, I stood and grabbed Ricky's hand.

As we stepped through the park, I peered down at him and saw the past return in one wonderful jolt. He was Aubrey, ten years earlier. His nose was running like a broken faucet, his shirt was untucked, and in his dirty face, there wasn't a worry in the world. Adopting his carelessness and surrendering to his imagination, I decided to forget myself and everything I knew as an adult. I still remembered the joy I'd shared with my daughter on a day no different from this. Now I'd been blessed with a second opportunity to view what was important, to be reminded of who I really was and what honestly meant anything in life.

The entire day was magical. Ricky told stories that made no sense. The three of us ate fast-melting ice cream and danced under the sun. For Ricky and my entertainment, Aubrey described each person who passed with great fictitious detail. One was a real princess. Another was an astronaut.

We lay in the grass, rolled down a hill and looked up to watch big, puffy clouds float by. We took turns pointing out the obvious pictures painted above. Ricky then diverted our attention to a colony of ants that worked hard, marching in a straight row, each carrying his fair share. We played so many games that I had forgotten.

As the day wound down, Aubrey led us under the fort. With her bare hands she dug in the very area that had been our special hiding spot. My eyes filled from nostalgia and love that gushed for my daughter. Minutes later she held up the treasure. It was our secret bottle cap.

Little Ricky went wild. "It's a real treasure!" he squealed. "Let's bury it for some other lucky kids to find thousands of years from now. What a treasure!"

As he and Aubrey picked another spot to bury it, I decided then that everything worth knowing is learned young and understood by children. Lessons like playing fair, the reasons not to fight and sharing, for example, were really all anyone ever needed to know. In fact, anything more than that complicated and confused things.

I was so blessed for the sweet reminder, something everyone could use from time to time. I swear I'll never pass on the opportunity to take a walk through the park ever again. There are so many treasures that wait to be uncovered and rediscovered.

Steven H. Manchester

"Of course I realize the importance of interactive play. Amy, change the channel."

The Fifty-Cent Sewing Machine

Give what you have. To some it may be better than you dare think.

Henry Wadsworth Longfellow

Today, as I dust furniture in my living room, I pause at the beautiful antique sewing-machine cabinet sitting in the corner. It's Victorian style and made of solid walnut. It has beautiful scroll work, and the grain is in diagonals and squares. The sewing machine quit working many years ago, and I now just use the cabinet for storage. The wood gleams in the sunlight. It is one of my most prized possessions. Every time I dust it or even look at it, it reminds me of my grandpa and my dad and the lesson I learned from them.

The first time I saw that sewing-machine cabinet, thirty-four years ago, I was a junior in high school. I was a home economics major and loved to sew. I was desperate for my very own sewing machine. My grandpa knew that, and he wanted to help me.

The local Singer Sewing Machine Center would sell

their trade-ins for fifty cents to the first customer in the store on a certain day of the month. The machines were all guaranteed to work, and it was a real bargain. One day when I got home from school, Grandpa called, so proud. He'd gotten one of those fifty-cent sewing machines, and it was beautiful. I couldn't wait to get it.

When Dad got home from work, Grandpa pulled into the driveway in his old green station wagon. Dad and I ran out to greet him. Grandpa recounted the story about how he had gone to the store a half-hour early and waited just so he could purchase the bargain of the day. He beamed, "It's a Westinghouse. I know you'll love it!"

Eagerly, I watched as Grandpa opened the back of his station wagon. My heart sank. The cabinet was filthy and scratched. The finish was cracked with huge water rings all over it. The sewing machine might work, but who would want to use it? There was no way I was going to put brand-new, beautiful fabric on that machine. My dad and grandpa kept going on and on about the beautiful cabinet and what a great bargain it was. I thought they were crazy. I politely thanked my grandpa, hiding my disappointment. Dad set the sewing machine in the garage, saying he would clean it up before putting it in my room.

I went on about my daily school life, still wishing I had a sewing machine besides the one in the garage. A couple of weeks later, my dad said he wanted to show me something. I followed him to the garage, and there sat the most beautiful sewing machine I had ever seen! The wood of the cabinet was a dark, rich walnut, smooth and shining. It looked brand-new, more beautiful than any in the magazines or catalogues.

I couldn't believe Dad had cleaned and polished that old machine and sanded and refinished the cabinet. Dad and Grandpa weren't crazy after all. They had seen beyond the filth and cracks and water rings. From the very beginning, they knew what that machine could look like; they knew what it could be.

I can still see the scene in my mind like it was yesterday—the day I learned that even when life looks bleak, we must look beyond the negative, see the potential in the positive.

Brenda K. Stevens

Lessons from a Teenager

The greatest happiness in life is the conviction that we are loved, loved for ourselves, or rather loved in spite of ourselves.

Victor Hugo

My dad retired young because of heart problems. To help fill the time, he volunteered at my high school as a hall monitor. He had been doing it for a few years before I entered into ninth grade. I told him I didn't want him to stay there my freshman year. I kind of wanted to go through the school year without having to be known as a daddy's girl because him volunteering there meant me seeing him every day before lunch. On the inside I was praying he would ignore everything I said and go anyway because I was a nervous wreck about going into high school.

I liked it when he was there because it kind of made me feel safe knowing he was going to be in the school if I needed him. I was a freshman and not used to the idea of high school yet. He waited outside the cafeteria when he knew I would be going to lunch. We exchanged smiles, once in a while a wave. On rare occasions we actually talked for a few minutes before I caught up with my friends for lunch.

Although in school I acted as though I barely knew him, I loved being known as his daughter.

"Courtney Soucy?" said my art teacher, taking attendance.

"Right here," I answered.

"Any relation to Wayne?" This caught me by surprise because although my dad had been at the school for a few years, he wasn't actually part of the staff, just a volunteer.

Through my first week as a freshman, almost every one of my teachers asked if I was Wayne's daughter. When I said yes, they usually replied with something along the lines of, "You'll be a pleasure to have in class; your dad's such a nice guy."

I never met any teacher, let alone any person, who said they didn't like my dad. He was very funny and always had a smile on his face. He was the life of every party we went to, always cracking everybody up with his witty remarks and corny jokes. His light blue eyes reflected his cheerful nature—he was never grim or gloomy. People in our small town referred to him as "the mayor" because on walks around our neighborhood, he made at least ten stops to talk to people. When someone needed a place for their kid to stay while they ran a few errands, my dad volunteered to be the baby-sitter. In the summertime, our pool became the community pool with my dad as the lifeguard. He was surrounded by screaming kids all day, but he loved every minute of it. My friends soon became my dad's friends; he was such a lovable guy.

I don't remember any specific time when I just came out and told my dad I loved him. Sometimes we'd get into stupid fights about why I couldn't spend the night at Chelsea's, or why I couldn't go to the movies with Kelsey.

Even though there was a lot of screaming and yelling, the disagreements never lasted very long.

One night I stormed up the stairs to my bedroom. "Dad, you're a jerk, and I hate you!" *Just another fight,* I thought as I cried myself to sleep.

The next day I got myself ready, not even thinking about our fight the night before. Come to think of it, I don't even remember what the fight was about. We always forgot about our arguments because they were pretty meaningless. This fight appeared meaningless, too, until around 4:30 that afternoon.

I had a softball game at 4:00. We warmed up as usual. My dad and sisters, Brianna and Angela, showed up a little early, ready to watch the game. My mom rarely got out of work in time to see my games, but Dad was always there to watch. About five minutes into the game, I heard my mom screaming for a cell phone. She'd gotten out early, only to find Dad unconscious on the side of the field.

The paramedics rushed Dad to the hospital in an ambulance. Mom and I followed them in a police car, holding hands and praying all the way. Ten minutes later, Dad was pronounced dead from a second heart attack.

It was the worst day of my life. I'm sure many people have said that on occasion when they have a bad hair day, when they forget to do their homework, sure it's a rough day. But I've had those days before, and they didn't compare to what May 6th was for me. My mind wandered, nervously thinking about the past weekend, what had gone on, what I did with Dad, trying hard to remember his last few days. My thoughts were blank until tears cascaded endlessly down my cheeks, remembering what my last words were to him: "I hate you." I hadn't realized until then how much I didn't mean that.

People live each day knowing there's always going to be tomorrow to make up for today's mistakes. I thought the same thing. Never did it cross my mind that I would get into another stupid fight and then never get the chance to apologize to my dad.

I'm not writing this for sympathy, because I have enough of that. I'm writing this as a warning to others who still have their dads. It's hard growing up as a young girl with a "crazy" dad. It can be fun at times, and terribly embarrassing at others. Nevertheless, cherish the times you spend with your fathers. There's a small chance that tomorrow *won't* come. That you won't get that chance to say your "sorrys," your "good-byes" or your "remember the time whens." Don't disregard this and think, *That will never happen to me.* I thought the same thing—and it did happen.

Please make it so it isn't too late to say your "I love yous" to your dad, your mom, your friends, your family; make it so they all know you love them. The world will be a better place when you do.

Courtney Soucy

"Take your time, Honey. I'll talk to your date
'til you're ready."

Hidden Wings

The darkness of death is like the evening twilight; it makes all objects appear more lovely to the dying.

Jean Paul Richter

Daddy wasn't just an ordinary man. He was my daddy, a special kind of person who could charm the whiskers off a cat with a back rub or cajole the birds right out of a tree with a handful of seed. In my mind, he could do anything, from delivering moonshine to resurrecting a doll from decay.

I always knew when Daddy had been reading the Bible because he would burst forth in song, belting out the lyrics with gusto as he melded two songs—"When They Ring Those Golden Bells for You and Me" and "Oh Lordy, I'll Fly Away" together into one harmonious array. He sang those two songs until tears streamed down his cheeks. With a powerful shout of "Hallelujah!" he'd slap his knee and say, "Praise the Lord for hidden wings."

One morning, while Daddy was at work, I found a crippled cardinal lying in our backyard near our old concrete duck pond. Its wing was broken, and one foot was withered and drawn close to its beautiful red breastplate. I ran to the house screaming for Mother to get a bandage to wrap the wing and cried pitifully as I looked at the glorious bird writhing in such painful distress. Mother took the bird and carefully wrapped the wing in an old dishtowel. Placing the bird gently inside a cigar box, she said, "We'll just have to wait and see if the bird wants to mend its wing." I was five years old and didn't understand Mother's profound wisdom. I wanted so desperately to see the bird fly again. I said, "Just wait till Daddy gets home; he can fix it!"

That evening, when Daddy came home from a long day's work on the railroad, I met him as he came through our front gate. "Daddy, Daddy, you gotta fix 'im!" Daddy was grungy with caked-on, greasy soot from wrestling with massive steel wheels and rails and was exhausted from miles of walking. Somehow he managed to delay his rest to soothe my fears.

Daddy lifted the bird and said, "Honey, he's already been fixed. His hidden wings have taken him high into the heavens. Jesus has a special place just for him. You just weren't able to see the wings unfolding, but the little bird released a hidden spirit and soared high into the sky." I stood there in silence as Daddy explained, "Everybody has hidden wings. You just can't see them right now. The wings only unfurl when Jesus rings his golden bell."

I stood there in complete confusion when Daddy reached over and touched me on the back. "This is the place where the wings are lying, right here, between the shoulders. It's very close to the heart, and when it's time to go see Jesus, the love you have in your heart awakens the spirit. The spirit *is* the wings. One of these days, when you are older, you will understand what I have told you." Although I did not understand, I was content with his explanation.

As I grew older and watched my parents age gracefully, Daddy's words resounded with a thunderous roar. It was not until my mother passed away that I fully understood the magnitude of hidden wings or the wisdom of two wonderful souls. When Mother died, a peaceful grace consumed her frail little body. The years faded from her face to reveal a beautiful glow, almost stating "perfection has arrived." It was as though I could feel her spirit swirl around me, dancing with excitement. She was at peace and, strange as it might seem, so was I.

Several years later, Daddy went to a nursing home. Dementia and diabetes had taken hold of him, and he needed around-the-clock care, which I could not provide. I visited him every day, and we shared many stories of his childhood and one particular story about hidden wings. Early one Sunday morning, as I approached Daddy's room, the nurse told me that he was not responding and warned me what to expect when I went inside. As I neared his bed, I heard the strangest thing. Down the hallway, inside a dining room, a quartet broke forth in gospel songs, transposing one with another. The harmony was divine and surely sent by God. The joyous sounds drifted closer and closer until it draped the two of us with solid words: "When they ring those golden bells for you and me, I'll fly away, oh glory, I'll fly away in the morning, when I die, hallelujah, by and by, I'll fly away."

As I looked at Daddy, a single tear dropped from his steel gray eyes. Then, as day turned into night, Daddy was gone. I knew immediately what Daddy had told me was true. His hidden wings had unfurled, and his spirit soared into the heavens. When I finally left his room that day, I slapped my knee and said, "Hallelujah, praise the Lord for hidden wings."

Joyce L. Rapier

Questions

The interests of childhood and youth are the interests of mankind.

Edmund Storer Janes

I've always loved to fish with my children. When I've been with them, especially my young daughter Stephanie, the sport has served mainly as a backdrop for an endless stream of questions she has asked me throughout the years.

I realized Stephanie had a penchant for off-the-wall questions when she was four and we took her to see Niagara Falls. After driving five hours and depositing our bags in our hotel, we walked to the falls and were mesmerized by their beauty. I asked Stephanie what she thought of one of nature's greatest views, and she replied, "Is this all we're gonna do, watch this water go over the hill?"

And so her inquiries would begin early on at the fishing hole. "Daddy, if you could be a bird, which one would you be? Daddy, if I catch a big fish, can I cut him open and get my worm back? Daddy, can I have a boa constrictor?" And on and on.

Stephanie's attention span wasn't very long, especially on our early trips. If she didn't catch a bluegill after ten minutes, she would wander away to the playground in the park where we fished. I would push her on the swings, then coax her back to the pond with vague promises of catching the Big One. And then, soon enough, the questions would come again. "Daddy, are there sharks in this pond? Daddy, how do tornadoes start up? Daddy, how old are you? Nine?"

These expeditions were precious moments in our relationship, for as she grew older, I felt things change too quickly. During these fishing excursions, I willed time to slow down so I could enjoy them all the more because I noticed the questions were changing, too. "Dad, how come the boys in my class are so weird? Dad, does it hurt the worm when you cut it in half? Dad, can I be a storm chaser when I grow up? The rain doesn't bother me, just the lightning."

I was a police officer, and early one morning I was called to the bank of the Allegheny River near Pittsburgh for a DOA. The victim, an elderly man, had been found at a popular fishing spot by a fellow fisherman at around 6:30 A.M. The victim was lying face up on the bank, a rod and reel propped up on a rock with the line in the water and a bucket full of live minnows by his side. I secured the area after medics verified he had no vital signs.

I spent about twenty minutes alone with the victim until the coroner arrived. I took his wallet from the rear pocket of his fishing jeans—I knew these were his fishing jeans because there were stains on the upper thighs from years of him wiping his hands on them when no rag was available. From the looks of these jeans, he had been a fisherman for a long time. The contents of his wallet revealed the man was from Pittsburgh, right across the river.

As I bent down to replace the wallet, I noticed a slight smile on his face as he stared up at me. I said a small prayer for him, glad that this elderly fellow passed away doing something it appeared he enjoyed. He had one last visit to his fishing spot, one last cast. A slight smile spread across my face.

In the past, I've been given sage advice from parents of preteens that I should appreciate these inquisitive fishing outings with my daughter while I'm still relevant in her grand scheme of the universe. In little ways, I've been feeling my importance slipping away already. I've given up answering the phone at home; it's Stephanie's hotline now, and friends call constantly to check up on what has happened since the last time they talked fifteen minutes earlier. I have to make an appointment a week in advance to get on the computer.

I recently took Stephanie fishing. Of course, as is our tradition, we had to stop at the grocery store to load up on fishing essentials such as bubble gum, Sweet Tarts, Pepsi and, yes, even bait. Sitting with her on the shore of the lake, I couldn't help but notice again how grown up she's becoming. In a lull of conversation, mostly one-sided with me doing the listening, I thought about the fisherman I found on the riverbank. I leaned back in my fishing chair and looked up, asking myself a question, *Do you think he's up there, looking down with that smile of his?* I answered my own question. *Yeah, he's telling me to hold onto these fishing days with my daughter for as long as I can.*

"Dad, do you, like, think I'd make a good veterinarian? Dad, don't you think *NSYNC are better than the Beatles? Dad, are we rich?"

Absolutely, Honey, beyond your wildest imagination.

Danny Dugan

"I cleaned my dresser, can I go
fishing with Daddy now?"

Bullfrogs, Butterflies and Dads

I placed my guitar on the park bench beside me and gazed at the Detroit River rushing past. Three weeks until Susan's wedding. She wanted me to write a song for it. My heart sank. I thought daughters were supposed to marry guys like their dads. Rich and I were nothing alike.

My beef wasn't with Rich. He can't help that he picked Michigan State University over my alma mater, the University of Michigan. But what was Susan's excuse? How could my first-born, die-hard Wolverine fall for a Spartan? I picked up my guitar and strummed, "Traitor."

I remembered the first time Susan brought Rich home. I clutched my heart and pointed at her sweatshirt.

"It's nothing, Dad," she explained quickly, checking the MSU logo on her chest. "I was cold, is all. Rich loaned me his shirt."

I immediately grabbed my favorite U of M sweatshirt jacket.

"Here ya go, Princess," I said, holding it open. "This will warm you up." She looked at Rich and shrugged her shoulders apologetically.

Then I ushered everyone to the kitchen for cards. While

they visited, I covertly ditched my wife's snack bowls and replaced them with my "Go Blue" party dishes. Later, I heard Mare quietly searching for her dishes. When she finally gave up, she poured the pretzels and chips into my bowls and plunked them down in front of me. I didn't need to look up. I could feel her and Susan giving me the evil eye. Rich just chuckled.

At last, they had to go. I smiled through gritted teeth as I spied the "MSU" bumper sticker adhered to his Ford Explorer.

"I don't believe it. He not only went to State, he drives a Ford."

Mare said she didn't think he meant anything by it. He might not have, but Susan knew better. It was my General Motors salary that helped pay her college tuition!

A few months later, Susan called to say Rich was loaning her some furniture. Could I help move it? *Rich?* Yikes! I didn't realize he was still in the picture.

"Sure," I agreed.

"Great! Rich will appreciate your strong arms."

I smiled and flexed my muscles as I hung up the phone. As a dad of five daughters, I was a pro at moving and setting things up. I'd show Rich a thing or two.

Moving day was muggy and rainy, and I felt sluggish. Rich, on the other hand, was raring to go. He perched boxes on his broad shoulders and took steps two at a time. *Show off!*

Afterward, Rich invited us to his house. I winced when he served us beverages in his "Go Green" glasses. If I hadn't been so thirsty, I would have declined.

On the way home I pumped my wife for information. "So what's the deal with Rich and Susan? Are they serious?"

"Susan says they're serious friends." I could tell she was being evasive.

"What does Rich say?" I queried further.

She started to cry. "He says he wishes he knew the way to Susan's heart. He says he loves her."

I was quiet the rest of the three-hour trip home. That MSU Spartan, arch-rival, loved my precious, prettiest-baby-in-the-nursery, first-born daughter.

A few months later he asked her to marry him, and she said "yes." When she came home to break the news, I noticed her car was sporting a "Go State" bumper sticker also. I'd lost my little Wolverine to the Spartan.

The years fell away as I held my guitar close and fingered a melancholy tune. Suddenly, I was recalling Susan's first day of kindergarten.

"Ready, Dad?" she asked as she hopped into our old blue 1972 Buick Skylark.

"Ready, Princess!" I said as I kissed her head and tossed my briefcase under her feet. We stopped three times to pick up kids in our carpool. "It's okay to talk," I told them. They looked nervously out the windows.

Susan pulled a cassette from her book bag. "Can we listen to this, please, Daddy?"

"Sure," I said. It was a song about Noah's ark. Susan hummed, Jimmy kept time with his feet on the back of my seat, and the other two bobbed their heads. Before long, we were all belting out, "Bullfrogs and butterflies, they've both been born again!"

A horn blast from a passing lake liner shook me from my reverie. Thanks to that memory, the words for Susan's wedding song finally came.

Three weeks later, the pianist began pounding out the wedding march. Susan looked up at me with watery blue eyes and whispered, "Ready, Dad?" I tucked her trembling arm under mine and steered her toward the open double doors. Flashbulbs popped and people "oohed" and "ahhed" as we started down the aisle. I glanced over to reassure her, but her eyes were locked on Rich.

At the altar, the minister asked, "Who gives this woman in marriage?" The church was so quiet you could hear the candles burning. "Her mother and I do," I said proudly, as if I had just handed over a priceless gift.

I got my guitar and began singing. Coming to the last verse, I started to choke up.

Because, like bullfrogs and butterflies and how they live two lives,
Little girls play; grow up one day, with hearts changed into wives.

At the stadium-sized reception hall, Susan rushed from one wedding custom to the next. Finally, the lights dimmed as the DJ announced the father-daughter dance. I couldn't believe my ears. "Bullfrogs and Butterflies!" I twirled her around, and she flapped her "wings," and we jumped at the part where the frog leaps onto a lily pad. Then, like her childhood, the dance was over way too soon.

Afterward, Rich shook my hand and thanked me for the wedding—and for Susan, the very best gift of all. Suddenly, I realized maybe we weren't so different. Maybe Susan had married a guy like her dad after all!

If God can change polliwogs to bullfrogs and little girls to wives, I guess he can change me, too. Okay, I'm probably never going to root for MSU, but I'll always be right there rooting for Rich and Susan.

Joe Strube
As told to Marilyn K. Strube

What I Learned at the Outhouse Races

My seventy-five-year-old father, Ed Kobbeman, is one of the all-time-great, get-it-done, do-it-now kind of guys. He built his own home in 1946, and it's a veritable showplace of repair and improvement. He's often out in the barn fixing things before they break, restoring antiques, building things from scratch or designing and creating amazing gadgets and gizmos.

It wasn't too surprising, then, when Dad proudly showed me his latest creation . . . the outhouse he'd built from the rough wood ripped from an old wooden crate. The traditional sun and moon were cut out of the front door, and the sloped roof had shake shingles. Dad had fashioned a fancy seat inside, within arms reach, of course, of the supply of corncobs dangling on strings. The dual-purpose Sears Roebuck catalog hung from a hook on one of the inside walls. There was even an American flag waving off the back end. It was, indeed, a fine outhouse.

Why a man, who built an all-electric home in the 1940s with a beautiful modern bathroom, would build an outhouse in the 1990s was something of a puzzle to me at first, until Dad explained that he intended to enter his creation in the First Annual Rock Falls Days Outhouse Races.

To be in this grand event, one's outhouse had to have wheels. These he found in his neat-as-a-pin storage area outside the barn, taken off some old contraption he'd worked on years before.

The day of the race, Dad's nephews arrived to load up his pride and joy into their pick-up truck. The four made up the outhouse racing team, along with one great-niece weighing in at under a hundred pounds, chosen to ride on the seat inside, per race rules. They all wore red look-alike, tank-style, T-shirts, looking so spiffy they could have been vying for a medal at the outhouse event at the summer Olympics.

The contraption arrived safely in the heart of downtown Rock Falls, Illinois. In the blazing sun of that scorching June day, the five outhouse teams lined up. The four muscular nephews in charge of the Kobbeman outhouse grabbed the pole handles and rocked ole Bessy back and forth, chanting, "Feel da rhythm, hear da rhyme, come on team, it's outhouse time!"

The starting shot rang out. The red-shirted Kobbeman clan, out in front by a foot, screeched around the markers thirty yards down the parking lot and turned 180 degrees to make their way back to the start/finish line.

Just then, disaster. The hard rubber on the wheels started peeling off. One at a time, hardened black tires split off the wheels as old rubber gave way to new asphalt. The nephews hung on for the last few yards, barely winning the first race by sheer strength of will and brute muscle power as they lifted that outhouse off the ground, niece and all, and drag-carried her across the finish line. But now there was no hope for the second heat.

I stood there, ready to cry. My father had put so much

time and talent into making what was obviously the most superior outhouse in the race, and now it was all over. Without wheels, an outhouse cannot run.

Out of the corner of my eye, I saw Dad walking like a mad man away from the race. I wondered if he, too, was as disgusted with those old tires as I. *What a shame,* I thought, *to lose the contest because of some stupid old wheels.* Considering the strength and enthusiasm of the red-chested man-power, it was a low blow, indeed.

Five minutes later I realized Dad hadn't come back. *Where is he?* I wondered. Thinking he'd gone off to the restroom at the corner tap, I suddenly realized that if he didn't get back soon he'd miss the rest of the races.

Minutes ticked by. By now my cousins were using the old standby, gray duct tape, to wrap the wheels in hopes that they could patch them together enough to at least try for the second race.

Five minutes later Dad was still nowhere to be seen. *Doggone, him,* I thought. *Where could he be? Gone off, upset at himself for using old tires on a new outhouse? How could he just leave like that? This was my dad, the man who spent a great deal of my childhood teaching me to be a good sport, to enjoy life, but to always play the game fairly. And now, just because the wheels fell off his outhouse, he's acting like a poor sport?*

The announcer was on the microphone telling the participants to get their outhouses lined up. Just then Dad ran up to outhouse row clutching four brand new wheels. He tossed me a few tools.

"Here, hold these. Hand me those needle-nose pliers."

Within seconds the nephews and Dad had that wooden, shake-shingled wonder on its back, ripping the duct tape off with the pliers, undoing rusty nuts and bolts, and attaching the brand new wheels. It was a scene straight out of a pit stop at the Indy 500. Fifty seconds flat and those new wheels were in place.

The Kobbeman clan won the next four races amid plenty of good-natured hooting and hollering from the folks on the sidelines. In the ceremony that followed, Dad, his nephews and his great-niece were presented with an outhouse trophy so spectacular it could only be given to the finest of privy makers. That shiny, blue-and-gold, two-foot-tall trophy even had a tiny little outhouse on top with the door wide open, as if to say, "Come on in, friend!"

After the presentation, photo session, lots of backslapping and congratulatory kudos from the townspeople, including the mayor, we headed home. In the car I asked my dad, "Where'd you go when you ran off like that? And where'd you get those new wheels?"

My father took a deep breath. "Well," he said, starting slowly, then speeding up his words as he told the story. "I ran two-and-a-half blocks to the car. Unlocked it, drove home like a bat out of Bangkok, ran in the house, got the key to the barn, ran out there, unlocked the barn, pulled my new lawnmower out on the grass, grabbed some tools, pulled off the first two wheels and threw 'em in the car. Then I decided I could take the other two off downtown while the boys were puttin' the first two on the outhouse. So I lifted that lawnmower into the back end of the station wagon. Then I decided that was dumb. I could take the wheels off there at home just as fast, so I lifted the lawnmower back out of the car and unbolted the second pair of wheels, threw 'em in the car, put the lawnmower back in the barn, locked the door, jumped in the car, drove back to town and just happened to find a parking place right in front of the start of the race. Must have been a guardian angel. Best luck I ever had findin' a parking place."

I couldn't believe my ears. "Dad, you did all that in the fifteen minutes you were gone, between the first and second races?"

"Yup."

I just shook my head. "Why? Why did you do all that in this heat? You had a heart attack ten years ago, remember? And how did you know you wouldn't miss all the rest of the races when you took off for home like that?"

He smiled, "Well, I just couldn't let the boys down. They worked so hard to win that first race, I just couldn't let those old rotten wheels ruin their chances for the rest of the races. Besides, there was a problem, and it just needed to be fixed, that's all."

Well, one thing's for sure. On that hot afternoon in June in the heart of middle America, my father gave a whole new meaning to the phrase, "Race to the outhouse." He not only saved the day for his nephews and great-niece, he also taught me a valuable lesson: No matter how grave or impossible a situation seems, just bulldoze ahead. Don't hesitate. Just fix it.

Follow this advise and, who knows? You just might end up with a two-foot-tall trophy with a shiny little outhouse on top with the door open, welcoming you inside.

Don't you just love America?

Patricia Lorenz

4

SPECIAL MOMENTS

There's something like a line of gold thread running through a man's words when he talks to his daughter and gradually over the years it gets to be long enough for you to pick up in your hands and weave into a cloth that feels like love itself.

John Gregory Brown

The Dad He Planned to Be

Michael was shocked when we watched a videotape of a baby's birth during childbirth classes. But I, like several classmates, got teary-eyed as the tiny miracle entered the world. Passing a box of tissues around the room, the instructor turned on the lights. My twenty-nine-year-old husband leaned over to me. "What have we done?" he whispered, his face pale with horror.

After seeing that tape, Michael was adamant about not viewing the birth of our baby. He conceded to coach breathing exercises during labor, but when it came time for the actual delivery, he envisioned himself seated in a chair at the head of the bed holding my hand.

"Delivery is the touchdown," joked our birthing coach. "You wouldn't sit through four quarters of the Super Bowl then go to the fridge if the score was tied, your team had the ball on the two-yard line and there was less than a minute left in the game, would you?"

Throughout my pregnancy, Michael was the "go-to guy." During the first and second trimesters, I felt too tired to do anything but work and sleep, so he did the grocery shopping, errands and household chores. Weekly, he read me excerpts about how both mother and fetus were changing. "Your body is growing precious cargo," he'd reassure me. "It's taking all your energy to make our baby."

When my back hurt, he rubbed it. When my feet ached, he massaged them. The first time we felt the baby move, he cupped his hands around his mouth and shouted at my bulging belly, "Hi, little girl. I'm your daddy!"

But incongruent as it seemed, Michael wanted to sit in the stands rather than be on the field during the actual birth. "In fact, I don't want to look at the baby until she's properly cleaned," he emphasized. "And changing a diaper is out of the question. I'll vomit." From my husband's comments and behavior, I knew he would love our child, but the hands-on care of the baby would be my job.

Finally, I was in labor—for twenty-three hours—and Michael was by my side the entire time. He coached my breathing and held my arm as we walked halls. When the time came for me to give birth, Michael walked over to the dry-erase board in the hospital room and wrote: "Happy Birthday, Micah." He then took his seat near the head of the bed and prepared to watch the labor-and-delivery team perform their magic.

A few minutes later, one of the nurses called to him, "Dad, we need your help with pushing." White-faced, Michael stood. A nurse positioned him at the edge of the bed, shoved my foot into his stomach and wrapped his hands around my shin. "There, now," she said enthusiastically. "This will give you a perfect view of the birth." Michael smiled weakly. I thought he might faint.

A few minutes later, Michael shouted excitedly, "I see black hair!" Our daughter, Micah, was born, and the doctor immediately handed the gooey baby to my husband. "Isn't she beautiful?" he gasped, cradling her tiny body in his strong arms. Tears of happiness pooled in his eyes. I began crying as well, not only because our baby was here, but because of the tender joy in my husband's face.

When the nurse wanted to put Micah under warming lights, he said, "Honey, I don't want to leave you, but I should go with the baby to make sure she's all right."

"Hey, there, little girl," I heard him coo from across the room. "It's okay. Daddy's here."

Moments later, our families came. Michael proudly displayed our newborn, even before she was bathed.

That night, a nurse took Micah to administer some tests, saying she'd be back with the baby in an hour. "Let me put on my shoes. I'll go with you," hollered my husband from the foldout couch.

"I'll change her diaper before you go," I said.

"No, Honey, you rest," said Michael. "I need to practice changing her."

I tried to look nonchalant as he gently lifted Micah's legs and fumbled to get the diaper around her six-pound body, but inside, I was amazed. *He's a hands-on dad, after all,* I thought.

Micah is now eighteen months old and the pride of her daddy's heart. She's baptized him in bodily fluids and blessed him with giggles. Michael's shared in the good (when Da Da was her first word), the bad (when, as a newborn, she had jaundice and had to be strapped to a light table for seventy-two hours) and the ugly (when six-month-old Micah caught a virus and vomited in Daddy's face) aspects of parenthood.

Michael admits there's a big discrepancy between the way he planned to be a father and the dad he's become. But daughters do that to daddies.

Stephanie Welcher Thompson

off the mark
by Mark Parisi
www.offthemark.com
HEY, HER DIAPER IS CLEAN, AGAIN... WHAT THE HECK IS GOING ON HERE?
NEW DIAPERS WITH BUILT-IN WHOOPIE CUSHIONS
ATLANTIC FEATURE © 1996 MARK PARISI
MARK PARISI
offthemark.com

Dad's Right Hand

I cannot but remember such things were,
that were most precious to me.

William Shakespeare

Many of us who grew up in the '50s had dads who were more shadow than real. They left every morning to go to work (a vague concept to us) and came home every evening to eat and fall asleep in front of the TV before going to bed. We knew they cared about us, but we didn't know much about them.

My dad hauled bread for a living. Six days a week, he left the house at 3 A.M. and returned in time to eat supper and go to bed. On Sundays when he stayed home, Dad was usually working on jobs around the house while I was busy playing. Our paths seldom crossed.

So went our shared existence until the summer I was twelve. That was the summer Dad "hired" me to go along on his bread route and be his helper. Fridays and Saturdays were my designated workdays. For the princely sum of three dollars a day, I would climb into his big truck before the sun made an appearance and set out on an adventure with my dad. Off we'd go, traveling to little country stores as well as supermarkets in distant towns.

Dad stopped at most of the stores before dawn and used a flashlight to peer through a window to survey the bakery displays, then decided if they needed anything to start the day. He'd yell to me to get a box ready to pack. I'd quickly assemble a cardboard box that was stored in the corner of the truck and wait for him to tell me what to put into it. Bread and sweet rolls to start the day were bundled and left by the door of the shuttered store. Later in the day, on the return trip, we'd stop once again to replenish the bakery supply, get payment for the goods and continue to retrace our morning run.

Dad never lost his patience if I made a mistake. If he sent me to the truck for a loaf of rye bread and I returned with whole wheat, he'd grin and tell me I got the brown breads mixed up again and to go back and get a loaf in the orange wrapper. If I brought in Danish rolls instead of Bismarcks, he'd say we needed the ones with the jelly inside. Eventually, I got better at knowing the stock and made fewer mistakes. I could even suggest what was needed. I'd beam with pride when Dad told his customers that I made a pretty good bread man or that I was his right-hand man. (This was years before any of us would have thought it more appropriate to say "bread person.")

Halfway through the day, we stopped at Gracie's store in a little country village called Shennington. That little store was always a welcome sight because it meant lunch. After we finished the business end of the visit, Dad would point me toward the meat counter along the old side wall and tell me to pick out the lunch meat I wanted. I'd usually choose the ham or big bologna, and then watch in anticipation as the loaf was placed into the machine that cut it into slices. I'd wait while our banquet main course was wrapped in white paper, then I'd grab a bag of chips and a soda for each of us. By the time I got to the lone checkout counter, Dad would be chatting with Gracie and digging out his wallet. Soon, we'd be on the road again, Dad driving while I slapped meat between slices of bread to make sandwiches for both of us. Seldom have I had any sandwich that tasted as good as those unadorned meals.

Since Dad's route was mostly rural, there was a good deal of drive time between stops. The truck was noisy, so conversation was minimal, but we did manage to make short comments to each other. Our conversations consisted mostly of gestures and facial expressions. He'd point out a deer along the road and smile as I gazed with big eyes. He'd laugh when I bobbed my head in time to the rhythm of the windshield wipers. We'd share a look of disgust when some careless driver almost cut him off while passing on a narrow, two-lane road.

My workday ended when Dad pulled his truck into our driveway to drop me off, usually around two o'clock. His workday wasn't quite finished, however. He still had to return the truck to the outlet garage, clean it out and make it ready for the next day, and do his daily paperwork. I didn't see him again until supper, after which he crawled into his old rocking chair to watch a little TV before heading for bed. Though he was the same as always, I saw him differently then—he was no longer a shadow, but real.

The years have flown, and I learned more about this mystery man as I got older. After I had children of my own, I understood the long hours he worked to support his family and the sacrifices he made. We shared many lovely times together, but nothing has ever recaptured those special days when the world consisted of Dad and me rattling around in an old boxy truck.

Lana Brookman

Trust Me

To be trusted is a greater compliment than to be loved.

James Ramsay MacDonald

I wasn't expecting the feeling of total panic that hit me as I watched my ten-year-old daughter walk alone to the microphone at the front of the stage.

She was running for student body president, which meant that she had to deliver a brief campaign speech during an assembly of the entire school. She was pretty, articulate, charming and poised. I knew she would speak well. What made me nervous was the audience. The principal had ordered that no one could applaud for any candidate until the very end of the program, and the students had reacted to the restriction with boredom and resentment. Several times the principal had returned to issue warnings to those too eager to shout insults at their peers onstage.

I hadn't panicked when she asked for my help with the speech two weeks before. I told her that if she really, really

wanted to win the election, the only way was to make all
the kids laugh. To do so, she'd have to do something unexpected. "Trust me," I told her, "if you follow what I tell you,
I guarantee it will go over well and you'll win." She had
chosen her words carefully and practiced often; yet, in
that moment of silence before she began speaking, my
heart stopped beating.

What if I was wrong? What if they didn't laugh at her
jokes? What if they ridiculed her attempts at humor and
put her down? How could I have violated her trust? I was
sure that I had thrown my oldest child to the sharks and
that her respect for her father would be lost forever. I
knew if she flopped and lost the election, she'd never
believe anything I told her again.

"My name is Brittany, and I'm running for president,"
she started calmly. "I think you should vote for me because. . . ."
She paused and looked around. My hand on the video
camera shook with fear as I waited for her to deliver the
punch line. She picked up a Tupperware bowl from a bag
behind her and put it upside down on her head. She
pinched her nose and spoke in a robotic voice. " . . . I am an
alien. I came to your planet to eat your cafeteria food!"

The audience was caught completely off-guard and
erupted with glee. It took several seconds before the
laughter died down enough for her to go on.

"But don't take my word for it," she continued, "ask
someone who has the same birthday as me, George
Washington." With that, she turned her back to her classmates and put a gray wig over her hair. By now the crowd
was squirming with anticipation. "Oh, my gosh, am I sore!"
she shouted in an old man's voice as she stretched. "I guess
that comes from being dead for a couple of hundred years!"

The hall erupted again. I knew her humor had tamed
the crowd and that the election would be hers in a
landslide.

When she finished her speech, outlining her agenda if elected, screams and shouts of approval filled the air. The children stomped their feet and pounded their fists on the chairs. It was pointless to attempt to contain the applause, and the principal was too amused to try. With every clap and yell, I thought my heart would burst.

I held the camera to my face to hide my tears. I was filled with love and pride for the daughter who had given her father her complete trust—and relieved that I had been worthy of it.

Lanny Zechar

Papa's Gift to Kelsey

I have often thought what a melancholy world it would be without children; and what an inhuman world without the aged.

Samuel Taylor Coleridge

My father was a very warm and caring man, quick to lend a hand to anyone who needed it. I always looked up to my father and deeply admired his way with people.

He was in a care center for years after suffering a series of strokes that impaired his ability to walk and caused his speech to be slow and slurred. It pained me very much to see him there, and we tried to visit him several times a month. My toddler daughter, Kelsey, read stories to him, and he lay listening as her imagination ran wild, pretending to read words from the books she held in her tiny hands. They loved each other dearly, and he was her "Papa."

Kelsey was only four years old when Dad died. I was distraught for weeks, and Kelsey tried to comfort me. Oftentimes she cried with me or tried in some way to make me feel better. Nothing helped. I needed my father on this Earth, and sometimes my heart ached so badly I thought it might burst from sadness.

While we were preparing to go to my in-laws' for Thanksgiving, I heard Kelsey talking to her daddy. They were chatting about Papa and how he had gone to heaven and was now watching over us. She said in the sweetest voice, "Daddy, since Mama doesn't have a daddy anymore, do you think you could just share yours with her?"

Laughing and crying, I thought my heart would burst.

From that day on, my grief eased. I knew my father had given Kelsey gifts of compassion, sympathy and concern for others.

He would live on forever, in her.

Sonja Walder

Humor Me

The thought of our past years in me doth breed a perpetual benediction.

William Wordsworth

"Hey, let's go to the beach before we leave," Dad said out of the blue.

Even though I had been raised in Florida, I never really liked the beach—too much sun and sand. "Why?" I asked warily.

"I just want to see the ocean one last time," Dad said wistfully. I couldn't think of a good reason to say no, so I decided to humor him.

The sun's rays beat down on the roof of the car. Intermittently, we were either at a dead stop or a slow crawl. I had forgotten how hot March could be in Florida. I had also forgotten it was spring break. A long line of cars filled with nubile young bodies stretched ahead of us as far as the eye could see.

Dad interrupted my thoughts. "Try the AC again."

"Donna said it doesn't work. Frank was going to get it

fixed, before . . . " My voice trailed off. To humor Dad, I flipped the dial. Hot air blasted us in the face.

We had come "home" to Florida to attend the funeral of my father's youngest brother. Ever since Frank's death, Dad was convinced he was going to leave this world next. On the flight to Florida, he again regaled me with all the little details he thought I needed to know—where his will was filed, who held life insurance policies, and other important information.

"Dad, we've been over this a thousand times," I reminded him. "I know where it all is. We've taken care of everything. I don't know what you're so worried about, anyway. You're as healthy as a horse. We walk every morning—you even do your exercises. *I* can't even touch my toes the way you can. I wish you would get this silly thought of dying out of your head."

"Both my father and his father died young," my dad reminded me.

"Yeah," I said, "and you were sure you were going to die at fifty-nine, remember? In case you haven't noticed, you're seventy-one!"

"Will you just humor me?" Dad finally countered. "This is probably my last trip home to Florida, and I want to enjoy it."

After Frank's funeral, Dad had taken the time to visit with each of his remaining cousins for the "last time." His father had been one of twelve children, so the task was daunting.

The whoops and whistles of the teens in the car ahead brought me back to the present. If my memory served me correctly, the bridge to the beach island was still a couple of miles ahead. I was tempted to turn around, but I knew this would be our last chance to make the pilgrimage before our return flight home.

We were moving slowly now, and after an eternity we

crossed the bridge to the beach road. "Take a left here,"
Dad suggested. I turned onto the main stretch that ran the
length of the island. We drove back and forth on that road
several times looking for a public parking spot. I spied an
opening in the back of a lot and made my way to the
space. It was marked, "Police Parking Only."

"I guess we don't have to stay," Dad grumbled.

"We came all this way, broiled waiting to cross the
bridge and braved the spring break crowds. We are going
to see the ocean!" I vowed.

It was then I saw a store right across from the beach.
"Maybe if we buy something, they'll let us park in their lot
for a few minutes."

"It's a tourist trap," Dad protested.

"Do you want to see the ocean or not?"

Dad's reluctance quickly melted away.

Inside, the store brimmed with shell dolls, starfish cre-
ations and dolphin candles. I bought a hair clip and
explained our situation to the proprietor. "We'll only stay
a few minutes," I assured him. "Dad wants to see the beach
one last time."

He eyed us up and down carefully, and then a broad
smile transformed his face. I realized then what a sight we
were, Dad and I. He was dressed in his regulation khakis
and a short-sleeved shirt. His required white T-shirt, a last
vestige from his Air Force days, peeked out at the collar.
Lace-up shoes and brown socks completed the outfit. My
ensemble was no less amusing—dark jeans, a long-
sleeved cotton shirt, socks and tennis shoes. "Go ahead
and go." The storeowner gave his permission. I think he
knew we wouldn't be staying long. We'd die of heatstroke,
dressed as we were.

We crossed the street and descended the stairs. It
wasn't the beach of Dad's childhood. The coastline had
been ravaged by progress. It wasn't even the beach of my

childhood. No, every square inch of sand seemed to be covered by towels, umbrellas and near-naked bodies. But the sand, the surf and the horizon were the same, timeless.

"Scoop up some of that sand," Dad suggested, pointing to the snow-white crystals on the beach below. He handed me a paper cup he must have carried from the car. I didn't want to walk across the sand. I was wearing sneakers—once sand gets in, it never gets out! But I decided to humor him. I filled the cup and handed it back to Dad. He poured a bit of it into his hand and let the silky granules slip between his twisted fingers. Then his eyes went to the coastline once more. "See those shells over there? The kids would like them. Grab a few, please." I went over and selected several pretty ones. Dad nestled them into the sand in his cup, and then turned to me. "We can go now," he said contentedly.

We headed to the car and made our way off the island and back to my aunt's house.

Not long after we returned home to Colorado, Dad was diagnosed with terminal lung cancer—the same monster that had killed his brother. He died six months later.

We were constant companions until the end.

The sand and shells we collected sit in a jar on my mantle. Sometimes, I take the jar down and let the sand trickle through my fingers as I remember Dad's last trip to the beach. I'm glad I humored him.

Lynn Dean

Baseball Game Plan

In his heart a man plans his course, but the Lord determines his steps.

Proverbs 16:9

When her father died of a heart attack, Kelli was a nine-year-old little girl with blonde hair and hazel eyes. She first came into my life when I met her mother in 1986. Carolyn and I were married that same year. I had one son, Kevin, from my previous marriage, and Kelli was the daughter I never thought I'd have. I never tried to replace her father, only to be her dad and a good friend. Over the years, she and I gained a closeness few step-relationships ever hope to attain. She and Kevin were by my side through the good times and the not-so-good. I watched her with pride through dance recitals and volleyball games, through high-school proms and college gradua-tion. I saw her grow from a little kid in pigtails to a beau-tiful, mature and successful woman. Even when she was twenty-five years old, living in Texas and in a serious rela-tionship, she and I were best friends.

That summer of 2002, I fulfilled a childhood dream—going to historic Fenway Park in Boston. A young man sitting next to my wife and me leaned over and politely asked if he could get us something from the concession stand. As a Texas sportswriter for over thirty years, I'd been to hundreds of games and *never* had a total stranger be so considerate. I was struck by the thoughtfulness of this twenty-five-year-old man from Maine. I liked Dave the moment we met. We visited throughout the game about sports, our families and my grandkids. Afterward, we continued to keep in contact through e-mails and phone calls. When Carolyn and I were in New England to visit our grandchildren, Dave and I got together again and became close friends.

In October the following year, Dave and I drove to Boston to watch the Yankees and the Red Sox in an exciting playoff game. After the game, I telephoned Kelli in Texas just to say "hi." During my conversation, for no reason, I handed my cell phone to Dave to say "hello" to her. It was the first time they'd spoken. Although he spent only a few minutes on the phone with her, he told me he felt like he had known her for years and remarked how he wished she wasn't married.

To his disbelief, I told him she wasn't. Two days later, he called her in Texas, and their relationship took off. Over the next three weeks they talked for hours late into the night, learning more about each other in a month than some married couples know in years. Dave and Kelli admitted then that they had finally found the person they had been looking for all their lives. We didn't take them seriously at first. But it didn't take long to see it was the real thing. Kelli eventually moved to Maine, and she and Dave got engaged on Valentine's Day 2004. One of the proudest moments of my life was when I walked her down the aisle of St. Patrick's Catholic Church in Portland,

Maine, and placed her hand firmly in the hands of Dave Walton for what I know will be a lifetime of happiness.

I know I'm not the reason they fell in love. God just used me and baseball to fulfill his game plan.

Larry Bodin

Who Giveth?

A father is always making his baby into a little woman. And when she is a woman he turns her back again.

Enid Bagnold

A cozy kitchen may not seem like the most romantic setting for a Christmas Eve proposal, but it didn't stop me from whispering "Yes" as Tom slipped a diamond ring on my finger.

But when he announced our engagement to my parents, the atmosphere in the living room was not quite as comfortable. After an interminably long silence, my father said, "I suppose she said 'yes.'" Tom, taken aback, nodded tentatively.

"Well, Tom," Dad said, "I think you should know I never give anything away cheerfully."

Although we realized his response had nothing to do with Tom but everything to do with a father's reluctance to part with his youngest offspring, it was definitely an uncomfortable moment. Mother broke the tension with expressions of joy.

Over the next months, Dad observed our wedding preparations from the sidelines. By May, he was fitted for his wedding attire, apparently reconciled to giving me away.

However, a month later, when our entire wedding party
gathered in the kitchen for a late-night snack following the
evening rehearsal, Dad was unusually quiet amid the chatter.

"I can't do it!" he finally burst out.

"Can't do what?" we all chorused. I caught my breath.
Surely he wouldn't refuse to give me away at the last minute.

At long last, his voice broke the awful silence. "When
the minister says, 'Who giveth this woman?' I can't say, 'I
do.' I think I should say, 'Her mother and I do.'"

With deep sighs of relief, we assured him that he should
say whatever felt right.

Our wedding day dawned bright and sunny. As we
waited in the vestry of the old, gray stone church, the clear
notes of my sister's final solo, "O Promise Me," rang out.
When the organist struck the opening chords of the wedding march, I took Dad's arm. Together we walked down
the center aisle.

Step, pause. Step, pause. A photograph of the moment
shows me as a radiant bride; Dad was not smiling. All eyes
were on us as we approached the altar and my handsome
groom.

"Dearly beloved, we are gathered here . . ." the pastor
began. Looking directly at Dad, he posed *the question.*
"Who giveth this woman to be wedded to this man?"

Dad was ready. He never missed a beat.

In clear, measured tones, he replied, "Her mother."

With that, he placed my hand in Tom's, turned and took
his place beside my astonished mother in the front pew.

Just as he'd vowed from the beginning, Dad *didn't* give
me away cheerfully. Or—for that matter—at all!

S. Maitland Schrecengost

Long-Distance Vitamins

Sweetest melodies are those that are by distance made more sweet.

William Wordsworth

We arrived at the hospital to find Dad exhausted and weak, but his smile was as sure as ever. It was another bout of pneumonia. My husband and I stayed with him for the weekend but had to return to our jobs by Monday morning. Local relatives would see that Dad got home from the hospital, and they would look in on him regularly and prepare his meals. They would make sure he got his daily medicine and take him to his doctor appointments. But I longed to be able to let him know that we cared, too, even when we weren't with him.

Then I remembered a family tradition I initiated when our children were small. When leaving their grandparents' home after a visit, each child would hide a love note in the house for their grandfather or grandmother to find after we were gone. They hid notes in the cereal box, to be poured into their bowls the next morning. They'd tuck a note under a hairbrush, in a deck of cards, next to the phone or even in the microwave. For days after our departure, their grandparents would smile as they discovered these reminders of our love.

So as I tidied Dad's kitchen and made up a bed for him downstairs in the living room, I began writing notes. Some were practical. "Dad, I froze the casserole that was in the fridge so it wouldn't spoil." Some expressed my love. "Dad, I hope you sleep well in your new bed." Most notes were downstairs where he would be confined for several weeks until he regained strength, but one note I hid upstairs under his pillow. "Dad, if you have found this note, you must be feeling better. We are so glad!"

While others cared for Dad's day-to-day needs, we, of course, would stay in touch by phone. But our notes were a tangible reminder of our love and concern for him during this recovery period. Just like his medicines boosted him physically, these "emotional vitamins" would boost his spiritual health.

Several weeks later, in one of our regular phone calls, I asked Dad how he was doing. He said, "I'll tell you how I'm doing. I just found your note under my upstairs pillow!"

Emily Chase

The Best "Father-Daughter Date" Ever!

Music is the art of the prophets, the only art that can calm the agitations of the soul; it is one of the most magnificent and delightful presents God has given us.

Martin Luther

In early May 1996, my twelve-year-old son, Bobby, and I took a two-week trip with my dad, Rev. Dale McClain. We drove from Venice, Florida, to Stone Mountain, Georgia, to visit my brother. I was recently divorced and considering a possible move to Georgia or North Carolina, depending on the outcome of several interviews I had scheduled during our time there.

What a trip that turned out to be! Bobby, Dad and I told jokes and funny stories all the way to Stone Mountain. I can't remember when I've laughed that much! Traveling with Dad was always a real treat. Unlike the stereotypical "man on a mission," Dad always took time to stop and enjoy the sights. A beautiful sunset? We'd pull over so we could really see it! If anyone even *hinted* at being hungry,

Dad immediately found a place to eat. He could turn getting a cup of coffee into an event.

After a few days in Stone Mountain, Dad and I left for
North Carolina where I had an interview at Montreat
College. Leaving Bobby with the family in Georgia, Dad
and I took off for another wonderful adventure together,
just the two of us on our "father-daughter date," as Dad
always called them. Our dates had spanned the globe,
from India to Hong Kong to America. Dad was there,
enriching me in every phase of my metamorphosis from
toddler to teen to woman.

Some missionary kids—or MKs as we are called—grow
up feeling a constant lack of their father's attention. I was
blessed as a child in that I didn't have that experience.
Dad was the most sentimental man I've ever known. No
matter how intense the schedule, somehow he always
took time to be with his children and, often, with each of
us individually. I never felt deprived. Dad could cram
more love and fun into one game of Monopoly than many
fathers do in an entire summer. He never communicated a
sense of obligation as a parent; on the contrary, I knew
Dad's greatest delight was to be with his family.

We shared memories like these and many more on the
scenic drive to Montreat College. As we walked up a steep
incline to the campus, Dad seemed very weak. I wondered
if his pulmonary fibrosis was acting up. His lungs were
damaged years earlier while ministering in the Philippines
where the air was thick with volcanic ash. He had already
lived about eight years longer than the doctors projected.
They had been good, strong years for the most part. But
on this day, he seemed especially weary, older than his
seventy-four years.

On our way back to Stone Mountain, Dad and I stopped
in at The Cove, Billy Graham's restful retreat tucked in the
mountains near Asheville. We particularly wanted to see

the prayer chapel, a beautiful two-story building built among tall pines and glassed in on the second floor. The receptionist told us it was almost closing time, but encouraged us to go upstairs and enjoy a few minutes together anyway.

We were the only ones in the chapel. A late afternoon sun bathed the quiet room in a warm, almost sacred glow. It was so peaceful. God's presence was there. As we walked hand in hand toward the front, we noticed a beautiful, old grand piano. Reading my thoughts Dad said, "Carol, I'm sure they wouldn't mind if you played something. It's just the two of us anyway."

That's all the encouragement I needed! The piano, shipped from Germany, was over one hundred years old. The wood was beautiful, as were the old ivory keys. It was almost surreal, playing that magnificent old piano for my dad in such a serene setting.

I deliberately played the hymns and choruses I knew he loved the most: "And Can It Be," "When I Survey the Wondrous Cross" and "So Send I You." When I looked out at Dad, my heart melted. He was sitting about four rows back, looking at me, tears streaming down his cheeks. Just then the receptionist came in the back and walked to join us.

"That is so beautiful, dear," she kindly said to me. "Where did you learn to play like that?"

"From her mother," Dad replied, with obvious pride. "Her mother plays like an angel and has blessed people all over the world with her gift. My daughter has it, too." Dad wiped the tears away.

"Would you mind if we sang a song together?" she asked me. "I love 'Amazing Grace.'"

And so the three of us sang all the stanzas of that great hymn. When the song ended, the presence of God was so real that we reverently left the chapel without speaking.

The rest of the drive blurs in my memory. I recall Dad holding my hand most of the time as I drove. But something he told me stands out as a bright jewel, a gift I will always cherish.

I said, "Dad, it was so touching for me to look up and see you crying. I knew you were missing Mother and remembering a lifetime of listening to her play the piano."

"Oh, no, Honey. That's not what I was thinking at all. While I was listening to you play, my mind traveled back over the years to the night I drove six hours from Ohio to Lexington, Kentucky." I knew this story well, but dearly loved hearing it again. "I had just preached the closing sermon in a week of meetings. Your dear mother insisted that I keep my speaking commitment, even though your birth was already two weeks late. A man walked up to me with a big grin, held his hand out, and said, 'Congratulations, Rev. McClain, you're a father!'"

Dad's hand covered mine as he continued. "I was remembering barging into the hospital where a very large nurse tried to catch me as I raced down the hall. She said, 'Excuse me, sir! You can't just come in here in the middle of the night to visit your wife!' I told her, 'Well, I'm Rev. McClain. My daughter is three days old, and I haven't seen her yet!' And that nurse said, 'Oh! We've been waiting for you, Rev. McClain. Come right this way.'"

Now *I* was the one crying.

"I was thinking about you, and how I've loved being your daddy. You could not possibly have brought me more joy than you have, Carol."

Holding hands, we drove and hummed and prayed on what would be our last date. What a legacy for a father to give his daughter.

Carol McClain Bassett

I'm Confessin' That I Love You

Music, in the best sense, does not require novelty; nay, the older it is, and the more we are accustomed to it, the greater its effect.

Goethe

It was 1957, and I was twelve years old. Dad, who was a music buff, took me to an early evening concert at Valley Junior College. This was a rare event because he was usually grinding out courses in management, hoping to advance his career at a local California aerospace company. His real passion was jazz, and this particular night gave us the exciting opportunity to see Louis "Satchmo" Armstrong. We fidgeted in annoying, fold-up chairs but counted ourselves lucky to be seated directly in front of a special platform built to accommodate the large crowd gathering to see Louis and his "All Stars."

Louis stepped casually onto the stage, chuckled slyly and pattered, "We really gonna lay somethin' on ya!"

I was mesmerized from the instant the first electric notes were struck. Dad had played Louis's records for me many times, but they paled compared to the real thing. The drummer shimmied as if in a trance when he beat his rhythm; the trombone player sent soft, slide tones soaring; the clarinetist oozed sweet melody and pitch. Added to this was the vivacious vocal performance of the hefty Vilma Middletown, who nearly brought down the house, as well as the makeshift stage, which wobbled precariously as she bounced and swayed to the beat of each intricate piece. Music came pouring out of them, exploding in tempo and energy. Dad's toes tapped wildly, and my heart pounded uncontrollably along with the pulsating tempo.

The perspiration on Louis's brow glistened almost as much as his battered but glittering trumpet. From the crack of the opening note, his performance was a dazzling display of virtuosity and inspiration, earning his reputation as an improvisational genius.

His endurance and power were legendary, his singing style as original as his trumpet playing. His lips were iron, and his lungs had the strength of a hurricane, blending and twisting notes in his unexcelled technique. He bent notes as he sang, just as he did when he played. He growled and grated, grunted and wheezed. And his gregarious spirit was nothing less than infectious.

Then, something extraordinary happened. Just as Louis lowered his horn at the end of a tune, a small object flew off the stage. I glanced down to see a burnished brass object laying at my feet. It was a trumpet mouthpiece. I sat transfixed, staring reverently at the object as though it were something sacred. This was not just any mouthpiece. This was the Hope Diamond of trumpet mouthpieces. It was Louis's, and through it, he shared his soul with the world. Dad urged me to pick it up. Slowly, I reached out and cupped it tentatively in my trembling hands.

As I lifted it from the floor, I heard a gravelly voice

above me say in a secretive tone, "Careful now, it's ver-ry hot!" I looked up into a face that seemed sculpted from the Earth's own clay, a pair of soft twinkling eyes and a generous mouth grinning fully at me. I nestled the mouthpiece into the handkerchief Louis extended to me. He enfolded it along with my hands and, with a gentle squeeze, cocked his head to one side, winked at me and purred, "This next one's just for you, Honey."

As he belted out, "I'm Confessin' That I Love You," Dad stretched his arm around me proudly and sang along unabashedly. I was spellbound—not only by Louis's song, but also by Dad's love for me.

Louis is gone now and so is Dad, but that melody and that magical moment still linger in my heart. I still hear Dad's jubilant voice, those golden notes dripping like honey from Louis's horn, and together we murmur the words that had become his signature expression: "Oh, yeah!"

JoAnn Semones

Father of Fortune

Once again, the Christmas season was upon us. And once again, my daughter Tania was asking, "What do you want for Christmas, Dad?"

"The usual," I replied. After twenty-three years, she knew that this meant boxer shorts and some happy socks, the kind that help that tender old bunion. These were Christmas rituals for me.

In the small town of Peterborough, Ontario, where we lived, life had a certain rhythm, and the festive season was full of ritual. After living in Calgary for many years, I had returned to my hometown to be near my own aging dad, and life took on a fairly predictable sort of rhythm. But this particular year, my daughter, Tania, and her young husband, Barry, changed all that.

Every day for two weeks prior to Christmas, unable to contain her excitement, she repeatedly said, "You'll never guess, but you're going to love what we got you for Christmas!" The girl was relentless in her teasing and her quest for my reaction. She was determined that I should be impressed.

Now, I'm no Scrooge, so please don't get me wrong. I'm simply one of those individuals who's been around for some time and who's gotten a bit cynical and hard to impress. I must admit, however, that it was fun to watch and listen to her excitement and enthusiastic teasing day after day. Her joy and anticipation of my reaction to this special gift was contagious. By the morning of Christmas Eve, I had become more than a little curious.

At 11:00 A.M. on the 24th, my wife and I were asked to join the kids for some last-minute shopping. We elected to opt out. My wife wanted to finish up her own festive preparations, and old Dad, well, I just wanted a cold beer and a snooze. Four hours later, the kids were back at the door, shopping mission completed.

"We have your gift out in the car, Dad," Tania exclaimed, "and it's getting cold!"

We were then not asked, but ordered to vacate the premises. No, not just to another room, but upstairs and out of sight with an emphatic, "No peeking!" command. Heck, my old army sergeant was gentler. "Get out! Get out!" Tania ordered.

So, obediently, we retreated upstairs.

The minutes passed in that odd kind of anxious, wondering, quiet anticipation that makes butterflies in your stomach. We strained our ears but couldn't hear anything.

"Big deal," I grumped to myself. "I'm still not impressed, but I'll play their silly game."

Then we heard them hollering, "Okay, you can come down now!"

Descending the stairs, we were directed into the front room where the surprise Christmas gift was waiting to be opened. Immediately, my excited daughter said, "No waiting until Christmas morning. Open it now!"

"Okay," I said. "This is highly irregular, this is breaking the ritual . . . but what the heck is it?" I wondered out loud. The three-foot-square, irregularly shaped lump over by the tree was smothered under blankets. Out came Tania's camera, and the guessing game started in earnest.

"Maybe it's a pinball machine," my wife offered.

"No, no," I said. "It's gotta be something perishable, otherwise they wouldn't have been so anxious to bring it in out of the cold. Maybe it's a crate of Florida oranges, or maybe it's a puppy!"

By now, my daughter was about to explode with excitement, and I, too, had passed the stage of mildly curious, feeling somewhere between inquisitive and demanding.

"What on earth can it be?" I asked as I felt the lumpy object, looking for a clue. My daughter sharply rapped my knuckles with a classic, "Da-ad!"

Finally, we arrived at the unveiling. "Okay," Tania instructed us, "on the count of three both of you grab a corner of the blanket." She stood by with the camera, and even though I was trying my best to remain unimpressed, I'd by now reached an emotional state ranging from paranoia to frustration. My heartbeat sped. My wife and I lifted the blanket in one fell swoop, and the gift was exposed.

The next few minutes were a blur. My heart pounded. The blood rushed to my head. My stomach contracted. My mind jumbled. Overwhelmed with astonishment, I thought, *I can't believe my eyes! Perhaps I am delusional! This is just not possible!*

The flash of my daughter's camera went off when, rising up out of that heap of blankets and wrapping me in an enormous bear hug was none other than my six-foot-two, one hundred and seventy-five pound first-born son Greg, home for Christmas for the first time in nineteen years!

Ted Bosley

Daddy's Little Tomboy

What gift of Providence bestowed on man is so dear to him as his children?

Cicero

Thanks to her father's coaching, nine-year-old Kathy could outpitch, outshoot and outrun most of her classmates in baseball, basketball and touch football. So when she was invited to be a flower girl at her cousin's wedding, no one was more surprised than her father that she accepted.

Up to then, blonde, blue-eyed Kathy showed little interest in dressing up. While she wore skirts and sweaters to school and church, she preferred wearing jeans and T-shirts and playing with neighborhood kids in the park across the street from our home.

Each time we shopped for her wedding attire, her enthusiasm for the impending nuptial ceremony increased while her interest in sports decreased. This prompted her father to comment, "I think our little tomboy is ready to be more feminine."

At the rehearsal party, Kathy listened intently to the bride's instructions on what was expected of a flower girl. All the way home, she bubbled with excitement. "I promise to make you proud of me tomorrow. I won't chew gum, make funny faces, get boisterous or act silly."

The next morning, decked out in new dresses, hats, shoes and gloves, we went outside and waited beneath the glistening August sun in the clear, azure sky while Jim went to get the car.

Smiling, Kathy waited expectantly while her father backed the car out of the garage. Her smile turned to stunned amazement when he backed past us, entered the street and took off without her!

"Daddy! Daddy!" Kathy's new shoes clomped against the sidewalk, and her curly hair bounced as she raced after his car, waving her arms and shouting, "Daddy, stop! Stop! You forgot us!"

She kept shouting until he disappeared around the corner. Tears streaked her cheeks as she sobbed and sulked back home. "How could Daddy pass by me when he knows what an important day this is?"

She had barely finished blubbering when her father pulled up to the curb and parked where we stood. "Sorry," he sheepishly apologized. "I'm so used to backing out and heading for the office, I forgot we were going to a wedding!"

Without comment, Kathy climbed into the car, smoothed the folds of her dress, straightened her hat and dabbed at her eyes with a tissue. Her father's efforts to engage her in conversation were met with sullen silence.

When we reached the church, Kathy quietly joined the bridal party, and her dad and I were escorted to a pew. When the organ music began, we glanced toward the back of the church where the nuptial entourage had assembled. Kathy looked radiant in her princess-style, rose taffeta dress that harmonized with the attendants' gowns.

Keeping perfect time to the music, she proceeded down the aisle carrying her flower basket. Smiling, she scattered multicolored rose petals onto the white runner.

"I sure hope my goof-up didn't upset her too much," my husband whispered as the procession strolled toward the altar.

Keeping time with the music, Kathy approached our pew. When her eyes met her father's, her smile faded and her eyes glared at him. Scooping her hand into the flower basket, she cupped her fingers around fragile flora and tightened her grip as if clutching a baseball. Then she raised her hand and drew it back as if preparing to hurl a fastball. Her father tensed and held his breath. Still keeping time to the music, Kathy gracefully opened her fingers and tossed rose petals into the air. As some cascaded over her dad's head, she winked, grinned mischievously and, without missing a beat, continued toward the altar.

Sally Kelly-Engeman

Father's Secret

Home is the seminary of all other institutions.
                                        Edwin Hubbell Chapin

I am frequently the brunt of family jokes because I have no sense of direction. Once, when we were discussing death and the hereafter, my son jokingly remarked, "Well, I certainly hope there are heavenly guides, Mother, otherwise, you will never find the way."

I smiled and assured him that I wasn't worried. "I'll just watch for the hill with the privet hedge," I said. When his eyebrows came together in a questioning frown, I hastened to tell him a story about my father.

Pop was raised in a fatherless home at a time when government assistance was unheard of. The family of five struggled mightily to survive. That Spartan upbringing caused my father to be extremely tightfisted.

When we children—two older brothers and myself— became aware that other children got spending money from their parents, we made the mistake of asking Pop for some. His face turned stone cold. "If you're old enough to ask, you're old enough to earn," he rumbled. And so, when the need arose, we scurried about the neighborhood seeking odd jobs or peddling produce from the garden.

His attitude didn't soften as we grew into adulthood and drifted away to jobs or college. There was a period of time when none of us had a car, so we had to ride the bus whenever we came home. Though the bus stopped about two miles from home, Pop never met us, even in inclement weather. If someone grumbled (and my brothers grumbled a lot), he'd say in his loudest father-voice, "That's what your legs are for!"

So when I went away to college, I knew I was in for a long walk whenever I came home. The walk didn't bother me as much as the fear of walking alone along the highway and country roads. I also felt less than valued that my father didn't seem concerned about my safety. That feeling was canceled one spring evening.

It had been a particularly difficult week at college. Tests and long hours in labs had left me exhausted. I longed for home and a soft bed. As other students were met at their stops, I gazed wistfully out the window. Finally, the bus shuddered to a stop at my destination point, and I stepped off, lugging my suitcase to begin the long trek home.

A row of privet hedge edged the driveway that climbed the hill to our house. Once I had turned off the highway to start the last lap of my journey, I was always relieved to see the hedge because it meant that I was almost home.

On that particular evening, the hedge had just come into view when a gentle rain began to fall. I stopped to put a book in my suitcase and when I stood up, I saw something gray skimming along the top of the hedge, moving toward the house. Upon closer observation, I realized it was the top of my father's head. Then I knew—each time I'd come home, he had stood behind the hedge, watching, until he knew I had arrived safely. I swallowed hard against the threatening tears. He did care, after all.

On subsequent visits, that spot of gray became my beacon. I could hardly wait until I was close enough to watch for its covert movement above the greenery. Upon reaching home, I would find my father sitting innocently in his chair. "So! It's you!" he'd say, his face lengthening into mock surprise.

"So you see," I told my son, "I'm not worried about finding my way to heaven when I die." There may be light at the end of a tunnel, as many who have cheated death have reported, but beyond that, I think I'll see a row of privet hedge climbing a hill, and my father will be waiting at the top. "So! It's you!" he'll say.

And I'll reply as I did then, "Yes, Pop, it's me. I'm home."

Betty Stanley

Two Fathers and a Bride

Remembrance is the only paradise out of which we cannot be driven away.

Jean Paul Richter

My daughters were ten and twelve years old when their father died. Among the shattered dreams was the reality that some day they would marry the men of their dreams, and their father wouldn't be there to walk them down the aisle.

My husband, Gerry, was a motorcycle officer in the Royal Canadian Mounted Police. In the spring of 1990, my worst fears were realized when he was hit by a car while driving the police bike. His injuries were extensive and included multiple broken bones, lacerations to his face, arms and chest, massive bruising and a severe brain injury.

Our girls, Myriah and Dale, braved the turmoil like little soldiers, though it wasn't easy for them. When Gerry first came home from the hospital, the girls understood that he wasn't able to go outside and play with them, or take them fishing in the creek, or help them with their math and reading as he had done in the past. But as the weeks progressed and then turned into months, it was harder and harder for them to comprehend. Then five months after the crash, he died at home of a heart attack.

After Gerry died, I doubted that the possibility of feeling joy would exist again. But it did. Within two years, I met and married Lyle, a wonderful man with three beautiful children. It was wonderful to be in love again, and the girls and I were thrilled to have a new family.

For the next ten years, the kids kept us busy with school, activities and all the usual trials and tribulations that go along with raising children. We eagerly assumed full responsibility as mother and father to all five of the children. Still, in the back of my mind I knew that one day, one of my daughters would take that special walk down the aisle of a church. And no matter how much Lyle loved her and did what he could to be a father to her, a void would remain because Gerry could not take her on his arm and walk her to the man of her dreams.

As expected, the day finally came when Myriah and her boyfriend of five years announced their engagement. Wedding plans consumed our days and our nights for the better part of the next eighteen months. All the while, I remembered the dreams Gerry and I shared of him escorting the girls on their wedding day—her wearing a magnificent gown and he fully adorned in his dress uniform of red serge, boots and breeches.

As the wedding quickly approached, I realized how sad I felt about Gerry not being there to participate. I knew, even after all these years, this sadness was as much about my pain and sorrow as it was about my daughter's. I was grieving that I would not dance with him or watch him waltz her around the ballroom. In reflecting on my feelings, I was astounded with an incredible idea for a beautiful ritual to include him in her wedding ceremony.

The day of the wedding was drenched in sunshine. Leaves of red and gold scattered, colorfully blanketing the ground. As I sat at the front of the church excitedly waiting for the spectacular event to begin, the harpist plucked away at the strings of her instrument. Soon, the wedding march commanded our heads to turn.

First down the aisle came the two flower girls and the ring bearer. Following them were the bridesmaids and my younger daughter, Dale, the maid of honor. Immediately following her marched Nathan, my brother, who was a sheriff, and next to him was Amelia, a close friend and officer that Gerry had trained, both wearing their official dress uniforms. Nathan carried the folded Canadian flag that had adorned Gerry's casket at his funeral, and Amelia held Gerry's Stetson hat. They reached the front of the church and reverently placed the hat and flag on a white pedestal. They turned to face Myriah and Lyle, as he walked her down the aisle.

When the bride's shoes made one final click on the shiny tile floor at the front of the altar, the officers raised their arms in a magnificent salute. At that moment, when their gloved hands graced the tips of their hats, I knew the hearts of two fathers beat as one.

Janelle Breese Biagioni

Roadside Rescue

The guardian angels of life sometimes fly so high as to be beyond our sight, but they are always looking down on us.

Jean Paul Richter

It's a good thing the summer wedding was beautiful, because the rest of the day was nothing but problems. My friend John and I had borrowed Dad's car to attend the wedding of our college friend 150 miles away. Shortly after our venture began, John discovered he had forgotten his wallet at home. Later, at the restaurant, I realized I had left my driver's license in the jeans I'd worn the night before. Then, on the way home, John got really sick. He took out his contacts and slumped in the seat next to me, holding his stomach and looking pale.

That's when the car died at the side of the interstate. Over and over again, I turned the key, pumped the accelerator and rocked with the sound of the groaning engine.

"Where's my guardian angel when I need her?" I moaned. Dad had recently shared with Mom and me two books he had received on angels working in our lives. Each of the stories was fascinating and believable. I always knew I had a guardian angel, yet questioned if I had ever personally experienced it.

"It's seven o'clock," John said, squinting at his watch. "We'd better walk back to that gas station before it closes."

So I led my visually impaired, nauseated friend down the shoulder of the highway. It was hard to tell if he was sweating from the ninety-six-degree heat or from his fever. My white high heels clicked on the pavement, and the strand of imitation pearls clung to my neck as we trudged along the roadside.

I called Dad from the gas station and listened to his mechanic's advice. If his suggestions didn't work, I'd have to call a tow truck.

"It's 7:15," Mom said into the speaker phone. "If you aren't back on the road in one hour, call again so we know how you're doing." She tried not to worry about me now that I was in college, but at times like these, I knew she couldn't help it.

John and I plodded back down the scorching pavement to the car and tried Dad's long-distance advice. The car coughed and choked, but refused to start.

I draped myself over the steering wheel. "What if no one stops to help us?"

"What if someone does?" John worried out loud. He propped his aching head on the dashboard while we swapped tales of horrible crimes along the highway.

At 7:50, we admitted our defeat and traipsed across the highway to walk back to the gas station. Just then, a white, dilapidated station wagon sputtered to a stop in front of our car. I could see the two male occupants through the missing rear window. The driver's long, stringy hair touched the shoulders of his ragged shirt. As we stood across the road from them, John and I agreed they looked pretty rough.

"And we look pretty rich," John said, motioning to our wedding attire. "Think they'll believe we're poor college students?"

"Need some help?" the driver hollered. His smile leered through his scraggly beard. "I know some 'bout cars." As we headed back across the interstate, we could see the sleeves had been torn from the denim jacket he was wearing. His tall, leather moccasins had fringe hanging just beneath the knees of his holey blue jeans.

"I always knew my guardian angel would be unique," I teased in a whisper. "Maybe he will help us."

"Or rob us," John cautioned as we crossed the highway.

A second unshaven man silently exited the car. I thanked them both for stopping and, with trembling hands, released the hood, hoping I wasn't making a big mistake in letting them help us.

The driver bent over the car engine. I read the back of his worn jacket: Christian Motorcycle Association. John and I beamed at each other. I nodded and winked—and breathed a sigh of relief.

Within minutes, the car was running, and the four of us stood together smiling and shaking hands. John and I each offered them the only money we had with us—five dollars each, some of it in change. They accepted it gratefully saying it was more than they'd had in a long time.

I drove home, collapsed in the chair and recounted my "guardian angel" story to my parents.

Mom's face was serious. "What time did they stop?"

I thought for a minute. "About ten 'til eight."

She smiled at Dad. "I looked at my watch at 7:50 and said to Dad, 'Let's pray an angel stops to help her.'"

Dad said, "That's when I sent you mine."

Christie Rogers

5

ON GRATITUDE

Grace and gratitude belong together like heaven and Earth. Gratitude evokes grace like the voice and echo. Gratitude follows grace as thunder follows lightning.

Karl Barth

Father Christmas

Presents which our love for the donor has rendered precious are ever the most acceptable.

Ovid

I didn't realize how much Carissa resented me until I became united with her mother. The sweet eleven-year-old did everything she could to sabotage my loving relationship with Paula. No matter what I tried, there were no signs of progress. Carissa would leave her bed at night, claiming bad dreams, and crawl in next to her mom. Each time, I was slowly pushed out, destined to sleep on the cold couch. It was the perfect metaphor for our struggling relationship.

I hung in there, though, doing all I could to stay nice and teach well. With Christmas quickly approaching, I knew I had the perfect opportunity to show Carissa an example of selfless love. I played Santa each year, the location depending on where I was needed most. On the eve of Christmas, without fail, I tore the red suit free from the dry cleaner's plastic wrap and fluffed up the white beard.

Through the years, I faced great criticism for interrupting my own holiday by doing volunteer work. "It's a night only to spend with family and close friends," some said. I chuckled silently. They didn't understand. Though I spent every spare moment I could with those I loved, Christmas Eve could not be any more magical when spent with children who believed in me, Santa. I was hardly being selfless. In fact, it was the opposite. It was a most selfish act. Yet, year after year, I allowed those who sighed heavily to believe I was giving something up. I never let them in on my secret. I never wanted it to end.

As fate would have it, I had two stops planned for this year and wanted to spend both with Carissa. Paula was more than accommodating and insisted on going along.

On our way, I told them about my secret love of playing the jolly fat man.

Our first stop was at a Grange Hall in the country. With a wolves' bite in the air, we hurried for the door. Before Carissa took the first step inside, Gene Autry's version of "Rudolph the Red-Nosed Reindeer" poured out. Paula turned to the fat man in the red suit and smiled. The entire night was going to be filled with magic. We could both feel it.

On the giant square-dance floor, a tight community of people celebrated the holiday the old-fashioned way. They strung popcorn and dried cranberries on a giant Christmas tree. Before anyone could spot me, I bellowed, "HO! HO! HO!" The children came running.

Paula and Carissa stood off to the side to watch. The excitement of the children was contagious and overwhelming. Carissa beamed with the joy, and Paula fought back the tears.

A kind-looking, heavyset woman approached and took my hand, leading me to a chair that had been decorated for Santa. Though the kids hadn't seen it, there was a bag of gifts already waiting to be handed out. I waved Carissa over, and with Paula's gentle prodding, she came. "Pretty girl, can you help Santa hand out the gifts?" I asked in my deep Santa voice.

With dozens of tiny eyes upon her, Carissa nodded and went to work. She handed me a present from the bag. I read out the name and then personally handed it over to the excited child it belonged to. Together, we handed out a bag full of wrapped presents. Toward the end, I caught Carissa staring at me. Seated by the frozen window, her heart was beginning to thaw. She actually smiled, and it made my eyes fill.

Santa and his helpers were invited to share dinner with the townsfolk, and they weren't about to take "no" for an answer. Even through the matted beard, I enjoyed the feast.

Just before I was about to pass out from the heat exhaustion I suffered in the thick suit, we bid our farewell. Walking out of the Grange Hall, the starry night ushered us back into the present. I hurried for the van and, under the cover of darkness, tore off my wig and beard. While Paula and Carissa giggled, I took in the fresh air.

Forty miles later, I donned my wig and beard again. We were in the city, at Santa's last stop of the night.

The snow-swept streets were alive with holiday magic as the three of us stepped out of the van. With the tall buildings blocking the wind, the night felt twenty degrees warmer. With Carissa by my side, we stepped into the Boys Club to meet another pack of underprivileged children. I laughed from my belly, listened to wishes and handed out presents. I looked up again to catch Carissa staring. I smiled, and to my surprise, she returned it. I'd finally made progress and gotten through to her. I wondered then if I'd ever make a real difference in her life.

Upon returning home from the incredible experience, I collapsed in the living room. While I wrestled the sweat-drenched outfit free, Carissa proceeded to the tree.

Escorted by her mother's gentle eyes, she reached under the soft pine, grabbed a neatly wrapped present and handed it to me. "I wanted to give this to you tonight," she whispered before quickly leaving the room.

I pulled off the black boots, wiped my hands on my pants and tore through the wrapping to find a framed essay. Through shocked and misty eyes, I read:

The Person I Admire Most
by Carissa Kennedy

The person I admire most is Steven Manchester . . . he is very funny and most of all he teaches me a lot about life . . . he is a United States veteran . . . he stood tall and fought with honor . . . honor is one of the things he teaches me . . . he also teaches me about respect at home and I think that is pure love . . . Steve teaches me friendship . . . not just with me but with everyone around him . . .

I wiped my eyes. I had already made a difference in Carissa's life. I just needed to remember that such truths are usually left unsaid and are normally invisible to the eye.

Steven H. Manchester

Solemn Images

Gratitude is not only the greatest of virtues, but the parent of all others.

Cicero

God was certainly gracious to us that Sunday. He exercised his authority over the outdoor wedding ceremony, creating the day beautiful and memorable, making all witnesses a bit godlier, the food a bit tastier, and the music perfect in tempo and tune. To answer our additional prayers, God painted the skies a delicate blue and accented them with billowing chiffon clouds. He spiced the air with September crispness. While most leaves were still anchored on their trees, a few strays floated to carpet the green grass with complementary and contrasting colors.

Jennifer had anticipated her wedding day since she skip-marched on other lawns, playing bride with a white pillowcase on her head and an incandescent little-girl smile on her face. She was always a very special daughter, a dependable "stand-up" kid, a great source of joy and pride as Elaine and I watched her grow. We shared Jen's birth cries and smiled through her first steps, her first words, her first giggles. We played tooth fairy and home-work professor. We beamed through school plays, bat mitzvah and graduations. We laughed with her and her little friends, and we shared their lives' anguishes.

My daughter deserved God's perfect day—a day she shared with her David, extended families and friends, a devoted teacher, and her heritage. After all, Jennifer, God and life itself rank high on our pantheon of blessings.

It was my serious, life-threatening illnesses that helped forge the steel of Jen's character and bonded us to life—and *for* life. While photographers captured images of the ceremony and reception on tape and film, Elaine and I revere mental images of the day. And they will warm us forever.

As I escorted my radiantly beautiful, white-gowned daughter to meet her groom, I thanked God for the day and for our good health. And I remembered so many stress-filled days and nights the three of us shared in hos-pital emergency rooms, a rehabilitation facility, nursing homes, a burn unit and two hemodialysis centers. The Gold family knows that life isn't always easy and fair. But Elaine and Jen were always at my side, cheering me on. They were there in the dark of my blindness, when my left leg was sawed off, and when my heart beat like a Buddy Rich drumming extravaganza. They were with me—twice—when caring doctors resuscitated me, and when I endured open-heart surgery and numerous infections, praying each time for God to allow me to share Jen's wedding day.

Jen and I smiled and kissed as I led her to David, under a ritual wedding canopy enriched by messages hand-printed, embroidered and painted by loved ones. Rabbi Peter Kasdan, Jen's longtime teacher, married the couple in an inspiring three-ring ceremony: the bridal couple's platinum wedding bands and a special community ring, one of a dozen saved from Jewish ghettoes of Eastern Europe during the Holocaust. (In those terrible times, new brides and grooms married their fragile communities as well as themselves.)

And so, that Sunday in suburban New Jersey, happy guests and God witnessed a solemn service uniting two lovers—the same God who saw me past death to become part of their living, loving glory during the autumn of my life.

Jen shared her second dance with me. The song was "You Are So Beautiful to Me." As we limp-danced, she smiled her grown-up incandescent smile.

"Life really is good, isn't it, Dad?"

I held back my tears and embraced the pretty white-gowned lady even more tightly in my arms.

Ron Gold

Spelling L-O-V-E

As are families so is society. If well-ordered, well-instructed and well-governed, they are springs from which go forth the streams of national greatness and prosperity, of civil order and public happiness.

William Makepeace Thayer

"Betty! Bonnie! Bob! Paula!"

I blinked awake. The house that a moment before slumbered in early Saturday morning darkness was now alive with lights and groggy children. I pulled the covers back over my head. But it was no use. Daddy had brought us his usual Saturday morning offering of love.

"Good morning, girls!" he boomed. Already dressed for his half-day at work, his cardboard-stiff white shirt, rosy cheeks, prematurely silver hair and beaming smile glowed.

"Here, Bonnie, this is your list of words for this morning. Betty, here's yours. If you learn them right away, you can have some more before I go!"

For in our home, the delightful, carefree wonder of Saturday began, not with a chance to sleep in for a spell, but with spelling itself. As in s-p-e-l-l-i-n-g.

Protests got us nowhere. "Don't worry, children," Daddy would assure us cheerfully. "You'll thank me when you're older. I wish I could have done this when I was your age." And, believe it or not, he meant it!

Harold Compton's love affair with learning began as a precocious four-year-old. Every morning his father, Charlie, left their hardscrabble farm in the hills of Eastern Kentucky for his teaching post at a nearby hamlet. In bad weather, when getting back home over the rutted, muddy roads was impossible, he would board with a student's parents.

The schoolmaster's lot back then was a lonely, hard and poorly paid one. But to his young son, getting to spend the day in a world of books instead of chores seemed the ultimate luxury. And soon Harold's persistent begging broke down his weary father's resolve. After that, Charlie's faithful mule carried both father and son off in the predawn darkness. And soon Harold was blissfully immersed in the three Rs: reading, 'riting and 'rithmetic.

Devouring every book available, young Harold dreamed of high school, Latin, Greek and Shakespeare, and college—and all the wonders such an education would bring. Meanwhile, he wrote poetry in the delicate Spencerian script his father taught him, an art form in itself. He taught himself algebra and geometry from ancient, taped-together books, saved for penny by penny.

Then tragedy struck—his beloved father died. And, in quick succession, so did two brothers and a sister.

As the new head of his family, Harold had four funeral debts to pay and a large family of brothers and sisters to feed. This meant leaving school after the eighth grade for twelve hours a day, six days a week of backbreaking, unskilled labor in fields and forests for fifty cents a day.

But he never gave up his dream. And years later, bypassing high school altogether, he went on to a teachers' training college and became a teacher himself.

Eventually, he left the hills and hollows of Eastern Kentucky for the bustling cities of Chicago and Cincinnati as a highly skilled building estimator for Sears Roebuck's booming ship-to-site housing industry.

World War II brought an end to the housing industry. Immediately Harold became part of the even more booming defense industry.

Then peace. And suddenly he was out of work, his lungs filled with metal shavings. Thus, twenty years after Harold left that Kentucky hollow, he found himself back in it, in poor health, and with a new family of children to care for. His own.

Even there, though, in our tumbledown log cabin near where he himself had grown up, he kept his dream alive. For crowded around its 150-year-old fireplace were our treasures: a piano, crammed-full bookcases, a well-thumbed Bible and a weighty *Merriam-Webster's Unabridged Dictionary.*

Besides running the farm, both he and my mother taught in schools much like the ones they themselves attended as children and taught in as young adults.

Even there, busy as we were, our Saturday-morning spelling tests continued. And so did Harold's self-education. He pored over that dictionary at night by kerosene light, after the last chores were done, memorizing word by word.

And that was not all. When he plowed or harrowed his rock-strewn fields, he grandly orated full Latin conjugations to his startled mules. He had finally taught himself Latin, too, from the hand-me-down textbooks we children used in high school.

We were still dirt poor when my older sister Betty graduated from high school.

Determined that she continue her education, Daddy drove her to Georgetown College himself in our wired-together '37 Chevy. Admitting that he didn't have a penny to put on her account, he promised the school that if she were accepted, he and Mother would pay all her bills somehow.

Many a night we would wake up to hear Daddy and Mother praying over how to make ends meet. But eventually all six of us went to college. And all of the bills were paid.

Of course, even with all of us working during college as well as taking full class loads, there was nothing left over for extras. One time I managed to stretch six dollars for laundry, clothes and all other incidentals for a whole semester. But we never dared give up, even at our most discouraging point. Daddy was counting on us to make it.

By the way, those Saturday mornings "took." From them we learned a world of words that helped one sister become a journalist, another a teacher, another a writer and our brother a lawyer.

But the word we learned best was: L-O-V-E.

Bonnie Compton Hanson

The Painted Tractor

Every child born into the world is a new thought of God, an ever-fresh and radiant possibility.

Kate Douglas Wiggin

The year was 1979, and my daughters were ages two, five and seven. Father's Day was approaching, and I was trying to come up with an original gift idea. Money was tight because we were in the process of renovating a barn into our home while we were living in it.

Suddenly, it hit me. "We'll paint his tractor!" It was Tom's first tractor, a used one he bought when we first moved to the northern Virginia countryside from Washington, D.C. "Yes, a new paint job for his tractor is what we'll give Daddy for Father's Day," I told my young daughters. They were delighted.

Off we went to the local hardware store in the nearest town. A salesman approached and asked if he could help me. "Yes," I said. "I'm looking for paint for my husband's tractor."

"What color do you have in mind?" the clerk asked.

I looked down at my daughters and asked each of them what color they wanted.

"I want pink," my oldest daughter said.

"I want yellow," my middle daughter said.

"I want blue," my youngest daughter said.

The salesman looked at me, barely able to hide his shock, and politely asked if my husband knew anything about what we were planning.

"No," I smiled. "We're surprising him for Father's Day. He's going to be thrilled!"

"I hope you have a strong marriage," the gentleman replied, genuinely flabbergasted.

We left the hardware store with several different colors of paint. I hired our favorite babysitter for a few consecutive afternoons after school to watch my youngest daughter while our masterpiece began. We started with the hubcaps. One soon had a big daisy in the center; another, a sunburst; the third, a smiley face; the fourth, a star.

We repainted the body of the tractor a pretty blue, and the headlights resembled happy eyes. We painted "We love you!" on the hood facing his seat, which we emblazoned with a big red heart.

When our job was finished, we were all thrilled! Father's Day couldn't get here soon enough.

The big day finally arrived, and we sent Tom on a mini treasure hunt. We handed him a written clue, which led to a spot where he found another clue, and so forth, until he eventually wound up in his shed. There he discovered the newly painted tractor.

"Did you girls do this for *me*?" Tom asked with a huge smile on his face.

The girls jumped all over him, no longer able to contain their excitement.

Each of them then took turns showing their daddy

which part of his tractor she had painted.

"Look at my star!" one chimed.

"And my daisy!" another squealed.

"I love it! I love it!" he laughed, hugging them all together. And he meant it. I knew he would.

We went back to the house together, and Tom put on his long-sleeve, black T-shirt designed to look like a tuxedo. He took an old top hat we'd stored away in the closet for who knows how long. "Can I have a picture taken with you girls?" he asked his daughters, now beaming with delight.

Tom drove his tractor closer to our house, and soon the girls were sitting on their father's lap or standing up next to him on his tractor. I snapped away with my camera.

The photo says it all: Tom, top hat, tuxedo, trio of daughters and a tractor, all saying, "We love you!"

Bobbie Wilkinson

"Happy Father's Day, Daddy!
I got you this card. What did you get me?"

Ethyl

What do we live for if not to make life less difficult for each other.

George Eliot

Ethyl entered my life on a bright July day in 1992, dressed in an aqua, polyester dress without a slip. Sturdy and scrubbed shining clean, she talked out of the side of her mouth, hiding eroded teeth in sad need of fixing. Ancient china blue eyes jumped out of a strawberry blonde haystack. Only in her late thirties, she was smart and slow, old and young—a garage sale of conflicting impressions.

My ad, which read, "Loyal, dependable, hard-working person to care for beloved, crusty, ninety-year-old grandpa," had attracted forty calls, ten of which I scheduled for an interview. My dad had taken to wandering, forgetting and losing his way home. I'd spent many hours driving up and down streets near his apartment house, asking anybody if they'd seen a distinguished old gentleman with a Sherlock Holmes hat, sport coat and white mustache who picked weeds out of street cracks and yards. Now something new had cropped up. He'd ride the number-ten bus to a grocery store, where he'd buy a bottle of booze. The day I got the "come-quick-I-think-your-father-had-a-stroke" call from the apartment manager, I found Dad in his underwear, drunk as a skunk, categorically denying he'd ever touched a drop in his life. He was skin and bones, a fact that his padded clothes had hidden. I sat there crying, feeding him bites of banana, anguishing over how I could keep him independent and on his feet as long as possible. Dad tried to wipe my nose and didn't have a clue as to why I was bawling.

"Well, what experience have you had?" I droned for the tenth time.

"I took care of my dad," Ethyl stated with obvious pride. "He lived in the Yukon and knew Jack London. You know—the writer of *Call of the Wild*. My last job was a logger in B.C."

"A logger?" I repeated incredulously. *Gosh, Dad,* I thought, *the things I've done for you these last years.*

"I really want this job," she said with a slight Scottish lilt. "I'm a hard worker, and I love crusty old gentlemen. I'm dependable. And clean. Just like this ad wants."

I told her I'd get back to her, then watched her from the porch. She hugged the steering wheel of a battered, rusty, belching fire dragon and departed in a cloud of black smoke.

I hired her. Something in me just believed her.

The next day we met at Dad's little apartment where I explained how Ethyl was going to come mornings to cook and clean a bit.

"I don't need anybody," he stated flatly.

"She's hard up and needs work," I whispered in *sotto voce* twice in his good ear.

"How much?" he cackled.

"She's free," I answered, adding "lying" to the "what-I-have-done-for-you-Dad" list. "She's a free service you get from the senior citizens."

He begrudgingly agreed, and Ethyl and I shared a stare and let out a long sigh of relief. We discussed how, along with her other duties and a daily 7:30 A.M. call to me, she'd be sly watchdog and shower-giver. That last one would be tough.

The next morning, promptly at 7:30 A.M., the phone rang.

"I'm using a phone in the lobby," Ethyl panted. "His door's locked, and I can't find . . . Oh, dear God! He's walking up the freeway. I gotta go!"

I yelled like a crazy person into the dead phone as my husband tried to calm me.

Ten terrible minutes later the phone rang. Breathless Ethyl stated she'd grabbed Dad by his coat on the on-ramp and dragged him home—his 124 pounds versus her 160. From the sound of things, it was a draw, and they'd stopped rush-hour traffic to boot. I could hear him roaring something in the background about picking up nuts and bolts, getting his hat run over, and who the hell was Ethyl.

Ethyl and Dad were together two years. He gained eight pounds because she fed him so well; she lost ten chasing him. Together we stopped his drinking. She found the bottles, and I gave them away to everybody I could think of. In time, Dad simply forgot about it. Faithful Ethyl walked with him in the mornings, avoiding the freeway. His little apartment shined. He shined, all cleaned and starched, glowing like a priceless antique.

Many mornings she'd hold the phone for me to hear. A musician in the twenties, Dad had played piano in the silent flicks for fifty cents a week. Now he plunked "Toyland" on the keyboard his granddaughters gave him for his ninety-first birthday. Ethyl, Dad and whomever, sometimes it was neighbors, warbled on one end of the phone, with me doing alto on the other.

One terrible wintry day, Ethyl willed her belching dragon of a car up the icy hill to his place when everything had been paralyzed by the storm.

"Ethyl, you're a prince!" I told her over the phone.

"George has got to have his breakfast," she stated with a slight lispy whistle through a sparkling set of dentures.

One Sunday I entered his apartment. "Where's Ethyl?" I asked.

"Down there," he said, gesturing to the Dumpster in the back of his apartment. He twirled his finger at his temple, making a crazy sign. There was Ethyl, up to her waist in trash, throwing everything out of the Dumpster. When she heard me tapping on the window, she turned.

"Teeth," she mouthed, taking out hers and waving them. "He threw out his teeth!"

She found them. But in the fullness of time, we lost his glasses and $1,700 worth of hearing aids.

When the time finally came for another care level, we settled Dad in a new place, and Ethyl and I took down his apartment and shared memories. Occasional tears turned to hooted laughter when we found one last bottle. As we clinked glasses, she pronounced, "We done right by George. God bless him, our bonny, crusty, old piece of work!"

The next day, the new place called to say Dad was missing. Ethyl, my husband, daughters and I combed the streets for two hours and ultimately called the police. Finally, the manager of the old apartment called my husband, who'd returned home for such an eventuality, and said Dad had thumbed a ride twenty miles across town to his old place, carrying family pictures and his keyboard. We all rushed over there, threw our arms around his neck and collapsed into tears. Of course, Dad didn't have the slightest idea what he'd done. For the next month, Ethyl and I took turns settling him into the new place.

Dad went to a full-fledged nursing home a year later when he didn't know any of us anymore, but Ethyl continued to visit him several times a week. He died peacefully at ninety-five. At his funeral, Ethyl stood in the family line with the rest of us, inconsolable.

Ethyl and I stay in touch and still exchange Christmas cards. I wrote her a reference when she applied for citizenship. And both of us have never stopped missing Dad.

Over the years, the one thing I know truly in my heart of hearts is, together, Ethyl and I kept that beloved, crusty old grandpa up, and independent, until the very end. We "done right" by George.

Isabel Bearman Bucher

Memorial Day Flags

After what I owe to God, nothing should be more dear or more sacred than the love and respect I owe to my country.

François Auguste de Thou

I served as a U.S. Army infantry squad leader during the Vietnam War. For many years the general perception of Vietnam veterans has been less-than-stellar, but I was always proud of my service and my three daughters knew it. Every year I marched in the local Memorial Day parade in full dress uniform, and I also prominently display my military awards in our home. About fifteen years ago, I joined a group of local Vietnam-era veterans who had taken charge of our town's Memorial Day parade. Our committee took a firm stand to eliminate activities that were not in the spirit of honoring the lives that were lost or disrupted in service to our country.

Besides organizing the parade every year, our group also placed American flags at the graves of our deceased veterans. I thought this simple patriotic task was something my three daughters should be involved with, so each year I took one of them along to assist. When my oldest daughter became a teenager, she no longer wanted to participate because to her it wasn't cool to be searching for gravestones with a group of old veterans. So I began bringing my middle daughter, but when she reached the same teenage threshold, she no longer wanted to help either. Undaunted, the following year I enlisted the aid of Ashley, my youngest.

For whatever reason, eleven-year-old Ashley seemed fascinated by the experience. She asked dozens of questions that ranged from what happened to the buried veterans to what was it like for me during the war. Needless to say, I was pleasantly surprised by her unusual interest in the people who served our nation.

As the years went by, Ashley did not display the same teenage aversion that her sisters did and continued to help place the flags. One damp, foggy weekend, however, she questioned whether we should wait for a nicer day. I explained that it was our duty to honor veterans no matter what the weather conditions because during wartime, soldiers were often stuck in the rain, snow or sweltering heat for several weeks and even months, with little or no relief. Ashley nodded knowingly and never complained about the weather again.

As my daughters were growing up, I began to give presentations about my Vietnam experiences to their schools and local civic groups. I also volunteered to be the main speaker for several Memorial Day and Veteran's Day ceremonies and was one of the founding members of our new veteran's museum. My continued dedication sparked something in Ashley—I could see that she had developed a genuine sense of appreciation for people who have served in the military. She made me feel proud because appreciation was the one thing that veterans covet the most, and it was especially gratifying that it came from one of my own children.

When Ashley was a college freshman, I thought her feelings might change somewhat, but surprisingly she still had more to offer. This past Memorial Day, our parade committee wanted to have a woman be the main speaker, but everyone we contacted declined. Then, from out of nowhere, eighteen-year-old Ashley asked if she could give the speech. Her request was very unusual because our speakers generally had a military background or were familiar longtime residents. However, Ashley insisted she wanted to do it, so we gave her the honor.

At the Memorial Day ceremony, I proudly watched Ashley walk to the podium and slowly adjust the microphone. She boldly faced the audience and began. "I'm reminded of a cold, foggy day when I was a little girl complaining about putting flags on veterans' graves." Ashley spoke with such confidence and clarity, as if public speaking was routine for her. "The one or two days a year that we honor deceased veterans cannot begin to compare to the absolute devotion of the Tomb Sentinels who guard the Tomb of the Unknown Soldier at Arlington National Cemetery. No matter what the weather, or if the nation is at war or enjoying peace, every minute of every day a guard is watching over soldiers who will never be identified."

To this proud father, that was the day my daughter became a true American patriot.

Arthur B. Wiknik Jr.

Struggle and Celebration

The fragrance always stays in the hand that gives the rose.

Anonymous

Where were you on February 21, 1976? How about the same date eighteen years later?

In my case, the answer to these questions is identical. I was at Grant Hospital in Columbus, Ohio. During both visits there were no broken bones to repair, wounds to mend or X-rays required. In fact, I left the hospital in the same condition I went in, perfectly healthy and blissfully happy! That was also true for my daughter, Shannon, who went with me. The first visit was the day Shannon was born. The second was to celebrate her eighteenth birthday.

I had been searching for a unique gift. The idea of returning with Shannon to the place she was born was my solution. The folks at the hospital loved the idea, and the party was on. They provided a cake and located two nurses still on staff who had helped bring my daughter into the world. I had cards made, with a newborn picture of Shannon next to one taken for her high-school graduation, which was coming up in the spring. Below the pictures it read:

On Feb. 21, 1976, at Grant Hospital, Columbus, Ohio, Shannon Leigh Snider was born. Today she celebrates her 18th birthday. Please accept this flower in honor of the occasion, and may God bless you and your child.

Sincerely,
Jerry Snider
"Shannon's Dad"

The cards and pink carnations were delivered to seven new mothers whose children now shared a birthday with Shannon. I said a prayer, we sang "Happy Birthday" and cut the cake. A local TV station recorded the event for the evening newscast.

"Proof," I said, "all the news isn't bad."

We had one more stop to make before the party ended. In the next room someone else was celebrating a birthday, too. Above a glass bubbled incubator hung a sign with pictures of hearts and rainbows: "Happy Birthday to me. I'm two months old."

The baby in the bubble, born prematurely, weighed only two pounds and was not much bigger than the hand of the nurse who held her. Eighteen years ago, children born in similar circumstances were not given much hope for survival. Shannon and I watched the struggle. Machines and monitors connected to the baby by wires and hoses, clicked and beeped. The little girl opened her eyes and wiggled her arms just enough to make us feel like she knew we were there. The nurse continued to gently stroke and cuddle her.

Shannon looked so worried. I soothed, "Science and technology can't invent anything more important than that nurse's hands." To the nurse I said, "Those might look like your hands, but they really belong to God."

Shannon and I hugged, knowing that in eighteen years this baby girl would be back to celebrate, too, with cards and carnations!

Jerry Snider

"Okay, let me get this straight; your friend Kristyn
is no longer coming to have supper with us
because Danielle told you that Tracy heard from
Holly that her sister Melissa thought she saw Kristyn
in the mall talking to your old boyfriend?"

A Decent Thing to Do

Virtue and decency are so nearly related that it is difficult to separate them from each other but in our imagination.

Cicero

Looking up at the big lettering on the garage building reading "Corr Richfield's Service Station," my father was a proud, happy man. It was 1935. He had built our house, a service station and mechanic's garage. Opening for business just five years after arriving in America from Northern Ireland, it was quite an accomplishment.

My father had two faults. The first was working too hard from sunup well past sundown every day. Second, he was very trusting and generous, helping anyone, always feeling sorry for those down on their luck. In the 1930s, people had little money, paying him with whatever they had to give. Dad trusted everyone, including strangers. Business was usually a handshake with a promise to pay. Mother often said, "Bill, do you think we're running a charity ward? We've barely enough to pay for our next load of gas." Nothing stopped him from helping people. He'd just shrug his shoulders, saying, "We'll manage." He was never too busy or tired, many times getting up in the night to help anyone who needed him, regardless of what it was. They knew he'd come.

It was a hot summer's day, and perspiration poured off him as he worked doing repairs in the garage. A car chugged up to the pumps. Going around to the driver's side, Dad asked, "Can I help you?" The panting, sweaty man looked at my father and said, "It's empty, but before you pump it, I've no money. I've a ways to get home. All I have is a gun to offer you in payment." He reached under the seat. "It's my army pistol." Slowly getting out, limping as he moved to nearby shade, he said he was a disabled war veteran who lived further down the valley.

Daddy walked over to his car silently and filled it up—as well as the gas can that he put in the back. He did the usual checkup, plus filled a water bag hanging on the radiator. "You're ready to travel," he said.

"Thank you very much." The man staggered as he started to move. Daddy grabbed his arm. "Are you all right?" he asked. "Better come inside for a bit. When was the last time you had a bite to eat?"

"Yesterday, I think."

"Good lord, man, no wonder," Dad said, pushing the buzzer for the house. Mother came. "Sadie, would you be fixin' this man a sandwich? Make it two, he's a ways yet to go."

Back she came with two wrapped sandwiches. Daddy pulled two cold drinks from the icebox outside. After enjoying the sandwich and a drink, the man stood, grabbed Daddy's hand and shook it. "Thank you again. Bless you and your wife." He took the gun from the car and handed it to Dad. "My name is George. I'll be back with the money," he promised. "Remember, Bill, I'll be back," he called, waving as he drove off.

Daddy knew two things as he placed the gun and the invoice for the gas in a locked drawer. One, he was going to catch the devil from Mother. Second, George would be back for the gun.

Right he was on number one. "Bill, the charity ward is running a bit dry," Mother scolded.

"Aw, Sadie, the poor man just needed a wee bit of a hand. It was a decent thing to do," he said.

"Before him it was that artist. The painting's on the wall—we can't eat it!" mother said.

Two years passed. The gun still lay in the drawer. Mother kept saying, "Sell it," but Daddy wouldn't.

One day a car pulled into the station. A man got out and walked toward the garage where Daddy was. "Are you Bill Corr?" he inquired.

"That I am," replied Daddy, extending his hand.

"Well, I'm George's son, the fellow who left the gun for gas. He's bedridden so I came instead."

"I knew he'd come or send for it," Daddy said, retrieving the gun from the drawer.

"Now what do I owe?" the man asked.

"One dollar twenty five," Daddy replied.

The man handed him a five-dollar bill. Daddy punched the register to get change. "Not on your life! Your kindness and trust cannot be repaid," the man said. "Keep the change." Then, smiling, he added, "Would you fill up my car? I'll pay you now."

After the fill, he shook Dad's hand again, got in his car, saluted and drove off.

Marking the invoice "paid," Daddy started to put it on the spindle, but didn't. Instead, whistling away, he headed for the house. Opening the door, he yelled, "Sadie, me dear, look what I have," waving the invoice and money. "The gun's gone. Got five dollars for it, plus another two for a fill-up. Do you not see? Good things come to those who wait and trust. You've got to put faith and trust in people. All I done at the time was the decent thing," he said.

Unfortunately, my father never fulfilled his dream of paying off the business. He died at age thirty-nine from a heart attack. His funeral was the largest in town, filling the church to standing-room only, then down the steps and into the streets. People he had befriended came from miles around to pay tribute to a man who never lost faith and who trusted them.

I have the framed photo of Dad, taken in 1935 in front of "Corr Richfield's Service Station," and the artist's painting he bartered in trade. Both hung on the wall of the station before Mother sold it. Now they hang on my wall as reminders to be honest, caring, hardworking and compassionate, and to have faith and trust in the goodness of people.

Isabel Corr Rizzo

$\overline{6}$

FROM THE MOUTHS OF BABES

There are only two things a child will share willingly—communicable diseases and his mother's age.

Benjamin Spock

READER/CUSTOMER CARE SURVEY

CE6G

We care about your opinions! Please take a moment to fill out our online Reader Survey at **http://survey.hcibooks.com**.
As a **"THANK YOU"** you will receive a **VALUABLE INSTANT COUPON** towards future book purchases as well as a **SPECIAL GIFT** available only online! Or, you may mail this card back to us and we will send you a copy of our exciting catalog with your valuable coupon inside.

(PLEASE PRINT IN ALL CAPS)

First Name _____ MI. _____ Last Name _____

Address _____ City _____

State _____ Zip _____ Email _____

1. Gender
❑ Female ❑ Male

2. Age
❑ 8 or younger
❑ 9-12 ❑ 13-16
❑ 17-20 ❑ 21-30
❑ 31+

3. Did you receive this book as a gift?
❑ Yes ❑ No

4. Annual Household Income
❑ under $25,000
❑ $25,000 - $34,999
❑ $35,000 - $49,999
❑ $50,000 - $74,999
❑ over $75,000

5. What are the ages of the children living in your house?
❑ 0 - 14 ❑ 15+

6. Marital Status
❑ Single
❑ Married
❑ Divorced
❑ Widowed

7. How did you find out about the book?
(please choose one)
❑ Recommendation
❑ Store Display
❑ Online
❑ Catalog/Mailing
❑ Interview/Review

8. Where do you usually buy books?
(please choose one)
❑ Bookstore
❑ Online
❑ Book Club/Mail Order
❑ Price Club (Sam's Club, Costco's, etc.)
❑ Retail Store (Target, Wal-Mart, etc.)

9. What subject do you enjoy reading about the most?
(please choose one)
❑ Parenting/Family
❑ Relationships
❑ Recovery/Addictions
❑ Health/Nutrition
❑ Christianity
❑ Spirituality/Inspiration
❑ Business Self-help
❑ Women's Issues
❑ Sports

10. What attracts you most to a book?
(please choose one)
❑ Title
❑ Cover Design
❑ Author
❑ Content

FOLD HERE

Do you have your own Chicken Soup story
that you would like to send us?
Please submit at: **www.chickensoup.com**

Comments

She Calls Me Daddy

Pretty much all the honest truth telling in the world today is done by children.

Oliver Wendell Holmes

Wendy and I had just started dating, and we were beginning to think that this could be "it." I was hesitant at first because Wendy had a daughter from a previous marriage, and I didn't know if I possessed the ability to love two people at the same time.

Shaina was two years old when Wendy and I first met, and her father had just been stabbed to death on a bus in San Francisco. I had been single for thirty-two years and was a bit frightened about my lack of ability to be a good father to this beautiful child whose father had just been taken from her.

The relationship between Wendy and I continued to deepen, and we set the wedding date. Even then I was still a bit frightened.

I was the youngest in my family by five years, and had never been around children, especially girls! The idea of becoming a husband *and* a dad on the same day had my heart conflicted between joy and excitement and fear and trepidation.

Wendy and I started spending even more time together and going to church. We noticed that Shaina was getting more comfortable with me in a paternal way. Wendy wanted to make sure that I would not feel unnecessary pressure, so she explained to Shaina that she should call me Johnny until the wedding, and then she could call me Daddy.

So, as the wedding day approached, I thought of ways to make Shaina feel a part. I had asked Wendy's father for permission to marry his daughter, so I thought it would be cute to ask for Shaina's permission to marry her mommy.

"No," Shania said.

Startled, I smiled and said, "Please?" But she was set on her answer.

"No."

My heart dropped, and all my fears and insecurities stuck in my throat, choking my words. I couldn't catch my breath. Wendy and I glanced at each other completely stunned and wondered together, "Oh my, now what?"

I finally spoke, "Why not?"

With a shy smile and a little embarrassment, she replied, "Because I want to marry you."

John Cox

Anna's First Cubs Game

Blessed be the hand that prepares a pleasure for a child, for there is no saying when and where it may bloom forth.

Douglas Jerrold

I can still remember the first Major League Baseball game my father took me to as a child, so I wanted my five-year-old daughter Anna's first game to be just as memorable for her. Two weeks before the game I purchased a kids' music tape filled with baseball songs. We endlessly learned the song "Take Me Out to the Ball Game" in anticipation of the famous seventh-inning stretch sung by Harry Carry and the Chicago Cubs' fans.

Decked out in her new official hat, shirt and oversized leather glove, we were ready for the game. Anna was enthralled with the field, players, game and happy fans surrounding us. Peanut, hot dog, popcorn and ice cream vendors filled her with treats, keeping her busy until the seventh-inning stretch. Suddenly, I had an idea. Turning to Anna, I asked her loudly, so everyone around us might catch on as well, if she would like *everyone* in the stadium to stand up and sing the song along with her.

Her eyes widened as she looked around and said, "You mean everyone will sing along with me? That's great, Dad!"

I answered, "No problem," and added that the man in the booth above us would not only join in, but he would help everyone as well.

Beckoning everyone to stand up and join us, Anna stood on her seat and sang as loud as she could. "Take me out to the ballgame . . . " We all joined her and cheered her on. She was beaming with pride, in love with the thought that the entire stadium was singing along with her.

When the song ended, we all applauded Anna and gave her high-fives. It was a magical moment; she was so happy. As I was about to sit back down, Anna had an even better idea. "Dad, make them do it again!"

People within earshot burst out laughing. Taking her hand, I said, "No problem, Anna. Next time we come, we can do it all again."

Louis Schutz

Owed to Joy

Man is the merriest, the most joyous of all the species of creation.

Joseph Addison

The year my youngest daughter, Shelly, was four, she received an unusual Christmas present from "Santa."

She was the perfect age for Christmas, able to understand the true meaning of the season, but still completely enchanted by the magic of it. Her innocent joyfulness was compelling and contagious and a great gift to parents, reminding us of what Christmas should represent no matter how old we are.

The most highly prized gift Shelly received on that Christmas Eve was a giant bubble-maker, a simple device of plastic and cloth the inventor promised would create huge billowing bubbles, larger than a wide-eyed four-year-old girl. Both Shelly and I were excited about trying it out, but it was dark outside so we'd have to wait until the next day.

That night, after all the gifts had been opened, I read the

instruction booklet while Shelly played with some of her other new toys. The inventor of the bubble-maker had tried all types of soaps for formulating bubbles and found Joy dishwashing detergent created the best giant bubbles. I'd have to get some.

The next morning I was awakened very early by small stirrings in the house. Shelly was up. I knew in my sleepy mind that Christmas Day would be held back no longer, so I arose and made my way toward the kitchen to start the coffee. In the hallway I met my daughter, already wide awake, the bubble-maker clutched in her chubby little hand, the magic of Christmas morning embraced in her four-year-old heart. Her eyes were shining with excitement. She asked, "Daddy, can we make bubbles now?"

I sighed heavily. I rubbed my eyes. I looked toward the window, where the sky was only beginning to lighten with the dawn. I looked toward the kitchen, where the coffeepot had yet to start dripping its aromatic reward for early-rising Christmas dads.

"Shelly," I said, my voice almost pleading and perhaps a little annoyed, "it's too early. I haven't even had my coffee yet."

Her smile fell away. Immediately, I felt a father's remorse for bursting her bright Christmas bubble with what she must have seen as my own selfish problem, and my heart broke a little.

But I was a grown-up. I could fix this. In a flash of adult inspiration, I shifted the responsibility. Recalling the inventor's recommendation of a particular brand of bubble-making detergent—which I knew we did not have in the house—I laid the blame squarely on him, pointing out gently, "Besides, you have to have Joy."

I watched her eyes light back up. "Oh, Daddy," she beamed. "Oh, Daddy, *I do.*"

I broke records getting to the store, and in no time at all we were out on the front lawn creating gigantic, billowing, gossamer orbs—each one conjured of purest Joy and sent forth shimmering in the Christmas sun.

Ted A. Thompson

Be Slow to Anchor

Out of the mouths of babes and sucklings has thou ordained strength.

Psalm 8:2

Shortly after my daughter Nicole was born, father-daughter fishing trips became a regular occurrence. We would most often fish from my little aluminum boat at a small, shallow lake near our house. By age three, Nicole had an uncanny ability to sit in our boat for long periods, certain that a fish would bite at any moment.

Our family has also always been actively involved with our local church. One Sunday when we went to pick up our daughter from her Sunday school class, the teacher asked if we could meet with her a moment after all the parents had picked up their children.

Every parent knows that instant of dread associated with wondering what your three-year-old may have said to someone. We mustered up our courage and waited.

Finally, alone with her teacher, the truth came out. The week's memory verse was James 1:19, "Be slow to anger."

When the teacher asked the children if anyone could explain what that passage meant, Nicole's hand shot up immediately.

"It means that when you go fishing, you crawl to the front of the boat and put the front *anger* down very slowly," Nicole said. "Then you crawl to the back of the boat and put the back *anger* down very slowly. That way, you don't make a splash and scare the fish away."

Dan DeVries

Moonshine

We are all here for a spell; get all the good laughs you can.

Will Rogers

Long before life took over and complicated things, I was once a princess and my daddy was definitely the handsomest man in my four-year-old world. I especially liked the way he winked and his sense of fun. Sometimes, however, it got us both into a spot of trouble.

One unusually warm fall afternoon, we were out for a ride, just Daddy and me. In the days before air conditioning, seat belts and car seats, I sat alone in the back enjoying the breeze that swept through the car's open windows. At the same time, I found myself mesmerized by a mysterious glass jug sitting next to me. Fascinated by the reddish glow that sparkled in the sun, my fingers lightly played over the glass container, feeling the heat that seemed to come from inside it.

"Daddy, what's this?" I asked, my curiosity getting the better of me.

"Moonshine." He winked at me in the rearview mirror.

"Moonshine?" I repeated the word trying to comprehend what he meant exactly.

"Just for you," he added with a grin.

Moonshine, I thought to myself as I carefully looked over the amazing jar. *It certainly looks like something that came from far away.* Suddenly, it all made perfect sense. My daddy had gone up to the sky and caught some shine right from the moon. He put it in this jug and brought it back to Earth for me. I bet no other daddy had ever done that before! I was one lucky little girl.

Totally awestruck, I clutched the gallon jug, amazed by the magical substance inside. It seemed to glow even brighter, glistening in the afternoon sun. *Just wait until everyone sees this! My very own moonshine in my very own glass jug!*

Wrapped up in my imagination, I absently felt the car come to a stop. Looking up and through the windshield, I could see a red light dangling above us on a thick wire. I let my jug go long enough to climb onto my knees and peer out the open window on the passenger side.

Two policemen sat next to us in their patrol car, also with their windows rolled down. As we all waited for the red light to turn green, I couldn't contain my excitement for another second, so I hollered out to them: "My daddy's got moonshine in the back seat!"

They both turned to look at me, and then they looked at each other. The driver peered at my daddy. "Pull the car over, sir." He wasn't smiling.

"But officer . . . ," my daddy tried.

"Just pull the car over, sir—now."

The two policemen parked directly behind us and asked my daddy and me to get out of the car. They then proceeded to search it, front seat, back seat and trunk. They even opened the hood.

"See, Daddy," I was hopping from one foot to the other, "the policemen want to see the moonshine, too!"

My daddy didn't say a word. He just closed his eyes and shook his head as we stood there waiting.

Finally, one of the officers held up my glass jug. "Sir, what's in here?"

"Just what the label says," Daddy sighed. "It's apple cider. Open it and have a taste if you want."

"But your daughter said . . . "

"I know. I told her it was moonshine," my dad admitted sheepishly. "She has no idea what that is."

Their serious faces suddenly turned into smiles and then peals of laughter followed. "Here you go, little lady." One of the officers held the door for me and helped me climb back into the car.

His partner handed over the glass bottle with a grin. "Take good care of your moonshine, Honey."

As we all drove away, I tightly held on to my bottle of moonshine. After all, it wasn't every princess whose daddy took a trip to the moon.

Debra Ann Pawlak

A Forkful of Humor

Children have never been very good at listening to their elders, but they have never failed to imitate them.

James Baldwin

If something has to go wrong, why does it have to happen while we're on vacation? It seems like every trip our family takes, we wind up making a visit to a hospital or clinic. It's one thing to visit these facilities while we're home and can utilize the comfort zone provided by our own family doctors, but while vacationing we are ultimately at the mercy of every student of the nearest medical school. It doesn't take a rocket scientist to diagnose an ear infection and prescribe some antibiotics. And it certainly was no rocket scientist who cared for my husband when our three-and-a-half-year-old daughter rammed the tines of her fork into his eye. For Dad and Elizabeth, it was no "tine-y" problem.

It was, of course, purely accidental. She's a sweet child who adores her daddy. However, she is animated, and she loves to talk. So while making conversation at dinner, her arms flailing to make a point, she pierced her father's eyeball with her salad fork.

"Owwww!" he screamed, pressing his hand to his instantly throbbing eye.

After persistent coaxing, I was finally allowed to look at the damage. There was obviously a serious problem at hand. My poor husband's eye was punctured and trickling blood. He needed immediate medical attention. Like rats in a maze, with our daughter in tow, we drove all over our tourist-infested region in search of a hospital or walk-in clinic. Soon we were seated in a nearby emergency room. The more seriously afflicted were seen first, and in comparison to heart attacks and severed limbs, a punctured eyeball was fairly low on the totem pole. Knowing we were in for a lengthy wait, we busied a guiltless Elizabeth with coloring books and crayons and waited. She immediately started drawing a stick figure of a man with a fork protruding from his eye. Her humor didn't go unnoticed.

"What seems to be the problem?" the male nurse asked when my hubby's name was finally called.

"My little girl stuck a fork in my eye," he explained.

"Any fever?"

"I don't think so."

"Any vomiting?"

"No, but I felt a little queasy when it happened."

"Any diarrhea?"

"From a fork in my eye?" my husband asked, partly amused, partly flabbergasted.

"Oh, that's right. Of course," the nurse jotted things on the chart and muttered constantly to himself.

Next he checked my husband's ears and throat, never looking at his eye, then turned and left the room. We assumed things would improve when the doctor got there.

"Looks like you've got a puncture wound here," the doctor said after a quick exam, indicating immediate pleasure in his quick diagnosis.

"Yes, I know," my husband said. "My daughter punctured my eyeball with a fork."

"Nope. It couldn't have been a fork," the doctor said, still peering from one eye to the next.

"I'm telling you, it was a fork," my husband said, by now becoming clearly disturbed.

"Looks more like a fishhook to me," the doctor said, ferociously scribbling his notes.

My husband shouted, "Look, I obviously was there when this accident happened. So was my wife. My daughter stuck a fork in my eye!"

"A fork!" Elizabeth chimed in.

The doctor didn't look up. He just kept writing.

"Does your husband have a drinking problem?" he asked me.

"What?" I asked. "No, he doesn't have a drinking problem. He hardly ever takes a drink."

By now Dad and daughter were headed for the door. I followed closely at their heels. We stopped by the desk and informed the secretary that since we'd received no service, we had no intention of paying the bill.

"Drinking problem," Elizabeth muttered, shaking her head like an adult rather than a child who had stabbed her daddy's eye.

As we headed out the door, the nurse stopped us once again.

"Here," he said, handing me a business card. "Please take this. And think about taking your little girl to Al-Anon."

On the card were the telephone numbers for the local human services office and the nearest chapter of AA. I couldn't believe what was going on! We were nearly at our car when we noticed a different nurse waving her arms frantically to get our attention.

"Excuse me, excuse me," she said.

"Yes?"

"I am so sorry. The receptionist mixed up your chart with someone else's. You were mistaken for a family where the father had repeatedly gotten drunk and drummed up a list of ailments a mile long," she explained. "Please, sir, accept our apologies and come back inside."

Everyone makes mistakes; we all have. We've always tried to practice the philosophy of forgiving and forgetting, so we went back into the hospital.

After waiting just a couple of minutes, the same male nurse came back out for my husband, greeting him with a smile and a profuse apology.

"It's okay," my husband said to him. "I just wish someone would do something for my incredible eye pain."

After we were made comfortable once again in a different examining room, we awaited the return of the doctor. When he arrived, he looked at my husband's chart and promptly asked how long his sinuses had been bothering him.

"They're never going to fix Daddy!" Elizabeth cried.

We quickly and quietly got up and walked out. There would be no looking back. There would be no going back. And there would obviously be no treatment for Dad's eye tonight.

A couple of days later when we were safely back at home, my husband, accompanied by Elizabeth, visited our family doctor.

"What seems to be the problem?" the doctor asked.

Elizabeth interjected quickly, "He has a drinking problem. What can we do to fix him?"

Kimberly A. Ripley

The Price of a Child

It's good to have money and the things money can buy, but it's good, too, to check up once in a while and make sure that you haven't lost the things that money can't buy.

George Horace Lorimer

"Daddy, how much did I cost?"

Perched on my parents' cedar chest in the bedroom, I listened to their casual talk about budgets and pay-checks—talk as relevant back in 1967 as it is today. My then-six-year-old mind concluded, wrongly, that my family was poor.

Dad stood at his dresser, looking at bills. He wore faded jeans, an undershirt and white canvas shoes stained grass-green from mowing our lawn. Mom folded laundry on the bed, making even towers of sun-dried clothes. I spotted my new shorts sets and thought about day camp.

Their money talk continued, and Dad joined me on the cedar chest. I plunked the springy metal watchband on Dad's tan wrist, thinking that the white skin underneath reminded me of a fish belly. Just as I started to ask him to "make a muscle" so I could try pushing his flexed biceps down, a thought hit me like icy water from a garden hose: *Dad had to pay for me.*

While the story of my birth ranked as a bedtime favorite, I had never considered hospital bills, or the countless meals I'd eaten, or the price of summer clothes.

"Daddy," I interrupted again, "how much did I cost?"

"Oh, let's see." He sighed in distraction and placed his watch on the safety of his dresser. "About a million dollars."

A light went out inside of me. *A million dollars.* Because of me, Dad worked two jobs. Because of me, he drove an old car, ate lunch at home and had his dress shoes resoled—again.

With my eyes and chin down, I inched off the cedar chest and shuffled into the kitchen. From a shelf, I took my granny-shaped bank, which held every penny I owned— seven dollars even. And not seven dollars in assorted change, but seven cool, shiny silver dollars, one for every birthday and one for the day I was born.

The bank's rubber plug surrendered, and the coins poured into my hands. I had often played with these coins in secret, jostling them in a small drawstring bag in my roles as gypsy or runaway princess. They had always been put back in the bank, though, and I felt secure pleasure in just knowing they were there. But that day, the "clink" of returning each coin sounded hollow.

If the topic had changed when I returned to my parents' bedroom, I didn't notice. Tugging on Dad's shirt, I held out my first payment on a million dollars.

"Here," I sniffed. "Maybe this will help pay for me."

"What?" Dad's confused look matched my own. Didn't he remember what he'd said? Didn't the sight of me remind him of how much I cost?

My tear-filled eyes, which I couldn't seem to take off the bank, finally made sense to him.

Dad knelt down and pulled me close. "You didn't cost a million dollars, but you're worth a *million*-million dollars. And if that's what I'd have to pay for you, I'd do it. Now dry those eyes and put your bank away."

Today, I often pull this memory out, turn it over and feel the warm satisfied weight of it in my heart. Back then, no price could be put on my worth to my dad. No price can be put on his worth to me now.

Debi Stack

Black and White

One day, while driving in the car with my seven-year-old daughter, we began talking. Somehow, the conversation turned into a discussion about my childhood. She was amazed when I told her that television in my day had no remote control and that the picture on the tube was only in black and white, no colors. She thought about it for a short time and asked me if I was in black and white then, too. I assured her that was not the case and went on to tell her that many changes and new things had happened in the world during my lifetime. I further explained that we could not imagine how the world might change during her lifetime.

When I told her I would probably not live to see all the things that would happen in the world while she was alive, she fell silent, digesting what I had told her. She thought for a moment and said, "Don't worry, Dad. When it's done, I will come to heaven and tell you all about it."

Al D. Luebbers

Dear Daddy . . .

Children have more need of models than of critics.

Joseph Joubert

My father was the gentlest, most loving and caring dad in the world—until we had an argument. During those moments, he transformed into an obstinate, unrelenting ogre who never considered that there could be a side other than his own. My words surely never reached his "open mind" because his ears were sealed. When he spoke, it was with such authority that it was easy to begin to doubt my own point of view. But I, my father's daughter, had inherited his debating skills and argued back with the passion of a court-room attorney, welcoming the battle of our wills. That was, until the fights became personal and our confrontations charged with emotion. There was no point trying to argue with my dad. He always had the last word. I could never win.

When my father refused to understand that I *needed* the privacy of a phone in my own room, my frustration turned to tears. When he sensed that I was gaining the upper hand in defending my case for wearing lip-gloss to school in junior high, he ended our "discussion," leaving me silently defeated and miserable. So when he refused to budge on letting me go on my senior class trip to Montreal, I could do nothing but race from his room in hysterics. And then came the epiphany. If I couldn't get him to *listen* to my side of our arguments, maybe I could get him to *read* it.

With the hope that his eyes would be more open than his ears, I began to plead my case—uninterrupted and uncontested—in a note that began "Dear Daddy" and ended with how much I respected his opinion, how much I hated to fight with him, how much I valued our relationship and, above all, how much I loved him. Following my exhausting catharsis, I folded my note into an envelope, slid it under the door of his bedroom and raced back to my own room where I collapsed on my bed.

It was only minutes before I heard a knock at my door. When I saw the look on my father's face, I knew that my note had melted his temper, softened his stubbornness and touched his heart. After all, there was never any question that I was Daddy's girl.

The victory of winning my dad's permission to go to Montreal was sweet. But even sweeter was the serendipitous discovery of a strategy that enabled me to have an argument with my dad that didn't end in tears, but instead with a hug. My "Dear Daddy" notes became a follow-up to many of our hotheaded confrontations. During our most emotional arguments, when his unyielding final word drove me to tears, when his "I'm your father, that's why!" left me speechless, I knew just how to get through to him. While my notes weren't a guarantee that I'd get my way, they did succeed in defusing the anger between us and paving the way for the truce—and hugs—that always followed.

Years later, when my father died, his memory lived on vibrantly through the many stories about him that friends and family continued to share. One of my favorites was the "Dear Daddy" notes. It always made me smile to remember some of our most passionate arguments and how my dad would become so pig-headed, until he read my notes. He surely must have seen through my calculating strategy, but he never let on; he savored every note that turned him to see my way.

When I first told my own children, then twelve and nine, about my emotional battles with their strong-willed grandpa, they thought that the notes were a silly solution. My daughter, also a recipient of the "skilled debating" genes, responded with, "What a cop-out! Why couldn't you just work out your issues face-to-face?"

But a few months later, when she became a teenager, she finally understood the frustration I had been trying to explain.

During the first major argument, I overheard protests of "Daddy, why *can't* I take the train to Manhattan? All of my friends are allowed to go—we're thirteen!" As I listened to their shouting match, I suspected that my husband, as stubborn as his father-in-law had been, was not about to give in. My prediction was confirmed when I saw my daughter bound out of our bedroom, sobbing. Knowing the two strong-willed contestants, I prepared to assume my role as mediator. In the privacy of our bedroom, I faced my husband and was all set to begin my speech, when out of the corner of my eye I spotted an envelope sliding under the door.

Linda Saslow

$\overline{7}$

ON HEALING

It doesn't matter who my father was; it matters who I remember he was.

Anne Sexton

Tearing Down the Wall

*He that cannot forgive others breaks the bridge
over which he himself must pass if he would ever
reach heaven; for every one has need to be
forgiven.*

George Herbert

There was a moment, a day, when I first discovered that
my father was famous. I was about five years old, and my
parents had taken me to Disneyland. We were waiting to
get on the Teacup ride when dozens of people realized
that Ronald Reagan, the host of *General Electric Theater*, was
there. We were suddenly surrounded by eager, smiling
faces and arms begging for my father's autograph.

I remember looking up at my handsome father and feeling frightened that he was being taken from me, claimed
by strangers, swallowed by the crowd.

Daughters lean toward their fathers in ways that they
never do with mothers: tenderly, with unrequited longing.
If that father is famous, the longing for him cuts deeper

until it is a river running through your life, drowning every other relationship.

I was fourteen when my father was elected governor of California; I knew there would be no turning back. Politics is a demanding mistress and for eight years, California was my father's other child. I was consumed with sibling rivalry; I was angry, petulant. I wanted more of him, his time, his attention. I lashed out bitterly, tearfully, hurting him with my defiance, all the while loving him desperately. My real fury was at the life of public service I believed had taken him from me.

When he was elected president in 1981, America was now the favored child, or so I believed. During his two terms in office, I felt that when I reached for him, all I could grasp was his shadow.

I got my revenge with other men. I frequently chose ones whose lives had no opening for me, oftentimes, married men. Or I would set my sights on men who had no ambition, no future. Either way, they were stand-ins for the man who once taught me to ride a horse and swim in the ocean, who climbed hills with me on windy days to fly a kite and who could find Pegasus in a sky full of stars. I used other men to act out my rage, but the two who really suffered were my father and me.

The problem was that I hadn't separated the private man from the public figure. I had been looking at my father's chosen profession and goals as a type of larceny; they were stealing him from me. It took me many years to understand that the shadow people cast in the world is a part of them.

All the while I thought my father had abandoned me. The truth was that I had abandoned him.

I returned as he was starting to leave, pulled away not by his duty or his country, but by a disease. I have returned with a reverence for the life he lived: for the persistence of his dreams and the unfailing faith that let him burn past his history as a poor kid from a dusty Midwest town, past those who scoffed about an actor becoming president, past those who said his passion was just pretense. He proved them all wrong, and his absence left a hole in the world now that he is gone.

History will immortalize Ronald Reagan as the president who helped end the Cold War, who stood in front of the Berlin Wall and said, "Mr. Gorbachev, tear down this wall." As his daughter, I immortalize him in the quiet passages of my heart. By instructing me in the rhythms of nature, my father taught me about life. By waiting for me, the prodigal child, to come back, he taught me patience. I live my life differently for having known him. As dramatically as the Berlin Wall came down, the walls between us crumbled and I stood on open ground, wondering why I had ever put up walls at all.

After the anger, after the ranting and acting out, we finally grow up and we realize it's a gift to be born to someone who dreams big and reaches far. It inspires us to do the same, because their blood runs through us, and the lessons they pass on to us are powerful.

Patti Davis

Advice from a Tree

Nature and revelation are like God's books; each may have mysteries, but in each there are plain practical lessons for everyday duty.

Tryon Edwards

There are two things I remember vividly on the way to the hospital—my pounding heart and the calm, guiding fullness of the silvery moon at midnight. Here, now, WOW, it was really happening! As we pulled up to the entrance, I don't know how my rubbery legs got us into the elevator. Our daughter was so anxious to greet the world, she nearly arrived between the second and third floors! She was born so quickly the word "push" never entered anyone's mind.

Then my heart was pounding for different reasons. My eyes fixed on this beautiful baby as I drank in the newness, the preciousness, the raw love. Early the next morning the nurse smiled and asked me if I would like to give Laurel her first bath.

"Would I!" I gleamed. Such tiny little feet and hands,

beautiful round, red cheeks . . . yes, yes, *yes!* One of the many firsts I would enjoy. The sound of the water, the sponge, the gentle instructions from the nurse are as vivid today as they were then. Once she was bathed and wrapped, I held my baby girl high above my head. The light that guided us on the way to the hospital gave way to her first fiery sunrise. We drank it in together, holding each other close.

Ever since that night, the beauty of nature has gifted our connection. Early along the journey of fathering, I heard some "mother's wisdom" that if you take a baby outside and show it the moon, it will quit crying. Those nights when she cried, I took her out onto the front porch, held her up facing the moon and let her soak up the calm night. Soon she calmed down, snuggled in and fell asleep in my arms. The crisp chill in the autumn air as the cotton-wood leaves swayed in the bright moonlight—those nights were my favorite. I celebrated how nature bonded us in this unique way.

I loved being a father. I cherished seeing the world anew. As my daughter and I grew together, my relation-ship with my wife grew apart. The healthiest thing for everyone was to let go and let love find a new way. The unknowns of the court system wore on me as I searched deep to keep the hope, love and joy of involved parenting alive. I tried my best to keep a positive attitude, but some days the river of grief and fear ran deep.

One particularly difficult day, I agonized about my three-year-old daughter and the strong winds of uncer-tainty. *Why me? Why this? How can I remain involved and be the father I want to be?* I just had to get outside to breathe and somehow find a way back to my center, to the peace and clarity of my soul. I managed to open the front door, and, with tears in my eyes, I began to move along the side-walk, shuffling one foot in front of the other without a clue where I was going. Halfway down the block, exhausted, I leaned against a huge cottonwood tree; the deep ridges of the bark supported me and held me close. I said, "I need your help! Can you help me? I need some advice."

I felt the tree reach out to me, wrap me in its branches to comfort me as I leaned against its steady trunk. This old and wise cottonwood seemed to speak to me with steadfast wisdom.

Dear Friend,
Stand Tall and Proud
Sink your Roots deeply into the Earth
Reflect the light of your own true nature
Think long term
Go out on a limb
Remember your place among all living beings
For each yields its own abundance
The Energy and Birth of Spring
The Growth and Contentment of Summer
The Wisdom to let go like leaves in the Fall
The Rest and Quiet Renewal of Winter
Feel the wind and the sun
And delight in their presence
Look up at the moon that shines down upon you
And the mystery of the stars at night
Seek nourishment from the good things in life
Simple pleasures
Earth, Fresh Air, Light
Be Content with your natural beauty
Drink plenty of Water
Let your limbs sway and dance in the breezes
Be flexible
Remember your Roots!
Enjoy the View!

I walked home feeling hopeful, renewed and loved.

Over the years I've walked by that old cottonwood friend many times as it reaches to the sky. I've always stopped, breathed in its fresh air and given it words of thanks for teaching me that it's the growth and change that make us strong; it's the gratitude that makes us tall.

Nearly a decade later, as my teenage daughter and I walked together, the moonlight reflected on the waxy leaves of an old, large tree. Laurel said with an excited voice and big smile, "Look at that tree, Dad. Isn't it amazing?"

Tears came to my eyes. "It sure is," I said. "It sure is."

Ilan Shamir

Taken for Granted

Doing good is the only certainly happy action of a man's life.

Sir Phillip Sidney

It's strange looking back on my relationship with my dad, because for the first thirty years of my life we didn't have much of one.

No, we weren't separated by divorce, long hours at work or even a grudge lingering from my not-so-pleasant adolescence. Over the years I'd developed a vague composite of my father—a tall, shy man who worked very hard.

I just never really paid him any mind. He was a fixture that I took for granted.

Then nine years ago, when I was pregnant in my second trimester and bleeding, my dad showed up to offer his help. I was surprised. Sure, in the past he'd given me financial aid, fatherly advice and fixed broken appliances, but money, words and tools weren't going to prevent a possible miscarriage.

Still, every day he came. He took me grocery shopping, did the heavy chores of cleaning and undeniably maintained my household.

At first I felt awkward having my retired dad around on a daily basis. I even felt guilty at times. I didn't know how to relate to this calm, quiet gentleman because at the time that's all he was to me, a nice, helpful man.

But, somewhere between folding laundry together and watching *The Oprah Winfrey Show,* we started talking. It seemed silly that it took a talk show's calamity to break the ice between us. Yet soon we were voicing our opinions on everything from politics to child-rearing. Then things got more personal, and we started swapping life stories.

My dad became a remarkable man who had a fascinating history—and a new granddaughter.

After the baby, Dad continued coming over and helping out. Our projects began extending beyond household chores, and he taught me how to hold a hammer "like a man." We built furniture, then a shed. To this day he arrives religiously at my door every other week to help me get ready for Girl Scout meetings in my garage.

My friends find it amusing that my dad is still helping out even though my two girls have started school full-time, but they don't understand. It's not just about the work anymore. Working together broadens our understanding of one another. I doubt the issues of race, religion and morality would have come up during a brief lunch at the mall. So you're more likely to find my dad and me complaining about the inflated prices of nails in a hardware store than having a polite conversation over a hamburger. He is my best friend, after all, and that involves more than talk of the weather.

Knowing him is to understand what makes a man noble.

When he reads this, he'll probably laugh and wonder

what the heck I'm talking about, but I know him now and that's an honor I almost lost.

So, to anyone searching for a true friend, I recommend starting with the person you may have taken most for granted.

Donna Pennington

Letter to a Stranger

Only the brave know how to forgive; it is the most refined and generous pitch of virtue human nature can arrive at.

Lawrence Sterne

"You've got a letter from your dad." My husband's words stopped me on my way into the bedroom to change clothes. It was late in September, and we were already running late for the Friday night football game where our boys were marching with their high-school band. We left the house a few minutes later, with the letter still sitting on the counter, unopened. I wanted to have a fun evening, yelling with the other band parents, not wondering and worrying about what the letter contained. And I did have fun—but I did wonder, and worry.

I had missed having my father in my life as a child. By all accounts, we had been extraordinarily close before the divorce. Most kids I knew in the sixties and early seventies had a dad, and being different was painful. Information regarding my father was always scarce. When

Mom said anything about him, she just told me that he was a good dad. But the question always plagued me: If he was such a good dad, why didn't he want to see me? Whatever the reasons, I had seen my father a grand total of three times since second grade.

As the years went by, the emotions I felt about him ran the gamut: hurt, disappointment, anger, indifference. At one point, in my thirties, I wished secretly that he'd just die so that I wouldn't have to worry about him trying to come back into my life. I was doing well—a happy marriage, two children of whom I was extremely proud, a job that gave me satisfaction—why did I need a father? But the years continued to pass, and though I still felt very angry at times, I found myself turning forty and wondering about him. Was he happy? Did he have other children? What had *really* happened between him and my mom? I asked a colleague who was visiting the town where I thought my father lived to check the phone book for his listing. She found his name and brought me his address. I carried it in my checkbook for six months.

A few months before my forty-first birthday, I wrote the letter I had been contemplating all summer. And rewrote it, and rewrote it. After all, the man was a stranger to me, and I to him. The finished product was short and matter-of-fact:

September 13, 1997

Dear Bill:

I apologize for calling you by your first name. I have no idea how to address you—everything I can come up with sounds too weird, so I hope "Bill" will be okay for now.

I don't have many questions, but they are the ones I need to ask. It may be that your ability to answer them is long gone—and if so, it's okay. You don't have to worry about starting something here that you might not want to finish. I really want nothing more from you than a few facts, but I'd particularly like to hear your side of things. But please, if you decide to answer, do it in writing. I don't think I'm ready for more than that right now.

It was a very self-protective letter, designed to minimize the hurt I felt sure was coming: no answer, or worse, a cool "thanks but no thanks."

That Friday night after the football game, I read:

Dearest Karen:

Wow, what a surprise to hear from you. . . . Your question about why I did not keep in touch—I made a decision that it was better for you and your brother not to be sent back and forth between your mother and I. . . . I now realize that was a wrong (underlined twice) decision. That was a long time ago. . . . I miss you so very much, and only hope that someday I could be a part of your life again.
My love,
Your dad

There was more, of course, but I focused on those two parts; he was sorry he hadn't been a part of my life in the past, and he wanted to be a part of it in the future.

It took me a month to sort out my feelings enough to write again:

October 29, 1997

Dear Bill:

Truthfully, this father-daughter thing scares me to death. What if you're someone I don't like? Worse, what if I'm someone you don't like? What if we write a couple of letters and then you quit writing and it's like I'm five years old again? I guess it's about forgiveness. It requires no action on your part; I will be satisfied whether or not you ever respond again because I made the effort. I hope God will take the effort and make it into something good. I'm sorry if a writing relationship is less than you were hoping for. A year ago, even writing a letter would have freaked me out . . .

November 5, 1997

Hi Sweetheart:

The fact that you wrote back makes me feel so good, like the void in my life is starting to be filled. I do understand your feelings about me, all I can hope for is our starting to learn about each other will hopefully become a comfortable situation for us both.

His future letters were full of details about his happily married life and his past. In each one, he reiterated his love for me. Mine were a little more restrained, full of questions and misgivings:

November 13, 1997

Dear Dad: (I had progressed!)

I have to tell you that it was kind of uncomfortable for me to read that you love me. I mean, you don't really know me, so how can you know that you love me? But then, I thought about my children at five years old and knew that I would love them if I never saw them again. So it's a different kind of emotion for me; I can't say yet that I love you, or if I will. All I can say at this point is I, too, am full of emotions and want to continue to learn about you. I will leave the rest to God to work out.

We continued to write to each other, usually within a week of receiving the other's letter. We decided to meet after the holidays, and on Christmas Eve I spoke to my father on the phone for the first time in more than fifteen years. We both cried. On January 9, 1998, when I walked off the plane and saw his face filled with joy (and looking so much like mine), I knew God had indeed worked it out.

Now, I speak to my father almost every day, and our lives have become irrevocably entwined. Each conversation ends with "I love you," and now I believe that he means it, as I do. The anger I felt so often has mysteriously disappeared, and a wonderful sense of peace has taken its place. My life has been changed, in joyous ways I could never imagine, by that letter to a stranger.

Karen L. Cooper

The Haircut

His heart was as great as the world, but there was not room in it to hold the memory of the wrong.

Ralph Waldo Emerson

The ringing telephone pierced my peaceful silence as I relaxed in my living room. It was the admitting clerk at the hospital, calling to tell me that my mother was being taken there by ambulance.

When I arrived, they were wheeling Mom in on the stretcher. Her eyes were open in a blank, glazed stare; she could not move nor utter a single word. Mom had suffered a massive stroke. The doctor told us that any treatment would be futile and that death was imminent. As we watched in disbelief, she slipped from life to death in three hours' time. I was devastated and delirious with grief.

My parents had been married almost forty-two years. My mother had spent most of this time raising their ten children and trying to survive my father's alcoholism. Dad's problem had plagued our family. Mother's only solace was her faith in God and her commitment to her children.

Four years prior to my mother's death, my father retired, his drinking subsided, and their lives seemed less tumultuous. Somehow, after decades of abuse, there seemed to be more peace between the two of them and a lot less anger. It was as though she forgave him for the many years of sorrow and remorse.

But years of living with an alcoholic father had filled many of the ten of us siblings with anger and animosity toward him. We had not been blessed with the forgiving heart of our mother. Dad had been our cross to bear; Mom had been our savior. When we went to their house it was to visit Mom; the fact that Dad lived there, too, was immaterial. When we called home, it was Mom we conversed with. We shared our hopes, dreams, future plans, sorrows, joys, heartaches and accomplishments with her. I guess we always knew she would relay all this information to Dad, but we never really sat down and had a meaningful conversation with him.

When Mom passed away, I was only twenty-two and living near my parents' home. It was difficult surviving without my vibrant mother. She had been the sun that could melt the winter snows, the electricity that could illuminate and enlighten my mind, the North Star as my guide to wherever life would lead me—and now she was gone.

Left here on Earth was my father. I had known for a long while that I was Dad's favorite. He was less harsh with me as a child than with my siblings. Perhaps it was because I was the youngest or maybe because I always tried to see a reason or find an explanation for the way he was. I prayed and trusted that God would make sense out of a senseless situation. As I grew older I learned to divide my father into two people: my sober father, whom I loved, and my alcoholic father, whom I treated as a stranger. This had become my key to survival.

One day not long after Mom died, I stopped by Dad's to see how he was doing. It was obvious that he was getting by, but not very well. He had learned to use the washing machine, vacuum, stove and microwave, but his menu included lots of hamburgers and hot dogs and barrels of coffee. It was also evident that he was in dire need of a haircut.

Mom had started cutting Dad's hair when they were first married. In forty-two years I don't believe he ever went to the barbershop. I spent hours watching her gently and lovingly cut and trim everyone's hair, with clippers, shears and comb in hand.

"Do you think you could cut my hair?" my father asked sheepishly.

Cowardly, I responded, "I've never cut hair."

"But you've watched your mother cut hair hundreds of times, so do you think you could try?" he pleaded.

I felt doomed. Why did it have to be me? Wasn't there anyone else who could fill these shoes? With grave reluctance I relinquished all my objections. I managed to utter only two words, "I'll try."

Dad retrieved the comb, scissors and clippers from the cupboard, and I began my feeble attempt. It occurred to me that I had never really "touched" my father, as we'd never been a hugging, touching family. I was even a bit embarrassed, not so much by my inept haircutting skills, but by my inability to cross the abyss that had always been present between my father and me.

Dad's graying hair was beautiful. Graceful waves gently covered up any mistakes I made. While I clipped away at his hair, carefully cutting around his ears and trimming with the clippers, we chatted about my son, my brothers and sisters, Mom, and the haircuts she had given over the years. This was truly the first real conversation I ever remember sharing with my father. As I finished, I trimmed his eyebrows and brushed the hair off his neck. He wet his hair and combed it—not a bad job after all.

Throughout the next few years, I became my father's barber. The job seemed to get easier with each attempt, and it was a ritual we both came to enjoy. Our conversations grew to include politics, religion, world affairs and what we would do if we won the lottery. He truly was a brilliant man and could talk for hours about the conflicts in the Middle East, China and Europe, giving insight into all the details and backgrounds of these events. He'd endured twenty presidential elections and subsequent administrations. His recollection of history and current world affairs was enviable.

Ten years passed. One day, when Dad was almost eighty, I visited him and cut his hair. When I had finished, he shyly asked if I might wash his hair in the kitchen sink. A bit embarrassed at first, I reluctantly agreed.

If I should live to be an old woman, I will never forget that day. It is forever imprinted in my mind. I can still see myself standing there at the kitchen sink, washing his beautiful gray curls, rinsing away all the many years of despair, anger and remorse. The washing, the touching, the healing, the forgiving between an old man and his loving daughter closed the abyss that had always been present between us. It would vanish that day like new snowfall on an early spring morning, to evaporate and disappear forever. The wounds that had festered for so long had finally healed; scars had been clipped, trimmed and washed away.

Margaret J. Wasilewski

Peela

The more we know, the better we forgive.

Madame de Stael

Up until she was five years old, my sister Peela (that's what I called her and still do) had my mom all to herself. Then Mom remarried, and Peela felt a little left out. Mom's new husband, my dad, adopted Peela shortly after, and she took his last name. When she was eight years old, I came along, and when she was ten, my little sister, Barbara, was born.

For her whole life, Peela felt like she was an outsider in our family. She got in trouble a few times as a teenager. She never felt like she belonged and thought that Dad never really cared for her. Even though her birth father had another family with several kids, and her visits with him were few and far between, she adored him in her own little fantasy.

Over the years, Peela always remembered our dad on Father's Day and his birthday with cards or letters. She began this as a young girl, with drawings and handmade cards, and continued into adulthood, never forgetting a special occasion. Still, she felt certain that he was untouched by her gifts.

Peela was fifty years old when Dad passed away. She couldn't bring herself to visit him in the hospital. She feared sarcasm or even rejection. But she came to support Mom the minute we called and informed her of his passing. She had no tears for Dad, only concern for Mom. Peela had lost her own husband a few years earlier, and so she was very helpful in guiding Mom through making funeral arrangements.

Mom and I decided that Peela could help us go through some of Dad's belongings during her stay. He had a big gun cabinet with several drawers on one side. As we went through drawer-by-drawer, paper-by-paper, we found out he was quite the pack rat. Then we saw it—a bundle of cards, pictures and letters all kept together—every single thing Peela had given him over the years. I'll never forget her looking at me with tears welling up in her eyes, then crying, "He really did care."

We should have known.

Donna J. Gudaitis

Father Knows Best

And be kind to one another, tenderhearted, forgiving one another, just as God in Christ also forgave you.

Ephesians 4:32

It went without question. I would take my walk down the aisle alone.

As a young girl, I daydreamed that my natural father would show up like "Wonderdad" on the day of my wedding, clad in a tuxedo, ready to walk me down the aisle. In these naïve fantasies, he'd have a justifiable excuse for not being in my life, and, of course, I'd forgive him.

During my teenage years, the fantasy changed somewhat. Focus on forgiveness for the father I'd never met was replaced by rebellion toward the father I'd been given.

I had chosen to call my stepfather "Dad," and he had gladly accepted that. But that decision was the only thing we ever agreed on. In the perfect vision of hindsight, the road of disagreement went both ways, but I only saw it as a one-way street—headed the wrong way.

In the teenage daydream, 1 would stubbornly march myself down the aisle, unescorted by anyone. It would be my proclamation: I was an independent woman. I didn't need to be "Daddy's little girl." Thankfully, I matured by the time I got engaged. "Revenge of the Bride" was not the theme of the day. Our differences had faded over the years, and we'd called an unspoken truce.

But the decision of anyone walking me down the aisle had already been made for me when shortly before my wedding, my dad had his leg amputated. He used a walker, unable to endure the painful chafing and soreness that occurred from a prosthetic leg.

Our marriage ceremony took place at a park in our hometown where my fiancé, David, and I had played as children. It had a picturesque bridge over a shimmering lake with two swans swimming side-by-side, and the lush, green grass and weeping willows gave it romantic appeal.

Arriving in the limo, I tried to focus on the beauty around us. I made the bridal walk down the path, past my seated family and friends—alone. Until that moment, I hadn't realized I didn't want to walk alone anymore. True, my dad was never Wonderdad, and we never resolved the issues between us, but he was the only father I had. The path seemed to go on forever, but finally there I was, standing beside David, ready to become his wife.

When the judge asked the guests who gave this bride to be wed, I literally stopped breathing. We never did this during the rehearsal. Would my mom speak up? She and I never discussed it. I sent a quick prayer up to heaven, begging to avoid an embarrassing situation.

"Her mother and I do." I turned around and saw my dad, pulling himself up to a standing position despite the obvious discomfort and attention it drew. I searched his eyes, but they only stared straight ahead. Could it be he had thought of this moment before? Had he been disappointed in not walking me down the aisle?

For the first time in over twenty years, I considered the feelings of this man who I never thought of as a person. I'd made him out to be a monster. But he wasn't a monster. He may not have been the perfect daddy of my dreams, but he was the father I'd been given.

When I realized my dad wasn't going to meet my gaze, I turned to David and his reassuring smile, but I still felt a wave of guilt. I reminded myself there was no physical way my dad could have walked me down the aisle. But it was more than that. I should have seen him before, as I did today.

As I stood at the base of the bridge, I noticed the sign across the lake: "Welcome to Lord's Park." The name hit me. We were in his park, in his hands. It was time to forgive both the father I'd been given and the father I'd never met. The Father in heaven knew what was best for me, even when I had no clue what that was.

I may have not been my daddy's little girl, but I had always been my Father's little girl. I hadn't made that walk down the aisle alone after all.

Abigail R. Gutierrez

A Piece of Chalk

Conversion is no repairing of the old building;
but it takes all down and erects a new structure.

Joseph Alleine

In our home it was natural to fear our father. Even our mother was afraid of him. As children, my sister and I thought every family was like that. Every family had an unpredictable dad who was impossible to please and a praying mama who was there to protect the children. We thought God planned it that way.

We were good children. Mama was always telling us we were, even if Daddy couldn't see it. Part of this was because we dared not do anything. We were quiet, timid children who rarely spoke, especially never when Daddy was home. People thought God had blessed Mama with the sweetest girls. She was always so proud.

Then came the day we found something new and fun to do. It wouldn't upset anyone; we'd never take the risk of doing that. We discovered we could draw pictures with chalk on our wooden front door, and it would rub right off.

We could have lots of fun, so we set to work drawing and making lots of pretty pictures all over it. We had a great time. It surprised us to see how talented we were. We decided to finish our masterpiece, knowing Mama would just love it. She would want all her friends to come and see it, and maybe they would want us to do their doors, too.

The praise we expected did not come. Instead of seeing the obvious beauty in our work, all Mama could see was the time and effort she would need to clean it off. She was mad. We did not understand why, but we knew all about anger, and we were in big trouble!

Off we ran to find a place to hide. In our wooded yard it was not hard for two small children to find safety. Together, we huddled behind a tree and did not move. Soon we heard the frightened voices of Mom and our neighbors calling out to us. Still we did not budge. They were afraid we had run away or drowned in the pond out back. We were afraid of being found.

The sun set, and it began to get dark. Those around us became more anxious, and we became more frightened. Time was slipping by, and the longer we hid there, the harder it was to come out. Mom was, by now, convinced something awful had happened to us, and she resorted to calling the police. We could hear all the voices drawn together in a group. Then the search was on again, this time with strong male voices overpowering the others. If we were frightened before, now we were terrified!

As we clung together in the dark, we became aware of yet another voice, one we instantly recognized with horror: our daddy. But there was something strangely different about it. In it we heard something we had never heard before: fear, agony and despair. We couldn't put a name to it then, but that's what it was. Then came his prayers, tears and prayers intermingled together.

Was that our daddy on his knees pleading with God?

Our daddy with tears running down his face, promising God that he would give his life to him if he would safely return his girls?

Nothing in our lives had prepared us for this kind of shock. Neither of us remembers making a decision to come out. We were drawn to him like a magnet, our fears dissolving into the forest. We don't know yet if we actually took steps or if God somehow moved us out and into Daddy's arms. What we do remember are those strong, loving arms holding us and crying, hugging us like we were precious.

Things were different after that. We had a new daddy. It was like the old one was buried that day in the forest. God had taken him and replaced him with another, one who loved us and was ever thankful for us.

Mama always told us that God was a God of miracles. I guess she was right. He changed our whole family with a piece of chalk.

Holly Smeltzer

Unpaved Roads

We pardon as long as we love.

François Rochefoucauld

Dad was a large-built man who stood six-feet tall and weighed 320 pounds. His voice was loud and deep and always gave the impression that you had better not mess with him. And nobody did! When he stood there with blazing, fiery eyes and blasted you with his short temper, you were sure to know the fear of God—a fear I came to know at a very early age.

Whenever I did something wrong, there was no conversation about what I had done or any reason given to help me change my behavior—just the belt, that hard, leathery belt. Since the very first time he whipped me, I knew that God came equipped with a belt.

When Dad and his buddies got together at our house, they'd start roughhousing while Dad reminisced about the days when he was the Golden Gloves boxing champ. Whenever he'd try to take on one of the guys, they'd back away. They knew they were no match for him because no one was rougher or tougher than my dad.

I felt fortunate that he was gone most of the time. He was a heavy equipment operator for a road construction crew, and his work took him on the road for a week at a time. But when Friday night came, and I saw Dad's car coming up the driveway, I'd run and hide. Then Mom would give him a full report about how bad I was during the week. Soon he'd yell my name and summon me to the kitchen. As he shouted in my face, the stench of alcohol and cigarettes permeated my nose and throat, nauseating me.

"I'm in no mood for this!" he yelled. "I've worked hard all week, and now I have to come home to this!" Then off came the belt.

What Dad didn't realize was that this method of discipline encouraged the kind of behavior he was trying to prevent. And whenever I would call him on it, he'd get twice as mad and shout, "Don't do as I do. Do as I say!"

This misguided form of discipline led to more problems as I grew older. And what made it worse was that I had no one to turn to. I was terrified of Dad and didn't know what to expect from his outbursts. I vowed that when I was old enough, I would leave home and stay as far away from him as I could.

My parents eventually divorced, and I didn't see my dad for years. My mother kept in touch with me and called one day to tell me that Dad went to the doctor and that he was very ill. I thought about what I should do or if I should do anything at all. We weren't close. How could we be after all those things he had said and done when I was younger? I didn't even like the man! Oddly enough, I felt this strange tug at my heart that wouldn't let up. I decided to give him a phone call.

"Dad, it's Lindy."

"Lindy?" he said, sounding as though he was scanning his memory for all the Lindys he'd ever known.

There was a silence as I hesitated, trying to carefully choose the right words. "I heard that you weren't feeling well and decided to give you a call."

"The doctor says I don't have long to live."

"What's wrong?"

He started to cry and muttered some words I couldn't understand, and then he hung up the phone.

A couple of weeks passed while I thought about Dad's situation and what role I should assume. I still hadn't figured it out when I received another phone call from my mother informing me that he had been admitted to hospice. Indecision led to desperation. I knew what hospice meant. I didn't want to believe that Dad was terminally ill. How much time did he have left? I had to know.

I jumped into my car and hurried over to the hospice care facility. When I got there, two nurses and the attending physician immediately consoled me. After reviewing Dad's file, I had all the information I needed. All those years of drinking had finally taken their toll. Dad had cirrhosis of the liver, which made him susceptible to the cancer that was spreading through his entire body.

I dreaded what came next. I felt as though I didn't belong there. What was I going to say to this man I hadn't seen for years? I felt like this was a scene from someone else's life, not mine. Uncertain of what I was doing, I walked toward Dad's room, pushed by some force I didn't understand. And even though I slowly paced my steps, I reached his room much too soon. As I peered around the doorway, he noticed I was there and told me to come in.

"Look at me, Lindy," he said as he wept. Then he held up his arm and showed me his sagging skin. "I'm wasting away, and there's nothing I can do about it."

"I know, Dad," I said, trying not to feel his pain.

Then I listened to him talk. He talked about my mom and how things didn't work out. He told me that he tried to do the best that he could for me, but everything always turned out wrong.

"I love you, Lindy," he sobbed. "I made mistakes, and I'm sorry."

I held him in my arms as he confessed his many regrets. And even though I didn't say it, my comforting gesture showed I forgave him.

My head was spinning after I left the hospice. All in one night I felt shock, fear, forgiveness and grief. My dad was a broken man, not the man I knew when I was growing up. Nothing could touch him then. He was the Golden Gloves champ.

My vulnerability let loose, and I began to wail like a little child. Not only did I cry for what we hadn't had in our relationship, I cried for what we could still have if he weren't dying. He seemed like such a changed man now and like a father I could have lived with. Now he was dying, and there wasn't anything either of us could do about it.

But there was still time.

For the next few weeks I visited Dad every night after work. We sat and talked. I even ran errands for him and bought him a few items he wanted. I was starting to see things about him I'd never seen before. I knew the bad side, all right. But now I was starting to see the good, and we were becoming friends. But just as our friendship was starting to grow, he took a turn for the worse.

One night, when I went to visit him, the staff said they didn't think he would last through the night. The doctor increased his morphine but it wasn't regulated yet, and he was in considerable pain. I was told that every fifteen minutes his beeper would sound, and at this time I could push a button that would send intermittent doses of morphine through his body. I decided to stay with him through the night. Dad talked very little. And every time the beeper sounded, I pushed the button, realizing that by doing this I was also making it harder for us to communicate any longer.

Dad held on for two more days, and I was with him when he died. As I held his hand, I kissed him on the forehead and said, "It's okay, Dad. You can go now. Grandma and Grandpa are waiting for you, and now you can build roads in heaven."

After all, Dad was good at road construction. He paved the road and bridged the gap between us.

Linda Poehnelt

Apology to a Child

By the time that you can read this
You may not know me well
But then again, we may be close
You can never really tell.

You used to call me "Daddy"
I used to hold you tight
I used to bathe you every day
And tuck you in at night.

I should have held your Mommy more
We should have sat and talked
The love grew cold, the words got hot
And then one day I walked.

I cried the night I left you all
I cried again today
It seems sometimes that's all I've done
Since that night I went away.

I hope you know I love you
Though I wasn't always there
I think about you constantly
And you're always in my prayers.

I hope someday you'll understand
That this thing hurt me, too
I hope you'll know, I always have
And always will love you.

Last night I drove to where you live
I saw your bedroom light
I sat and watched and thought of you
Until the sky grew bright.

I'm not the man I used to be
I've learned a lot since then
I wish that I could turn back time
And live with you again.

But I can't change the things I've done
Or take back things I've said
All I can do is write these words
While lying here in bed.

I hope that when you read this
You will know this one thing's true
That no one else in this whole world
Means more to me than you.

Ron Wutka
For Daniel, Jacob and Rebekah

I Want My Daddy Back

God gave us memories that we might have roses in December.

James M. Barrie

A few years ago my beloved daddy had to be placed in a nursing home. Alzheimer's disease stole his memories and ability to function on his own. I was heartbroken— I knew it was the end of the daddy that I'd known. I couldn't conceive of him not being there for me like he'd always been. Always cheerful and happy, he had a "Howdy!" and a kind word for everyone he met.

Even though the staff at the nursing home was kind and treated him very well, he always asked Mom when he was going to be well enough to go home. It broke her heart for her to explain—again and again—why he could not do that. He'd frown and get sad, but would acquiesce.

I grieved when I saw him. Daddy was no longer a vital adult male; he was a young boy again in his mind. I'd frequently leave the nursing home in tears. I missed him so much. I wanted my daddy back.

One Christmas I reminisced about the days when my parents first moved to Florida. For many years, Daddy had played Santa Claus during the holidays at various shopping centers. He loved to watch the eyes of the kids as they sat on his knee and recited their wishes for Christmas.

Since I live in Orlando, where Walt Disney World is located, I went shopping for a Santa hat and found one with Mickey Mouse ears. I brought it to Daddy at the nursing home. To my surprise, he sprang from his chair, grabbed the hat and placed it merrily on his head. He insisted that Mom help him on with his red flannel shirt, exclaiming, "I've got to go entertain the girls!" He then shuffled out to the nurses' station. He grinned at the nurses and proceeded to do a little jig.

"Ho, ho, ho!" he bellowed, his eyes twinkling. One nurse pretended to sit lightly on his knee. Another grabbed a camera and snapped pictures. Mom clapped her hands and nearly squealed with delight.

For one fleeting Christmas moment, I had my daddy back.

Deb Haggerty

Daddy's Story

The only things that count in life are the imprints of love we leave behind us after we are gone.

Albert Schweitzer

Once, when we were children, my sister said, "Daddy will be home today."

"Who?" I questioned.

"Our father, silly. Remember, the man who's never here?"

"So what! I'll hardly see him anyway. How long will he not be here this time?" I said sarcastically.

"Who knows? You know Daddy," Bette replied.

And I thought to myself, *No, I don't.*

Noteworthy events of our lives are not the usual ones like birthdays and anniversaries. Sorrow sculpts us more than joy. Sorting through our lives we stumble upon the tough times—the times that teach us how to forgive.

My relationship with my father is one area of my life where I struggle to recall more than just a few happy times together. My sister, Bette, remembers good times with Dad. She was older, and I think he knew how to relate to an older child. He taught her how to play golf and gave her driving lessons. She thought he had something to do with hanging the moon. Their times together almost never included me, his other daughter. But the past can't be changed, just forgiven.

When I really needed a father's guiding hand during my teens, Mother and Dad divorced, then he was gone for good. Eventually, he remarried, and a great person was added to our lives: his wife, Elizabeth. Leave it to a woman to know how to rebuild a relationship with a man. And Liz did.

When he was diagnosed with cancer, I faced it knowing that the time left was precious. Deep within, I yearned to share some close, intimate time with my daddy before it was too late. I loved my father and knew, in his way, he loved me, too. But for both of us it was an undeclared love.

We asked Liz to tell us the best time for Bette and me to fly to California to see them. I definitely wanted to visit before it became a deathbed scene. Unfortunately, that happened sooner than I expected.

My heart was in my throat when I walked into Dad's living room and saw him sitting on the couch, frail, shaking and gray with weakness. The golfer, the World War II dollar-a-year man, the successful business tycoon, had been transfigured by illness. His strength was so depleted that Liz had to help him back to bed almost immediately upon our arrival.

On and off all that weekend we spent time at his bedside, discouraged. My plans for a one-on-one talk with Dad were fading fast, and I was sorely disappointed.

On our last evening there, Elizabeth came back from Dad's room and told us he was getting up, getting dressed and wanted to speak to us all together. I was unprepared for the man who, with good color and great strength, walked unaided down the hall toward us. His stride was sure and straight, as though some unseen power propelled him. It was hard to believe it was the same bedridden man I'd seen only hours before.

He took a deep breath, and when he spoke his voice was strong and steady. His eyes, no longer cloudy, were clear and direct as they fixed intently upon Bette and me.

Pausing cautiously between each sentence, he said, "Somewhere I've heard you can't change what you don't acknowledge. So here goes. I know I've fallen way short of being a good father to you. My own life and desires got in my way. I owe you an apology. So, before the man upstairs lets me go home, I need to say: I am so sorry. There are so many things I should have done that I didn't. I'd like to lay the blame on someone else—but there isn't anyone. The buck stops here. I can only hope you have enough love to indulge me and forgive your old man for all the times he's failed you. I know I don't deserve it, but I need your forgiveness." Then he paused, and for a minute tears choked his voice. " I've always loved you. It's a love you can take to the bank." Then he whispered, "I guess that's all."

We couldn't have taken more. Speechless and in tears, we hugged and patted him, mumbling our love. In the next minute, like flipping a switch, Dad again became the fragile, terminal patient. He was totally spent. I began helping him back to bed, almost carrying him down the hall, and for some reason Liz and Bette let me do it alone.

When we got back to his room, he sat on the edge of the bed as I knelt on the floor beside him. In a hushed voice he whispered, "Ruthie, did that help? Do you understand how much I love you?"

"Oh, Daddy, of course, I understand. I've never loved you more in my life." And for a little while we simply sat in the quiet. Finally, the child in me was holding tightly to her daddy's hand—an unforgettable moment.

Exhausted, he slept, and I lingered at his bedside, not wanting to break the newly found connection we'd made with each other. None of it completely answered my childhood questions of why he'd found the demands of fatherhood so difficult, but the adult daughter, mother and wife I'd become could understand what the child could not. His words had been like a medicine to me. I felt healed.

I'd had my longed-for special time with him. I wouldn't ask for more. There was forgiveness, and there was love. It was enough.

Ruth A. Hancock

Time to Forgive

Life that ever needs forgiveness has as its first duty to forgive.

Bulwer Lytton

I am my father's only daughter, but I always felt far from being Daddy's little girl. Growing up, I often felt judged against impossible standards to prove my worthiness. I can't remember how many tears stained my cheeks, pillow, and Mom's and friends' shoulders from the many thoughtless and harsh things my father said.

As I grew older, the already large rift between us grew to the point that we knew very little about each other. We could say that we were related, but that was about it. It got so bad that when he came to visit, we had nothing more to say beyond the usual small talk: "Hi, how are you?" and "So, how's the weather been?" He never understood me and, as I ventured off into the performing arts, he understood me less.

When I announced my major in college would be musical theater, he attacked my dreams with a tirade of insults about my talent and common sense. I knew from then on that it was pointless to try and make my father see my side or change myself to make him happy. The distance between us was seemingly unbridgeable, with little to no chance of us ever meeting on the same level again. I cannot lie; it pained me to be without a father in my life. He was physically present some of the time, but emotionally unavailable otherwise.

Our nonexistent relationship tormented my mind; my soul moaned quietly, aching to be healed. Finally, on the day I turned twenty-one, the pain welled up with such intensity I could not hold it back. It held me captive until I could find a way to heal it. Unsure of what to do, I decided to meditate and see if anything came to me on how I could begin to mend my bruised and broken soul. Nothing came but a deep sense of peace. Then, as if mental clarity just knocked me over the head, I got pen and paper and began to write. I wasn't even sure what I was going to write, but then pen met paper and the words, like the tears from my eyes, poured forth.

I wrote a letter to myself from my father in which he apologized for ever hurting me, and he told me what he could never say in real life: I love you and am so proud of the beautiful young lady you have become. I cried for what seemed like days. I cried until my chest hurt, my vision blurred and there were no tears left. I wailed in a voice wrought with twenty-one years of buried pain and hurt. I cried for every time I wouldn't allow myself to cry for the injury my father had caused. For all the times I wanted him there and he wasn't. For all the words I wanted to hear that he never said. For all the birthdays, recitals, plays and award ceremonies he missed. I cried the well of tears my soul had saved, until it was dry.

Physically and emotionally spent from the act of forgiving through the deluge of tears, I collapsed on my bed and fell into a deep sleep. When I awoke, it was late evening, and a peace I had never known my entire life until then filled me. I said my father's name and felt not even a flicker of anger or hurt, but instead felt a love I had never known for him.

From then on things changed immensely, and I worked on bridging the vast rift that had existed between us for far too long. My dad and I became friends and went from talking every couple of weeks to talking every night. We were determined to break the cycle of dysfunction that began in his childhood.

We decided to start over as father and daughter and do all the things we never did when I was younger. In fact, we compiled a list, and we work on checking off things every year. We have planted a garden together, made dinner together, walked hand in hand and gone to see a Disney movie in the theaters. He has read me a bedtime story and tucked me in, told me how beautiful I am and that he loves me. We've shot some hoops together, gone jogging together, worked in his store together, laughed and cried together.

Now when you ask my dad about me, he'll proudly tell you I'm his little girl—well, big girl now. Everything has changed because I decided to forgive a man who had caused me so much pain. I learned to love unconditionally, and it is a lesson I am sharing with my dad. He's a great student and puts his heart and soul into it. We're more than just related now and even beyond father and daughter. He is healing my wounded soul, and I am mending his broken heart. We are growing up together all over again.

Yes, there is a time to forgive, and the time is always now. In forgiveness I gave myself the gift of having the father I always wanted—and he got a daddy's girl.

Tracy Ryzan Ross

Closer and Closure

Music moves us, and we know not why; we feel the tears, but cannot trace their source. Is it the language of some other state, born of its memory?

Letetia Elizabeth Landon

Hardware. Replacement parts. A man's domain of shiny knobs, hinges and screws. I eased uncomfortably around the display in the aisle.

I heard, "Can I help you, ma'am?" Brushing a hand over his fringe of cottony hair, the clerk looked up again. "Say, aren't you one of Mac's daughters?"

I nodded.

"Sorry I couldn't make it to his funeral. Sure will miss him. He liked to stop in each time he drove your mom to her volunteer shift at the hospital. Just to shoot the breeze, you know."

I knew. Daddy loved people, sharing with them, helping them.

"Say, don't think I'm weird or anything, but Mac came to me in a dream the other night."

I lowered my eyes.

"Yeah, well . . . sure will miss him." He cleared his throat and glanced away.

What had made me seek out the hardware store? I wondered hours later as I headed back to Colorado from Kansas. Closure? Or was the better word "closer"? Maybe simply to feel near Daddy just once more by prowling one of his favorite places?

His unexpected death left me reeling, feeling fragmented, incomplete. Now I recognized a new emotion creeping in: jealousy. Envy that a near stranger had dreamed about my daddy, felt close to him. *Why not me, God? I feel cheated. I just need . . . something, anything, a second chance to say good-bye.*

Blinking away treacherous tears, I steadied the steering wheel and turned on the car radio, searching for music to keep me alert on the long and lonely drive home. An "oldies" station played "Goodnight, Sweetheart" and I sang along. " . . . Although I'm not beside you, still my love will guide you . . . " I choked out the words.

I want him back, God. I need him to be part of my life, I thought.

I had been away six weeks, helping with the funeral and settling my mother. Back in Colorado, I tried piecing together my old routine. Eagerly, I reclaimed my longtime volunteer work at a local nursing home. It was a safe place to both give and receive love.

Although I hadn't inherited his talent, I certainly had acquired Daddy's love of music—and the powerful desire to share it. Playing the piano and leading the music midweek in a casual sing-along never failed to lift my spirits. A genuine love for each of the elderly residents radiated joy in my life.

However, there were some songs I avoided. Songs I had heard over and over again until the words were a part of my heart and mind: "Green Grow the Lilacs," "Now Is the Hour" and "Moon River." And, of course, there was Daddy's all-time favorite, the hauntingly tender "Oh, Danny Boy." Songs that reminded me of him serenading us during the lazy Sunday afternoon car rides of my youth. Songs that painted powerful portraits of Daddy with his harmonica. The memories were tender. And precious.

So I surprised myself that day at the nursing home when I pulled out the dog-eared sheet music for one of Daddy's more rollicking choices, "Shoo-fly Pie." My fingers flicked out the light melody. "Do any of you recognize this one?" I began to sing.

Falteringly, by ones and by twos, age-rusted voices joined mine. Their words rattled like corroded screws in a battered cigar box. But as creaking memories hinged open, the song gained strength.

And then I heard it: Daddy accompanying me on his harmonica. The lively strains, the breathy notes, even his upper and lower dentures clacking a syncopated rhythm all their own against the shiny metal of his best "mouth organ." His presence was real. Tangible. I could *feel* him standing right beside me. He was with me. He was part of me.

Eyes swimming, voice cracking, I sang haltingly to the song's end. Limp-wristed, I paused to let the merry music wash over me, to save and savor the last lingering notes, to preserve the sacredness of both the moment and the memory.

Then I swiveled around on the walnut piano bench and came face-to-harmonica with matted-haired, pajama-clad Paul. The snaggle-toothed new resident grinned and wheeled closer. Broad fingers fumbled with an oversized red harmonica. A trembling hand tapped out the spit against his thigh.

"How's about we try another?" Paul cackled and lifted the harmonica.

My heart sank. *So much for a touching, spiritual moment.*
Swiping at my damp cheeks, I took a deep breath, closed
the sheet music and put it beside me on the bench.

Then, I glanced around the wheelchair-lined room
where aged human beings—dented and scarred—were
parked bumper-to-knee, like idling taxicabs waiting at a
busy airport. There was blind Alma, well-groomed Irene,
pain-filled Eleanor, Jim and Hazel and Florence . . . row
after row of the people I loved. All of them waiting
patiently, expectantly, for me to lift their spirits with
another song. And I smiled—inside and out—right into
Paul's grizzled, grinning face.

So we made music together: Paul with his harmonica,
me with my piano, and all of us singing and winging our
way through the sunny autumn afternoon. I knew I didn't
need a momentary sign or vision. Daddy was as much a
part of each note as he was a part of me. That was better
than a final good-bye.

For the last song that day, I chose the melancholic and
gently lilting strains of "Oh, Danny Boy." My daddy's
favorite.

Carol McAdoo Rehme

Secret Tears

The gods conceal from men the happiness of death, that they may endure life.

R. Lucan

"I know you don't believe this now, Nancy, but time will heal," my friend Jean said, as she hugged me a few minutes before my father's funeral. "It will get better. I promise."

During Daddy's funeral, tears fell freely down my face, but Jean's words continued to echo in my mind. During that hour of intense sorrow, I thought back to the days when I was a child. I remembered watching out the picture window waiting for Daddy to come home from work. I thought of the times that I was sick and Daddy was with me, holding a cool cloth on my head. When I had problems as a young mother, I called on Daddy. *What will I do now that he's gone?* I wondered.

For the previous four years, my father had lived in a nursing home. Parkinson's disease destroyed his muscles, and dementia had taken away his mind. The ongoing stress of losing him had taken a toll on my health. I knew my blood pressure was high, but I didn't take the time to go to the doctor for treatment. I pushed myself to the limit and, suddenly, it was all over. Daddy was gone, and I would never see him again.

Each night when the house got quiet, tears filled my eyes and I cried myself to sleep. I tried to keep my secret tears bottled up inside of me. I wanted others to think I was in control of my emotions and that I was handling the grief.

One month later, I felt lightheaded and dizzy at work. I had my blood pressure checked and discovered that it was soaring well into the danger zone. My pulse was racing as well. I wondered if I had waited too long to seek medical attention. I went to the doctor immediately, and he placed me on a medication that would control my blood pressure and heart rate. He encouraged me to take additional measures to control the stress in my life.

I might be able to control the stress, I thought, *but I cannot control the grief.* The secret tears remained with me, night after night. Even the closest people to me were not aware of the number of tears I had shed. Many times I remembered Jean's words and wondered when and how the grief would end.

Nine months passed. With every special occasion, I grieved. My birthday was very difficult, but Daddy's birthday was even harder. Father's Day was pure torture. Even Memorial Day brought grief and gloom, since Daddy was a veteran honored in a special Memorial Day service.

One November night, I went to bed dreading Thanksgiving Day. What did I have to be thankful for? I was too sad to be thankful. I woke up at six o'clock that morning. I realized that I had been crying in my sleep. I was too tired to get up and eventually fell back asleep. During the next two hours I had a dream that turned my life around.

I was sitting alone in what appeared to be a waiting room. The walls were white as snow. Empty chairs lined the four walls. In my dream I wondered why I was waiting. Suddenly, the front door opened. A bell was hanging from the top of the door. As the door opened, the bell jingled. I knew that someone was coming inside. I looked up and saw my daddy. His body was perfect. He was no longer crippled. His white hair glowed. He smiled at me. He was wearing the suit that he was buried in.

I jumped up from my seat and ran and hugged him. He felt the same as he did when I was a little girl and I ran to meet him when he arrived home from work. I recognized his scent. He hugged me back and kissed me. For a few seconds, he held me tightly.

"Please don't ever leave me again, Daddy," I cried. "I have missed you so much. Please stay with me forever."

Daddy broke our embrace and looked into my eyes. I felt a peace that I hadn't felt since Daddy became ill some five years earlier. "I will be with you forever, Honey," he whispered. "I will be living right here in your heart," he said, as he gently touched my chest. "As long as you continue to love me and want me to be with you, I won't ever leave. But you must take care of yourself. Always remember that I love you."

Just as quickly as he had appeared, he was gone. I opened my eyes and even though there were tears on my pillow, I also felt a sense of peace that I hadn't felt in years. I jumped up to tell my husband what I had just experienced. I called my mother to give her the assurance of my dream, too. Seeing him, hearing him, smelling him, all proved that he had surely been there with me.

I don't understand exactly what happened that morning, but I do know that the secret tears are now gone. Since then, I have been able to cope with the loss of my father. When I think of him now, I don't remember his illness or the difficult days preceding his death. I think about the good times. I remember the glow of his white hair, the smile on his face and feel the love in my heart the last time that I saw him in my dream. My blood pressure is now under control; my cardiologist gave me a clean bill of health.

Occasionally, I think back to Jean's words. I realize that time does heal many wounds. In my heart, however, I know that the real healing came to me through a dream— and that my tears were not a secret after all.

Nancy B. Gibbs

8

TRADITIONS

*What an enormous magnifier is tradition!
How a thing grows in the human memory
and in the human imagination, when
love, worship, and all that lies in the
human heart, is there to encourage it.*

Thomas Carlyle

Smeared Ink

*The manner of the giving shows the character
of the giver more than the gift itself.*

John Casper Lavater

My dad has been writing me letters every Thanksgiving
and Christmas since I was able to read. When I was little,
I would always find three letters taped neatly in a row,
sorted by age, on the bathroom door. First Kenneth, next
Kristina, then me, all sealed with our names scrolled
across the white envelope neatly in blue ink. Every holiday I eagerly anticipated my letter.

"Amy, I'm so proud of you," he wrote to me when I was
in fourth grade. "I know you will make a wonderful
Paddington Bear in your class play.... I pray for you every
day. I love you, Daddy." The blue ink has smeared and
faded over the years. The paper is tattered and torn
because I crammed most of the letters into my childhood
junk drawer.

"Amy, you will always be my baby . . . ," Dad told me
once after a very stressful teenage year. "I love you, Dad."

I remember that year. I was sixteen. A sophomore. And I wanted freedom. One thing that Dad was not ready to give me.

Then one year Dad hung our letters up on the bathroom door early—before Christmas dinner, instead of after. I tore mine down, put it in my pocket and went to my bedroom to read it.

"Amy, you're growing up so quickly. I can't believe you're in your third year of college. You're turning into a beautiful woman. . . ." I continued to read the neatly scrolled blue ink. "God has been good to you with the many gifts you have. Always use them for his glory. . . . I love you, Dad." I wiped my eyes, folded the letter and crammed it in my top dresser drawer with his other letters. I opened my door, headed downstairs and met my dad on the landing of the steps.

"Thank you," I said. He smiled and continued walking. I had never thanked him or written him back. I had always expected his letters and assumed he knew I looked forward to and appreciated them.

We opened our Christmas presents after our turkey dinner. As we were cleaning up gifts and the wrapping paper that was strewn over the living room floor, Dad announced that he had one more present for the three of us.

"You can't keep them, though," he said, as he reached behind the tree and pulled out three, small, neatly wrapped boxes. "This one's for Kristina. Here's Kenneth's. And Amy's," he said, as he handed us each a shiny silver box with a blue bow on top. "Now open them together."

We eagerly ripped off the paper. Inside each box there was a Waterman pen, each a different color. We all looked at him, confused.

"Every letter that you've gotten from me has been written with your pen," he explained. "And when I die, I hope you will take these pens and write to your children."

I stared at the pen. Its tip had been cleaned; the ink removed. I knew I probably wouldn't see the pen again until after Dad had died. I snapped the box shut and handed him back his pen.

That night I ripped my drawer out of the dresser and dumped all the contents on my bed. I fumbled through junk that I had kept over the years, wishing I had put all the letters together in a safe place. I knew some were missing and that they were irreplaceable.

I reread the letters. Each ended with "Amy, I love you, Daddy" or "I love you, Dad." I wondered when he stopped being my daddy and started being just Dad. And I wondered when he had noticed the change, too.

I remember when he was Daddy. I used to grab my daddy's hand in parking lots, to cross the street, and simply just to slip my hand into his. I wondered if Dad missed those days as much as I did.

The letters not only marked the transitions of my life, but also ultimately reflected my relationship with Dad over the years. He didn't see my fourth-grade play. But he knew that when I was ten years old, Paddington Bear was very important to me. And even though he wasn't there to see it, he was praying for me. And continues to.

Years have passed since I last saw my Waterman pen. But the letters keep coming. And now I am about to become a parent. I know that someday I will hold the Waterman pen, just like Dad did, and write to his grandchild.

And one Christmas, my Waterman pen will once again be under the tree, neatly wrapped in silver paper tied with a blue bow.

Amy Adair

Across the Pond

Letters are those winged messengers that can fly from east to west on embassies of love.

Jeremiah Brown Howell

A blue-collar worker with a young family to support in the 1950s and '60s in England, Eddie Knight was very much the breadwinner, while his wife, Alice, took care of the home and the children. While Eddie worked, the day-to-day dealings with his two daughters and his son were mainly Alice's domain.

As the children grew up and left the nest, it was Alice who wrote the letters to keep in touch. Imagine then how delighted his eldest daughter, now living 200 miles away in London, was, when on her twenty-first birthday she received a letter from her dad. He finished the wonderful letter by writing, "And don't expect a letter every twenty-one years!"

As time passed, Alice did sterling work, writing letters and staying in touch with the children. In 1983 the news came that the eldest daughter, now married with two small children, was leaving England with her family to move to the United States, to Rochester, New York. Alice's letters became even more important and were like a lifeline as the little family struggled to settle in a new land and a new culture. Hearing about familiar things quelled the homesickness they all felt at first.

Three months after they had moved, the unthinkable happened. Alice had a fatal asthma attack. Family on both sides of the Atlantic were devastated at the shocking loss. Struggling with his grief after losing his beloved wife of forty years, Eddie made a decision. The way he could honor Alice's memory would be to continue her writing tradition. So he picked up his pen, and a remarkable correspondence began that would span fifteen years and thousands of miles across the Atlantic.

Every week, letters between father and daughter would wing their way between England and the U.S. Each contained as many pages as the weight limit for a regular airmail stamp would allow, and every bit of white space on the paper—both front and back—was completely covered with writing. The writing was never a chore but became an important part of the lives of both father and daughter. Imparting as well as receiving news became an eagerly anticipated activity each week.

At first their letters were full of feelings of their sad loss, but soon the daughter was giving much-needed advice, as Eddie learned how to keep house like Alice had. He wrote of some laundry disasters and asked how to get once-white underwear, now pink, white again. He courted advice about how to iron shirts, what cleaned the bathtub best, how to clean windows without streaks, and he asked for recipe tips. He always kept his sense of humor, and the letters were a joy to read.

That first Christmas, Eddie decided to make "Alice's Shortbread," a family tradition. His letters caused great merriment in Rochester as he relayed tales of the dough falling apart, or of it sticking to the pan, or any other malady that can befall shortbread. Finally, he triumphantly wrote of his success, a perfect shortbread, and enclosed the winning recipe. His daughter immediately sent a Hallmark card to congratulate him.

For Eddie it became a ritual each evening to sit down and write about his day. It didn't matter how uneventful it had seemed, he always found something of interest to impart: a lovely bird he had seen at his bird feeder, a neighbor he had bumped into on his grocery shopping expedition, news of his English grandchildren or a wonderful sunset. His letters were always interesting; he always found life a joy.

Across the pond, his eldest set aside each Sunday afternoon so she could fill her six sides of paper telling Eddie all about her family's new life. She wrote of the adventures they were having in their adopted country and of her husband's new job, of an unfamiliar school system, of different customs, strange food and great adventures. She described their exploration of the local beauty spots, as well as taking him on their journeys to Florida and the sunny Caribbean. She sent photographs of the children so he could see them grow. She showed him the beauty of a New York fall when Mother Nature dons her most beautiful colors, and of the huge snows of winter, courtesy of Lake Ontario. Through her letters he experienced their new lives and learned so much about a different land.

Eddie cut articles and photographs out of the local and national newspapers to keep the family in touch with their homeland. He wrote of his trips to Ireland, and of a fortnight spent cruising along the Danube River. He told her about his choir concerts and the thrill of performing. When Torvill and Dean turned the ice dancing world on its head at the Olympics with "Bolero," father and daughter watched on both sides of the Atlantic, and afterward each rushed to write to share the thrill of it all. They talked of politics and the ups and downs of family life. He kept her in touch with home; she showed him a whole new world. And they knew that despite being apart geographically, very few dads and daughters had the opportunity to "talk" as they did. He once wrote that he felt that he knew his American grandchildren far better than his English ones who lived only a few streets away.

In 1996, the blue envelopes from England stopped. Eddie fell down the stairs at home and moved into a nursing home. The weekly correspondence from America continued to arrive each week, and the nurses delighted in reading the letters to him. Eddie was no longer able to write, but he still eagerly awaited the arrival of the familiar blue airmail envelope. In Rochester, the absence of the envelopes signaled the passing of time and the inevitable aging of a beloved father.

Two years later, Eddie died peacefully in his sleep. When his son went through his things after his death, he discovered boxes and boxes of letters. Eddie had lovingly kept them all. Across the Atlantic, in Rochester, there were more boxes of letters, for she had kept all of Eddie's letters, too. They had amassed a fifteen-year history of a family and a father, both struggling with new lives, but with this loving lifeline between them.

I am the daughter, and Eddie was my father. Even now when something exciting or interesting happens to us, I have a strong urge to pick up my pen and tell Dad all about it.

For someone who once wrote not to expect a letter every twenty-one years, my dad certainly stepped up to the plate after Mum's death and achieved his aim of keeping the whole family together. His letters—his legacy of love—will connect generations.

Linda Bryant

Christmas in a Nutshell

Though the gods feast on ambrosia, I savor the sweet meats of trees. I first encountered walnuts in the net stockings distributed by a jolly, red-suited man. Together with tangerines and candy canes, the English walnut became a Christmas treat—until the year there weren't any.

The hustle and bustle of preparing for Christmas put the purchase of those relished walnuts at the bottom of my list. After dinner at my relatives' home one Christmas night, Uncle Richie asked, "Can I get anyone anything?"

Without even thinking twice about their availability, I said, "Do you have any walnuts?"

He looked surprised. "Walnuts . . . hmmm . . . I'll look." Having searched the kitchen cabinets, he returned and announced cheerfully, "I guess I'm going shopping."

Store-hopping on December 25th proved to be a futile event. Empty-handed, my red-faced uncle sighed sheepishly. "The stores are closed. I'm sorry."

From that moment, my father took it upon himself to be an annual walnut-bearing Christmas elf. Each year, those special treasures prompted promise and laughter, camou-flaged in a brown paper bag, crowded into a red-and-green stocking, crammed to abundance in a shoebox lined with tissue or wrapped in dainty holiday paper. This con-tinued every year until my dad died.

An emptiness pierced the Christmas of 1985 even amid the joy of sharing gifts. Wrappings from all the opened pres-ents cluttered the living room. A sudden stillness accompa-nied a final gift my unusually quiet brother, Doug, presented to me. My unsteady hands reached out to touch the shirt-sized box, as my eyes searched the pain in his hazel eyes. It was a moment that lasted a lifetime, filtered through shared experiences, hopes and dreams. Indecision was trapped in the tender but cautious presentation of my brother's gift to me. "I almost forgot this one," he whispered.

Five pairs of anxious eyes focused on the shiny, dark blue paper punctuated with dainty white snowflakes. Their ice-cold appearance must have frozen my fingertips, which carefully untied the curly silver ribbon. There in the box were three pounds of walnuts encased in wrinkled, woody shells. The room held its collective breath, treasur-ing the tears that trickled down my cheeks and mirrored by those in my brother's eyes.

No gift was ever more precious. No walnut dessert has ever tasted as sweet or as palatable as the memories of my father. Every crunch imposed by the nutcracker echoes his love for me. It is impossible for me to shell or chop wal-nuts without sensing a delicious presence that warms my heart.

It's been eighteen years since that Christmas when Doug continued Dad's tradition. No Christmas goes by without a "nutty gift," and year after year, I'm touched by love that comes in a nutshell.

Bobbie Bonk

Slow-Dance

The CD player blared the voice of Luther Vandross singing "Dance with My Father," as my husband attempted to teach our fourteen-year-old daughter how to slow-dance, in preparation for her first formal school event. He gently gripped her waist with one hand, while holding her hand in the other. They stepped from side-to-side and back and forth to the rhythm of the music.

At first, she stumbled and wanted to lead rather than follow his guiding footsteps. "Oops, Pops—I'm bad!" she remarked each time the heel of her shoe clumsily mashed his toes. Smiling, he said, "It's okay, Boo. If these big feet could walk through the jungles of Vietnam, they can withstand the test of a dance with you." Then, one more time they commenced to step and slide.

I grinned and watched them, recalling a time when my father taught me how to slow-dance.

I remembered that at the dinner table one evening, I told my parents about the high school sock-hop to be held the following week. Bashfully, I said "I want to go, but I don't know how to slow-dance with a boy." My two younger sisters, one in elementary school and the other still in preschool, just stared at me blankly while my parents sympathetically smiled.

After the meal had ended, my dad beckoned me to follow him into the living room. While I sat on the sofa, he opened the door of the stereo console underneath the record player. He glanced through the record covers of Ella Fitzgerald, Sarah Vaughan, Duke Ellington and Etta James—until finally selecting Nat King Cole's 1956 "After Midnight" album.

He carefully removed the vintage vinyl record from its cover as if he were handling a priceless china plate. Then, holding the wide shiny black disc between the palms of both hands, he delicately placed it upon the turntable and set the needle on the first band. As the record spun around, the music began to play, and my mother entered the room with my sisters trailing behind her. She had an illuminating beam of pride and affection on her face. Dad turned to me and said "Now, watch this, Puddin'." He then politely took Mom's hand, and they began to dance in a jazzy sequence of two-steps in the vacant area between the stereo and the coffee table.

Dad gazed into Mom's dark-brown eyes while she gazed back into his with complete adoration. I was embarrassed to look at them because they were so absorbed in each other as they paced to the musical vibrations of sentimental merriment.

I thought to myself, *Who are these people? I have never seen them hold hands before, much less dance together.*

Before Dad and Mom had stepped halfway through "Just You, Just Me," they lost some of their audience. My two sisters left for other parts of the house to whirl hula hoops and play with their jacks rather than witnessing our parents' odd movements to strange melodies.

When Dad and Mom noticed I was still in the room,

they suddenly emerged from the trance they had fallen into and stopped dancing.

Wow! How do I follow that high-stepping act? I thought.

Mom quietly smiled at Dad, then left the room to check on my siblings.

Clearing his throat, my father said, "Does that give you an idea of how to slow-dance?

"Yeah, Dad. That was boss!"

"Your mother and I could really cut the rug in our day."

What a crack-up, I thought. *Cut the what?* Quickly, I blurted out, "Daddy, could we dance to something groovy?"

"I thought you wanted to learn to *slow-dance,*" he replied.

"I do, but that music is too lame. Nobody I know will be groovin' to Nat King Cole!"

"I see. Well, what do you suggest we dance to? There's Ella, Etta, Duke. . . ." Then, he began to search through the stereo cabinet again.

Before he could pull out another of his all-time favorites, I said, "How about dancing to some of my 45 records?"

Momentarily hesitating, he said, "Okay, bring them out here and we'll see what we can do."

Clearly, that was all he needed to say for me to hurry off to my room and retrieve the records. I brought back my entire collection of Motown 45s that were single recordings by Stevie Wonder, The Temptations, The Supremes, Aretha Franklin, The Miracles and Marvin Gaye.

As Dad sifted through my sounds from Hitsville, U.S.A., he said, "Which do you think we should play first?"

"Well, they're all out of sight, but maybe . . . I know, let's start with this one."

I tossed Aretha Franklin's record "Ain't No Way" onto the player and turned the knob to "45." I grabbed my father's hand and said, "Let's dance, Dad."

As Aretha belted out the words to the song, Dad

showed me how to do the circular two-step. This time I could sense he was embarrassed.

"Is this the kind of music you listen to?" he said.

"Yeah, Daddy. This is what all the kids listen to nowadays. Doesn't it just blow you away?"

There was no response from my father. He just stared into each corner of the room, at every turn of our dance.

Inevitably, the soulful cry of lyrics set to notes attracted the rest of the family into the room once more. This time, my sisters were trying to imitate the movements our father demonstrated as he slow-danced with me.

Dad shouted to Mom over the music, "This is what they dance to these days. Can you believe it?"

Now, as I watch my husband and daughter sway to Luther Vandross's song "Dance with My Father," I treasure this father-daughter ritual.

The beat goes on.

Stephani Marlow James

"Dad, tell me again how you
used to just *listen* to music."

Eat Dessert First

Everyone whose deeds are more than his wisdom, his wisdom endures. And everyone whose wisdom is more than his deeds, his wisdom does not endure.

The Talmud

My father had his own way of imparting wisdom. He handed down stylish phrases when I least expected it. They burst forth suddenly and always came as a surprise.

One hot July Saturday morning when I was a little girl, my dad asked me to join him for lunch. This particular day, it was just the two of us. My mother, also invited, declined the offer for nobler pursuits: a manicure and wash and set at the beauty parlor, where her standing appointment would never be sacrificed for anything as mundane as lunch.

"It looks like it's just you and me, Missy," Dad said with a twinkle in his eye, followed by one of his pat remarks. "So, let's go and raise some hell."

The restaurant was bustling with people, providing

enough background noise to add an air of merriment to our meal. My dad and I parked ourselves in a booth and were handed menus so large they reached over the top of my head and offered a dizzying array of choices.

Over grilled-cheese sandwiches and french fries for me and a fat hamburger, charcoal-burned and blood-red for him, my father revealed a most alluring confession: "You see that woman over there?" he pointed to a table a few feet away. I surreptitiously snuck a look. "That's Marion, the gal who had a crush on me all through high school and into my law school years."

With that came a wink of an eye to Marion, whom I could hear giggling all the way across the room. I, the budding adolescent, sat on the edge of my seat as he regaled me with this top-secret piece of news.

"But," my father said, moving his head so close it was practically touching mine, "she couldn't hold a candle to your mother."

And so began our luncheon rituals, where we broke rules, recounted anecdotes and shared secrets. Months later, I perused the menu at a different restaurant, this time in Manhattan, twenty minutes from our home. On this particular Saturday, I couldn't decide what I wanted to eat. My father, realizing my dilemma, summoned the waitress. "Bring us the dessert menu," he said.

Obligingly, she returned with a small, leather-bound book, edged in gold leaf with a list of desserts that had my mouth watering. Profiteroles, chocolate mousse, chocolate cake and chocolate soufflé were mine for the asking. I felt as though I had entered chocolate heaven.

"But, Daddy, we haven't even had lunch."

"Even better," he winked, that same Marion wink. "When in doubt, eat dessert first!"

"What will Mommy say?"

"It will be our little secret," he said.

And there we sat on that chilly autumn afternoon in a cozy French restaurant. He, dipping a long silver spoon into a parfait, and I, gorging on layers of chocolate cake oozing raspberry and covered in a white chocolate sauce. I remember wondering if life could get any better than that.

There were to be many more lunches and dinners in our future. I accumulated a wealth of knowledge from our talks, and I was privy to personal insights and private thoughts he loved sharing with only me, mainly because my reactions were always so spontaneous and sincere. I was genuinely interested in everything he had to say, which made me, his audience of one, a perfect dinner companion. Sometimes Mother asked half-teasingly, "Whatever *do* you two have to talk about?"

My dad also had a reflective side that felt protective and nurturing. He took me seriously, too, by paying credence to my individuality and giving me room for self-expression. As a lawyer, he was accustomed to problem solving. Our meals provided a venue into which I could retreat and unload my worst trepidations or, conversely, share my happiest moments. Without judging, he gently guided me through childhood, adolescence and young adulthood, and served as my one-man support system and guardian of my soul.

Even after I was married and living in Manhattan, Dad and I had a standing weekly dinner date that I came to rely on and treasure. He never once canceled out, despite his busy schedule, teaching me to honor commitment and value the importance of keeping appointments. The only Tuesday we didn't meet at a restaurant was when I delivered my daughter. That night, Mom, Dad, my husband and I dined together in my hospital room. My father brought the champagne that he had been saving for this occasion.

"Even my new granddaughter can't get in the way of

our Tuesdays." And there was that wink as we clicked glasses and toasted the birth of Elizabeth.

My father was in his sixties when it abruptly ended. His death brought with it a sense of longing I have never yet been able to relinquish—longing for something that would never be the same again.

Dad died too young and had a lot more tasting left to do, but I revel in the fact that we savored much of life together. We went on for years enjoying each other's company. After his parting, despite my sadness, I was energized, knowing how lucky I was to have shared the Tuesdays of my life with him and the great life lessons he passed on to me.

I now take my two grandchildren, Andrew and Caroline, out to dinner weekly. They can choose any restaurant they want, as I was privileged to do so many years before them. Recently Andrew sighed, perusing a menu too big for a seven-year-old's eyes. "I don't know what I want to eat."

Caroline chimed in, "I can't make up my mind, either, Grandma."

My father's voice came echoing back. "Then, I guess we'll have to eat dessert first!" I told them.

And they, sitting back in wide-eyed disbelief, broke out in smiles, and "eating dessert first" was exactly what we did.

Judith Marks-White

My Father's Chair

*Children's children are a crown to the aged,
and parents are the pride of their children.*

Proverbs 17:6

Somewhere between the first Christmas carol of the season and the exhausting shopping, baking, decorating and wrapping that follows, the true meaning of Christmas slowly slips away—until the moment I walk through the door into my parents' home.

When my husband, Ken, our daughter, Megan, our granddaughter, Hailey, and I walk inside, we are greeted by a sensory explosion of sights, sounds and fragrances of the season, and the spirit of Christmas swells up in my heart once again! What evokes this feeling the most is not the music and the decorations, but the sight of my father's chair. It was here that I first heard the Christmas story and was instilled with our family's faith and traditions.

"Have a seat," the courtly Southern gentleman whom I call Daddy offers, as he springs from his chair. I sink into the cushions, which have been recovered; the fabric of the furniture changing over the years along with the lives of the people who once occupied it.

Early on, my mother taught us children that Father's chair was a sacred seat of honor and respect. Even the family pets learned the unspoken rule in our house: Without an invitation, father's chair was off limits. My mother created this special haven for her husband as a shelter from the storms of life. His chair also became the nucleus of our family life. Here we learned lessons, celebrated joys and solved problems.

Although I have no recollection of my first days spent in the chair, I've seen the black-and-white photographs of my dad cradling me while sitting in it. My first memories of him in his chair are the stories he told me, and the songs he sang to me there.

Life with father was idyllic my first few years of life, until the day I was forced to share his chair with a baby sister. There was no place in my heart for this creature, but there was always enough room in my father's chair. Sharing this sacred space helped me accept this visitor, who obviously had come to stay.

Throughout our childhood, when the clock struck 5:00 P.M., my sister and I eagerly anticipated Dad's arrival. Peering out the window until his big black car came tooling around the bend, we squealed, "Daddy's home!" Then my mother, my sister and I, joined by a menagerie of family pets, rushed out to greet him.

After dinner each night we gathered around my father's chair for the nightly news, from which Dad derived his lessons in politics, current events and humanity. Later we watched television, read books or played games, learning to be good losers or gracious winners. We also learned all about sports from this armchair quarterback. Every Saturday our family studied our Sunday school lessons around Father's chair. Mother often raised an eyebrow

over his version of the Bible stories, but the Heavenly
Father who Dad presented seemed far more approachable
to me.

Special healing powers exuded from that chair whenever my father lifted us up there with him to kiss a scrape,
and it became a magical place for mending broken hearts
as he wiped away our tears with the monogrammed
handkerchiefs we'd given him at Christmastime.

My sister and I raced to collect the loose change underneath the cushions that had fallen from his pockets when
he vacated his seat. He doled out candy, gum and other
goodies from the treasure trove in the chest next to it for
special achievements or simply to say, "I'm proud of you."

Yet not every memory around the chair was so pleas-
ant—it could quickly become the hot seat, since Mother
sent us there for discipline, to learn right from wrong. We
also had to obtain permission from the man in the daunting chair to go out with our friends.

My brother was born when we were teenagers, and the
early activities of the chair were repeated, but soon afterward, my sister and I left for college. Life continued with
all its twists and turns, and it wasn't long until we were
bringing our future mates home to meet our parents. If
father offered a young man his chair, this was a sure sign
of approval.

When my siblings and I eventually married and left
home, the family dog, Chip, grew decrepit, and Daddy
often found another seat so as not to disturb his faithful
friend curled up in the chair. The house grew quieter, but
not for long. Laughter filled it again when the grandchildren arrived. What a beautiful sight as my mother sat
on the arm of the chair while my father lovingly held each
one of his grandchildren, recalling the same stories and
songs he had read and sung to us as children.

It's been years since the laughter of young children and

the bark of a dog have been heard around the chair. The grandchildren are grown and our dog, Chip, is gone, but at Christmas, history once again repeats itself as Hailey discovers all the joys of her great-grandfather's chair: the stories, the songs, the goodies and the coins.

This Christmas, like all the others before them, we gather around my father's chair to hear the Christmas story. It's livelier than ever, filled with the banter of four generations.

Susan Wales

Donuts

What an enormous magnifier is tradition!
How a thing grows in the human memory and
the human imagination, when love, worship
and all that lies in the human heart is there to
encourage it.

Thomas Carlyle

My mother passed away when I was six, and my dad became the only parent for my siblings and me.

Every morning before Dad went to work, he frequented his favorite neighborhood donut shop. He always left with a bear claw pastry and a cup of coffee. Occasionally, Dad would take me fishing on weekends or to his work during the summer, and we always stopped at Dad's morning hangout, where he would share conversation and jokes with the employees and customers alike.

When we left, accompanying the bear claw in a small box was a chocolate-covered donut for me. Dad would help me up and into his truck. My ankles just cleared the seat as my shoes stayed clear of dirtying the upholstery. I sat close to Dad, just under his wing, feeling honored, safe and comfortable. My job during the journey was to hold Dad's coffee between my knees to keep it from spilling. Even though the cup had a lid, I did my job well; the coffee never did spill.

After catching my first rainbow trout, Dad was so proud, we stopped by the donut shop on our way home to show off the trophy. The applause they gave me felt good, but to see how proud Dad looked was the real gift.

As time passed and I grew older and bigger, the donut shop became a special place for us to celebrate my wins from swimming and downhill skiing competitions. Even if I didn't win or place, Dad would still take me to that familiar place of sharing. We always left with the little box holding one bear claw and one chocolate-covered donut.

Eventually, I grew up and left Dad's home. On my wedding day, before he walked me down the aisle, Dad handed me a small gift box. When I opened it, I found a small chocolate-covered donut. My heart melted quicker than the chocolate frosting would have in an oven. We held each other and both cried. He told me how proud he was of me and that I would always be his little girl.

Dad continued going to his favorite donut shop long after I left. I only returned there once, with my first baby daughter. Dad glowed with pride, holding what seemed to be the best trophy yet to share with his friends.

In October 1989, Dad found out he had inoperable cancer. We lived an ocean apart, and our visits were few.

A year later, I was attacked and beaten, landing me in the hospital, undergoing three back surgeries for crushed vertebrae. Dad's cancer had progressed so much that his body was barely able to hold him up. Against doctor's orders, he flew to the hospital to comfort me. When he arrived, I was in traction and barely able to move. Dad's frail body lay over my chest, and with his skeletal arms he hugged me, saying if he could give me any gift in the world, he would trade places with me at that very moment.

As they prepared me for surgery, I watched Dad's eyes pour tears that would fill a dam. He asked the anesthesiologist to take care of his little girl. They wheeled me out of the room and into surgery. When I woke up, I was back in my room. Nobody was around. As I reached for the telephone to call Dad, I saw a paper plate holding a donut covered with chocolate.

I never saw Dad again. He'd become so weak he had to return home. The cancer took him just days after he left my bedside.

Now when I drive past donut shops, I can't help but smile, recalling those memories, my greatest trophy.

Gail Eynon

Wedding Day

She slips toward him
all dressed in white.
Never before has he
beheld such a sight.

His throat closes tight,
not a word can he say,
to this precious daughter
on her wedding day.

She floats even nearer,
a smile on her face.
Her small, dainty hand
on his arm she does place.

The organ notes swell,
the doors opened wide,
he'll soon give away
this vision, this bride.

In step to the music
they head down the aisle.
Why does he sense
it's at least a mile?

He wants to go back
and run for the door,
to return to their life
as it was before.

She was his first-born,
the apple of his eye.
When had the years
so quickly passed by?

He looks straight ahead,
plants a smile on his face,
for the sake of the man
who will soon take his place.

The last steps approach,
he starts to pray,
"Lord give me strength
to give her away.

He kisses her hand
and squeezes her arm,
whispers to the groom,
"Protect her from harm."

The young man nods slowly,
tears fill his eyes,
as he receives the hand
of this treasured prize.

Pamela G. Smith

$\overline{9}$

ACROSS GENERATIONS

The words that a father speaks to his children in the privacy of home are not heard by the world, but, as in whispering-galleries they are clearly heard at the end and by posterity.

Jean Paul Richter

Apa's Motto in Life

God is our refuge and strength, a very present help in trouble.

Psalm 46:1

In Hungary, before World War II put an end to it all, my grandparents, who raised me, and I had a prosperous life. Apa, which means Dad in Hungarian, was the only father I knew. He was a judge in the village where we lived, and my grandmother ran the general store. They owned a farm where I often watched Apa till the soil with the help of his two oxen. He never shrank from hard work and took great pride in providing well for his family.

It is still so hard to believe that everything we had, everything we knew, could change so dramatically. When the war finally ended, life did not improve for the people of Hungary. Soviet occupation and the new communist government brought with it new atrocities. Because Apa spoke out against these, he was soon in danger of being imprisoned. In late fall of 1947, we fled to freedom.

A refugee camp, or displaced persons camp as it was

called, in neighboring Austria became our new home. *Spittal an der Drau,* on the Drau River, housed hundreds of destitute refugees. Although dismal and crowded, the camp provided a roof over our heads. We were clothed with donated goods, fed cabbage and potato soup each day, and we were safe and protected from communist rule. So what did it matter that we were penniless?

To Apa, it mattered a great deal. He hated living off the charity of others and not being able to buy me the book I would glance at longingly when we passed the bookstore in town. Of course, the first thing Apa did at the camp was to sign us up to immigrate to the United States of America, where we would have a better chance at a new life, but he also looked for ways to make our life easier at the camp while we were there.

Just beyond our dismal home was another world. It was a beautiful, natural world of mountains, clear, cold streams, rolling, flower-carpeted hills, and small farms dotted with grazing animals. It was this other world that ignited my imagination with its beauty and gave me hope. Often I would slip away from the confined world of the camp, roaming and exploring the hills and valleys, and filling my stomach with wild blueberries. One day while out walking, I discovered the beautiful river, the Drau, just a half-mile from the camp. I returned often to the river where I sat mesmerized, gazing at the surrounding mountains and dreaming of better days. It became my favorite retreat, and one day I told Apa about it.

"A river?" he asked with great interest. "How far is this river from the camp?"

"I don't know. But it takes me a half hour to walk to it," I replied.

"Good. I will go with you to the river tomorrow."

"Oh, you will love it, Apa," I said enthusiastically. "It's the Drau River, and it is so beautiful!"

He replied thoughtfully, "I have always loved rivers. Rivers benefit animals and people."

The following morning, Apa and I set out on our walk to the river Drau. Once we reached it, I splashed around in the shallow, clear, rushing water, while he walked up and down the bank. Soon, I noticed he was cutting some branches from the river willows growing all along the bank. By the time we headed back to the camp, he had a large armful.

"What are you going to do with them?" I asked him as we walked together.

"I will make some baskets," Apa replied. Then I remembered that in the past his hobby had been weaving. He had made a beautiful settee for my grandma, and an adorable table and chair for me when I was five. But in the course of the war, all that had been forgotten.

"And what will you do with the baskets?" My curiosity was aroused.

"I will try and sell them to the Austrians."

Soon, Apa found some old boards and bricks, and set up a worktable in front of the barrack. Then, after peeling the willow branches, he began weaving his first basket. A large crowd soon gathered around to watch him, and some boys volunteered to get more willow branches for him.

"Good," Apa told them. "And when I sell my baskets, I will pay you for your help."

Within a short time, there were six beautifully woven baskets ready for market. Apa hung them on a long stick, flung them over his shoulder, and headed to town, much to my grandmother's dismay, looking more like a hobo peddler than a village judge. He returned a few hours later with an empty hobo stick and a gleam in his eye; each basket had been sold. Then he reached into his pocket, pulled something out and handed it to me. To my surprise and wonder, it was the new book I had been longing for!

"Oh, thank you, Apa!" I shrieked, giving him a hug. "I can't believe you were able to buy it."

"You are very welcome. And never forget, the Lord helps those who help themselves. Where there is a will, there is always a way," he said. Then he went off to pay the boys who had helped him gather the willow branches.

Apa continued with his new venture all summer, and even gave free lessons in basket-weaving to anyone interested. After he sold the next batch of baskets, he bought himself a fishing pole, too, and a large frying pan. He built a fire outside the barrack, cooked a batch of the large fish he'd caught, and shared it with our neighbors. (Later, he shared the fishing pole and frying pan as well!) The camp, with its barracks lined up like soldiers, was a dismal place, and it was most unusual to have the aroma of that frying fish wafting through it. This small thing was so uplifting to the helpless camp residents who hoped and prayed for something better.

Apa was the best father any girl could ever ask for. His example was an inspiration to many at that camp. His motto became my motto in life, and it has always served me well—the Lord helps those who help themselves. Where there is a will, there is always a way.

Renie Burghardt

Punch Lines

Wit is not leveled so much at the muscles as the heart; and the latter will sometimes smile when there is not a single wrinkle on the cheek.

Lord Lyttleton

My dad is an hour late when he shows up at my house for dinner.

"I can't believe the traffic," he says, as he takes off his coat. "There I was, stuck behind a huge mattahue. What a nerve-wracking experience."

He follows me into the kitchen and accepts a ginger ale.

"I'm sorry the drive over was so hard," I say. "By the way, what's a mattahue?"

"I don't know. What's a matta you?" he says.

If restaurants were divided into joking or nonjoking sections, I know where my father would sit every time.

As a child, I did not appreciate my father's persistent sense of humor. He lay in wait for me every morning. Wearing a respectable gray suit, reading the newspaper and drinking coffee, he looked like an ordinary adult. I knew better.

"Want a bagel?" he asked, as I dragged in.

I analyzed the question, wary that a joke lurked in its shadows. "Okay," I answered. I had learned monosyllabic replies made me less vulnerable to the pitfalls of punnery.

My father calmly sliced, toasted and buttered a bagel for me. I took a bite and relaxed. "Interesting article about the space program," he said. I nodded and kept chewing. He continued, "Johns Hopkins is doing a study on the nutritional impact of space. Do you know what those fellows eat?"

"Some sort of capsule or algae," I said.

"According to this article, all they eat is launch meat." One bite later, the pun sunk in. He'd gotten me again! I clutched my stomach and groaned. Dad smiled and returned to his newspaper.

Every neighborhood gathering, every family social, every Sunday school picnic, my father rolled out his stories and jokes. I envied my friend Susan whose dad quietly flipped hamburgers and freshened drinks. I wished for a father like Camilla's, who puffed on his pipe and occasionally interjected a philosophical comment. I yearned for a parent like Uncle Frank, who inconspicuously lounged on the sofa, absorbing wrestling matches. My father was at the center of every event, milking the crowd with the expertise of a Wisconsin dairy farmer.

When I reached high-school age, I avoided outings with my father. Why did such a smart man stoop to such fourth-grade humor? And why did the adults all eagerly wait for that lull when my father said, "Oh, by the way, did you hear the one about . . ."?

I dreaded a new boyfriend walking into my father's web. My father would be sitting there, looking middle-aged and innocuous in his La-Z-Boy. My friendly father would then gently draw out the boy until he found what he was looking for: the excuse for a joke.

"So where are you taking Debbie tonight? Dinner and a movie? You know, I recently ate at a Howard Johnson's. I ordered soup. The waiter brought my soup, and there was a stick right in the middle. 'Waiter,' I said, 'what is this twig doing in my soup?'

"'Oh, that's nothing, sir,' the waiter said. 'We have branches all over the country.'"

I'd enter the room just in time to see my potential Romeo roll his eyes and clear his throat. Then he'd crank out the smile. "Good one, sir. Do you think Debbie will be ready soon?"

Recently, my friend Philip dropped by to meet my family. My mother offered him a glass of orange juice, and my father graciously weaved Philip into the conversation. Philip told my father how he loved the desert, and my father listened attentively. After a pause, Dad said, "Speaking of the desert. . . ." Mom and I glanced at each other. The joke unfolded as casually as white bread. At the end, we all laughed and my father settled back, like a chess master contemplating his next move.

"Your father is great," Philip said afterward. "I never felt so at home meeting a new person."

"Well, he goes overboard sometimes with the humor," I said.

"I loved it," Philip said.

Suddenly, I realized my father does not just work for laughs: With his jokes and stories, he makes people feel welcome, comfortable and part of the group. My father has been quietly accomplishing the things I've been reading and studying about for years.

I often attend seminars on how to network. I read books on how to bring people together in groups. I attend conferences on speaking and storytelling. Yet I'd been in the presence of a master all these years without even realizing it.

One night, my daughters and I were gathered around

the supper table. I passed the baked potatoes and said, "I got a speeding ticket today."

"Mom, I can't believe it. You just had one last month."

"The policeman who stopped me was nice—and a real body builder. I asked him why he was so strong." I lowered my head and sliced my tomato into quarters.

"So, what did he say?" Sarah asked, taking a sip of iced tea.

"He said he's strong because he's constantly holding up traffic," I answered.

My daughters stopped eating and gave me "the look." They raised their eyebrows and shook their heads.

"You're as bad as Grandpa," Jessica said.

I smiled and basked in the praise. Then I wondered if they'd heard the one about . . .

Deborah Shouse

Like Riding a Bike

*K*ind words produce their own image in men's
souls, and a beautiful image it is.

Blaise Pascal

I sat watching Dad one afternoon while Mom shopped.
He was unable to walk since his stroke and had to rely
solely on others for most of his needs. As he slumped in
his wheelchair with his head hanging down, he seemed to
be off in another world, content and yet somehow
defeated. He wasn't his smiling self today; I wondered
what he was thinking.

Sometimes he'd get so frustrated with himself and with
me because all he saw were his weaknesses, and all I still
saw were his strengths. I was compelled to remind him of
all that he had done as I tried to encourage him to do all
that he could still do. It was a battle of the wills. He'd get
angry when I coaxed him to exercise his legs, but that was
a small price to pay if I could motivate him.

So in another attempt I quietly said to him, "Hey, Dad,
do you remember the day you taught me to cross the big

street on my bike?" His focus suddenly broke, and he laughed heartily.

His speech was slurred. "Yeah, I remember," he proclaimed, raising his head. "You got to the middle of the street and froze." His face lit up; his eyes and mouth smiled.

Ahh, there's my dad, I thought. "Remember, I was so scared and frustrated I couldn't move. You walked with me from one side of the street to the other, time after time, with your strong arms holding on to me, guiding me. With your gentle voice and calming smile, you repeated, 'It's okay, you're doing fine.'" Dad nodded and grinned. "And I was; I made it to the other side. You opened up my world, Dad, helping me to be all I could be."

And as we recalled the day, he held his head up higher, and soon he was ready to exercise his legs. With a gentle voice and a calming smile, I said, "It's okay, Dad, you're doing fine."

Linda Ferris

Reel Event

Remembered joys are never past; at once the fountain, stream, and sea, they were, they are, they yet shall be.

James Montgomery

"Do we have to watch that one again?" I pleaded as the rest of the room erupted in laughter. There I was at nine years old, dancing in front of the camera, with gangly arms and legs, straight bangs and a wide grin showing an embarrassing gap in the front of my mouth.

"Look at you, B.J.! Your two front teeth are missing!"

"Yeah, yeah, yeah," I said to the room filled with relatives. "You say that every time."

Watching those old home films was like watching the *Wizard of Oz* before they added color. And there wasn't any sound, either. Dad had the camera in his hand at every Christmas, birthday, picnic and family event. When it was turned on, everyone seemed to be possessed. They jerked around like marionettes on strings, pulling their lips wide with their fingers and grinning up close to the camera, or putting two fingers in the shape of a V behind their sister's or brother's head just to make Mom yell at them to stop. Nothing missed the eye of the camera, not even Uncle Frank walking out of the bathroom trailing toilet paper stuck to the bottom of his shoe.

Later, when color film came out, we'd howl with laughter as we watched Dad in his plaid, polyester pants and thick, black-rimmed glasses. Mom was no slouch in the fashion department, either. Dad captured her perfect 1960s image in a teased, upswept hairdo with her version of plaid played out in shorts with matching blouses.

It took Dad a while to get everything set up the night of our big movie-showing event. He lugged out the heavy projector and placed it on a card table, then used books under the feet to prop it up just right. We walked around the room pulling the shades down and closing the drapes. Dad tested the square beam of light as it hit the living-room wall where just moments before a picture of the Grand Canyon hung. We gazed in amazement as he moved the card table forward then back, getting the image to just the right size and the focus as clear as he could make it.

These nights were as special as the movies we came to see. The ladies brought cold cuts, potato salad, pickles, olives, cut-up veggies and brownies for dessert. While Dad reloaded the projector between flicks, we could sneak into the kitchen to reload our plates. "Come on!" someone would shout from the living room. "It's starting!" The cold-cut grazers would dash to the doorway as the characters flickered to life.

We shared laughter and tears while we watched reel after reel of film showing old pets, old houses and old friends. The threads of our lives were captured in each metal can with a white label on top. There was "Connie's First Birthday," "Joey's Baptism," the "Family Vacation to Disneyland." But the one we all clamored to see was the one labeled "Station Demolition." It was the razing of Dad's old building on his corner lot to make way for a new building. He stood across the street and filmed the implosion. The first time we saw the building crumble down as it played out on the wall, we let loose with *oohs* and *aahs*. But then someone had the bright idea to play it backward. Throwing the projector into reverse, we all watched as the building rose from the pile of rubble to become whole again. Oh, it was great, and we all hollered, cheered and clapped. "Play it again, Daddy!" And he did, first forward with *oohs* and *aahs,* and then in reverse with cheering and clapping. Dad showed incredible patience, but finally ran out after the fifth or sixth time, so we watched the building collapse and it stayed that way.

It was the saddest part of movie night to hear the final reel play out with its *flap, flap, flap* as it spun until the projector was turned off. "That's all, folks," Dad would say as he shut it down for the night.

Each round, metal can held yards of memories and were treasured, as family mementos usually are. Kept in a cardboard box tucked in a corner of the basement next to the projector, we always knew right where they were for the next time movie night rolled around.

Then one day the pipes burst, and water flooded the basement. "Oh, Dad, all our movies are ruined. We'll never see the station demolition again!" I cried.

"Don't you worry, Sweetheart. We can replay that movie forward and backward right up here," he said, tapping the side of his head, "right up here."

It's been many years since that day we lost all our old film, and many more years since Dad died, too. Even though we may lose something we treasure and love, even when we cannot touch it or feel it in our hands, it is still there—in our minds and in our hearts. Now that's a REAL event.

B. J. Taylor

Connected by Love

Let this be written for a future generation, that a people not yet created may praise the Lord.

Psalm 102:18

"Dad, it just doesn't get any better than this, does it?" I leaned over his shoulder as he rocked my three-month-old granddaughter, his great-granddaughter, Elizabeth.

"No, Sis, it sure doesn't."

It was the day of her dedication, and my house was filled with family and friends, all coming to meet our newest family member. As we admired her, my husband, Neal, and daughter, Amanda, walked over with a family friend.

"Okay, Charles," said Neal with a grin, "my turn." Dad handed her up to Neal so our friend could get a better look. The friend stroked her cheek with his finger and said, "She sure looks like you, Neal. She has your eyes." Then he nodded at my dad. "Great-grandpa, you can't deny her either. She has your mouth and chin."

We smiled and gave each other a knowing look—neither man was a blood relative to my daughter and me.

Mom married Dad when I was three. I married Neal when Amanda was two. And yet, I had to agree with our friend that Elizabeth did look like them both.

That evening Mom and Neal stayed in the kitchen to finish straightening up, but Dad and I opted for coffee on the porch. We sat in the rockers and enjoyed the twilight as the soft breeze caressed our faces. After a while, Dad broke the silence.

"You know, Sis, today reminded me of when our family would gather at the farm."

I nodded. "Yes, it does."

A cicada began his raspy call, taking me back to my dad's old home place, where we would visit his mother and father, known to me as Granny and Granddaddy. While rocking, lost in memories of days there as a child, I remembered a conversation Mom had with Granny in the kitchen back then. I sipped my coffee and rocked. "Dad, isn't it funny how people have always thought I looked like you?"

"What's that, Hon?"

"I remember Mom remarking to Granny how surprised she was that I was so tall since Mom was only five feet tall. Granny, never looking up from her biscuit bowl, said, 'Why, she got her height from Charles.'"

Dad chuckled. "She never thought of you as anything but my biological child. As a matter of fact, I haven't either." Tears began to well in my eyes.

Then Dad asked, "Do you remember at Granny's funeral when I introduced you and Neal and Amanda to my cousin, and she said Amanda was the image of me and Neal?"

"I'd forgotten that." I patted his knee. "Well, Dad, I guess you and Neal have such strong genes that they leap genetic barriers with a single bound." By now fireflies lit the night while crickets and tree frogs sang in full chorus. "More coffee?" I asked.

"Sounds good, Sis."

I took the cups and went inside to refill them. When I started back outside, I saw Dad through the window. With tears freely running down my cheeks, I watched him as he rocked, and I thought how lucky I was to have such a man for my father.

Then it hit me. When fate dealt the same blow to me as it did my mother years ago and I was left a single parent, there, waiting in the wings, was Neal—a man who would love my daughter as fully as my dad loved me. The power of love knitted three generations together so much so that we even look alike. Although life didn't connect us genetically, love did.

Linda Apple

Cash Rewards

Writing is like religion. Every man who feels the call must work out his own salvation.

George Horace Lorimer

The student intern hovered around my desk. Deep into the process of sending out résumés and developing a portfolio, Lisa wanted to see my clippings. She was determined to find the perfect presentation and most effective samples to get her a high-powered public-relations job with big cash rewards.

As I flipped through the pages of ads, annual reports and news releases, a yellowed news clipping slipped out of the lining of my portfolio. The weathered paper was a relic from my own student intern days, over a quarter century ago. I had kept it as a reminder to myself that no matter how important the cash rewards seemed, there were other, more important benefits to a writing life. In this case, it was the ability of my writing to draw me closer to someone I loved.

That summer of 1971, most of my assignments were the

routine stuff a rookie in the newsroom would expect to be doing: proofreading endless columns of type, pounding out obituaries of local businessmen or matrons, and crafting cookie-cutter "bridals." Those were the days when we announced weddings with a good twenty inches of type: The bride carried stephanotis and baby's breath. The bridesmaids wore empire-style gowns of lavender voile, the sleeves trimmed with broomstick lace.

One of the choicest assignments was reviewing shows at the nearby Saratoga Performing Arts Center, with a free pair of tickets going to the reviewer. Seniority determined who got their pick of the tickets, but since the only other person in the newsroom under thirty was the police reporter, he and I divvied up the coolest groups. He took Chuck Mangione and Joe Cocker; I got Arlo Guthrie and Judy Collins. The older staff snapped up the crooners, big bands and symphony orchestras.

Now one pair of tickets was making the rounds of the newsroom without any takers—*The Johnny Cash Show*. The managing editor was getting nervous. The unspoken agreement with the arts center was they provided a season's worth of tickets, and we delivered a season's worth of reviews. How could we miss one of the opening acts?

I knew my father would love to go. *The Johnny Cash Show* was his new favorite television program, edging out *The Lawrence Welk Show* and *Hee Haw* for his loyalty. Still, I hesitated to ask for the tickets. I was only a summer intern, after all, and I did have Arlo and Judy already tucked under my desk blotter and a date for both shows.

I had other reasons to drag my feet. I was twenty-one, cool, a college junior—not the type who fancied herself at a cowboy concert, even for dear ol' Dad.

Then there was my dad himself to consider. In his younger days he was eager to trip the light fantastic to the likes of Tommy Dorsey and Glenn Miller, but of late he'd taken to finding his entertainment in quietly hoeing his garden or welding parts for the army surplus Jeeps he loved to restore. He had become a bit of a homebody. A man who'd left school after the sixth grade to support his immigrant parents, he was now struggling to put his child through journalism school. A proud veteran of World War II, he was troubled by my generation's opposition to the war in Vietnam. I sensed that the father who wanted me to get a good education and fulfill my dreams was also a weary worker and a loyal American who couldn't help but wonder sometimes if it was all worth it.

I mulled over these things as Father's Day approached. Then, since I had no budget for a gift, I got those tickets and slipped them into a homemade card with a silly hand-written verse.

As we headed to the concert, I began to have my doubts again. Would my tie-dye and jeans fit in with the cowboy-shirt-and-boots crowd? Would my VW Beetle look out of place among the pickup trucks in the parking lot? Would I be the only person under fifty there? I was surprised to see as many young hippies as I did older country-western types in the audience. I learned Cash's views on the Vietnam War had earned him a young following I hadn't known about.

Then Johnny Cash came roaring onto the stage with all the force of a locomotive engine. I surprised myself again by being caught up in the energy and power of his perfor-mance. That locomotive image would become my lead for a powerful and positive review.

My dad and I had a great time that night and left know-ing we would both remember the concert for years. He bought me a souvenir music book, and I regaled him with my versions of "Folsom Prison Blues" and "I Walk the Line."

But the biggest thrill of all—and my surprise "Cash" reward—came the next day when the newspaper hit our doorstep. My review, pulsing with the energy I felt in Johnny Cash's performance and painting a colorful word picture of the crowd and performers, struck a note with my dad. At that moment, I think he finally understood me. He now knew why I just had to be a writer. Dad had shared in the experience that created the piece, and it made the concert live again for him.

He smiled. "Very nice, Doll," was all he said, then he solemnly cut out the review and folded it to fit into his lunchbox and took it to the rug mill to share with his friends.

I've published a lot of writing since then, getting paid for most and honored for some. But no paycheck or award I ever get can make me feel better than my father's simple show of pride in my story.

I still have my copy of the Johnny Cash review, but I don't still have my dad. Yet the memory of his love for me and of his pride in my work carries me away—like a roaring locomotive—every time I reread it.

Michelle Bazan Reed

That Dang Horse

Remembrances last longer than present realities.
                                    Jean Paul Richter

I was seven years old and clinging to my dad's hand as we walked toward the mercantile store. My other hand was holding my piggy bank that contained my life savings. Dad sneaked a peak at my determined face, knowing I was about to make the biggest purchase of my life—a bridle.

As we entered the front door, I made a beeline for the farm-and-ranch section. As usual, Dad stopped to pull two bottles of Coke from the cooler near the front. The tall clerk was used to me hanging out in the tack department while my dad shopped. He smiled as I approached, nervously chewing the ends of my long pigtails. Spotting my piggybank, he said, "So, today must be the big day. Now let's see, it was this one with the buck stitching, right?"

That night I proudly hung my new bridle on the bedpost. My dad came to tuck me in. He should have known why I was spending my life savings on that bridle.

"Now I lay me down to sleep and pray the Lord my soul to keep. If I die before I wake, I pray the Lord my soul to take. God bless Mommy and Daddy and Annie and Dadua. And God, please bring me a horse of my own to wear this beautiful bridle."

Now I'm a little fuzzy about just how my prayer was answered, but it wasn't too long afterward that a big white horse named Babe came into my life, which was no easy task since we didn't exactly live in the country. My dad owned a movie theater, and we lived smack dab in the middle of town, so we boarded the horse. Dad was smart enough to know that a seven-year-old girl and a thousand-pound horse would need all the help they could get. He promptly dubbed Babe "that danged horse," but he always said it with a smile.

Dad was amazing. This man who had never even been on a horse became a 4-H leader. This man who lived in a nice house in town became an expert on the rural lifestyle. He even had a trailer hitch welded on to his convertible so he could haul me to 4-H clinics and the county fair. This man who knew lawnmowers and edge trimmers became an expert on bales of hay and sweet feed. This man who wore suits and ties suddenly had a wardrobe of cowboy boots and bolos and sported a Lyndon Johnson cowboy hat with pride.

"Horses still make me nervous," he admitted, "but that horse is important to my daughter, so I hold the dang thing while Annie gets on."

Somewhere along the journey he recognized that horses and kids were a good combination, so he campaigned to get riding paths and outdoor arenas added to the plans for the new fairgrounds. As a city councilman, he seemed to spend just as much time with the county commissioners, talking about their projects that affected his daughter, her friends . . . and that dang horse.

But that dang horse brought us all so much joy. For the next ten years I raced my bike home from school, threw down my books, changed into my jeans and was out the door to ride Babe. No boys. No fast cars. Just that horse—and my father, doing what he could to support my love affair with it.

When I graduated from high school with straight A's and nary a trip to the principal's office, my dad whispered to my mom, "It wasn't us—it was that dang horse."

A generation later, my husband, Dick, and I were unpacking boxes in the living room. After ten years of living in a ski area, we'd just moved to the foothills along the Colorado Rockies' Front Range. The front door slammed, and our seven-year-old son, Richy, flew into the room, hollering. "Mom! Dad! You'll never guess what! Our new neighbor's got a great horse that he'll sell us for only $250—and he'll throw in the saddle!" Our delighted son was already back out the front door, red hair flying, yelling, "They call him an Apple-Sassy, but I'm gonna call him Dusty!"

Dick and I looked at each other and sighed. Dick said, "Good grief, we haven't even been here for an hour yet, and he's already found a horse!"

I thought of Dad and smiled, "Well, we should have known—he already had the bridle."

Ann Clarke

In My Dad's Boots

If a child lives with approval, he learns to live with himself.

Dorothy Law Nolte

They hung on the basement wall, surprisingly small for a big man. As a daddy's girl, I hoped I might be able to fit into them some day, perhaps with the help of an extra pair of thick socks. I treasured my dad's dusty old cowboy boots with their engraved leather design.

Dad told me how, as a young man, by moonlight, he had driven wild horses at top speed through rough western canyons, hanging on, as he said, "by the seat of my pants and a prayer." I wondered what he meant by that, not realizing I would soon find out for myself.

A city family, every summer we visited our Southern farm with its vast expanse of forest, meadow and bayou. As any curious child would, I tried to make friends with each strange creature I encountered.

When I was five, I climbed under a fence rail to pet the "pretty tail" connected to a huge bull! Somehow, Dad's soft voice gently wooed me out of the pen and into the safety of his arms without disturbing the bull.

At six, accustomed to my graceful, well-groomed collie, I was intrigued by a limping, bedraggled mutt. As I stroked him, he lifted his drooping head, not to lick me as I had hoped, but to bite me! Dad held me in his strong arms for the painful rabies shots.

As a seven-year-old playing by a pond, I was inches away from sitting on the head of what I thought was a statue of an alligator. When its jaws opened to take a bite out of me, fear jet-propelled me right back into my dad's loving arms.

Having survived to age eight, I felt indestructible when my older brother and I mounted horses to ride slowly along the dusty farm roads. With my flat-soled tennis shoes slipping in the stirrups, I imagined wearing Dad's sturdy, wooden-heeled cowboy boots.

When we turned in the direction of the barn, our ride done for the day, my horse decided he was in a hurry to get home. Without warning, he took off running, his mane blowing and my pigtails flying. "Pull back on the reins!" my brother yelled.

The reins? I looked around for them. Too late! I had let them drop out of reach so both my hands would be free to clutch the saddle horn. The louder I screamed, the faster the horse ran. With my brother left in the dust behind me and the barn way ahead, I was alone in a no-man's land. A hundred times a minute, I felt like I would fall. I thought, *Now I know how Dad must have felt chasing wild horses—terrified!*

Dad! If only he were here to rescue me. I gripped the horn until my knuckles blanched. Then I saw it—the high, wooden farm gate looming ahead. But the gate was closed, forming a barrier between my horse and the barn where he was headed. I'd seen enough cowboy movies to be pretty sure this wild ride was not going to end as gracefully as a Gene Autry scene. *Whether my horse jumps the gate or stops suddenly in front of it, either way, I am about to be launched like a Fourth-of-July rocket!*

"Help!" I screamed over and over. Unaware the saddle beneath me was slipping, I just sensed I was sliding off the horse. I squeezed the horse's sides with my thighs, hugged the saddle with my body and hung on "by the seat of my pants and a prayer," just as Dad had done.

Like frames in a slow-motion movie, I saw my knight in a white shirt taking long strides to reach the gate just in time. *Dad!*

Miraculously, the gate swung open the moment my horse and I flew through. When the lathered horse stopped at the barn, I slid onto the ground, crying. In a moment, I was swept up into the secure arms of my cowboy hero—Dad.

"I guess I won't ever be good enough to ride with wild horses in the moonlight wearing your boots," I said to him, sniffling.

"I wouldn't be so sure," my dad replied with his sparkling eyes and impish grin. "Anyone who could hang onto a saddle that had slipped partway off the horse, at the speed you were going, should be a rodeo rider!"

Back home a week later, there they were, freshly polished and standing at attention on the floor beside my bed—Dad's cowboy boots.

Margaret Lang

Daddy's Gift

It is the will and not the gift that makes the giver.

Gotthold Lessing

I sat glumly on the living-room couch, thinking back to Mother's call the night before for a family meeting. Beside me, the Christmas tree lights sparkled brightly, dancing joyfully off the windows and onto the mirror. There was no joy in my heart, however, because for the first time in my fourteen years, there would be no Christmas this year.

I was raised in a big family in eastern Montana. In summer, there was always someone to slide down the creek bank with and grab tadpoles in the water. With nine kids, we could split up into teams and play "anty over" the roof of our house or call in a few friends for a softball game.

Winters brought us "crack the whip" on the pond Daddy had iced over with water from the hose for the cow's trough. My twin sister and I joined our brothers and sisters *swooshing* down the hills on tin-bottomed sleds Daddy designed and built for us.

But Christmas was the best. Each year, Daddy selected

one or two of the oldest kids to go with him on a Christmas tree hunt, a hundred miles away where the Badlands cedar grew. There they tromped the coulees until they found the perfect tree, invariably one ten feet tall that had to be sawed off to fit under the living-room ceiling. Then we kids decorated it with construction paper chains of red and green and cranberry strings we threaded from cotton spools fished out of the drawer of Mother's old Singer sewing machine.

After school, we crowded around the kitchen table as Mother sprinkled tiny red and green candies on leaping reindeer and stars cut out of soft cookie dough. Presents covered the floor beneath the tree, just waiting for Christmas morning.

All that changed in 1960 when my father suffered a heart attack that nearly killed him. The tall, handsome cowboy, who had chased wild horses and won track meets single-handedly, slumped over behind the wheel of his well-drilling truck and plunged us into a world of poverty and loss. With one shrill phone call, our carefree days were over.

With Daddy weak and sick for the next two years, an invisible cloak of darkness settled over us, stifling our natural gaiety and culminating in the somber words Mother had spoken the night before. "Kids," she said, "we don't have enough money for presents this year, so why don't we draw names for Christmas instead?"

Draw names? We'd never drawn names! Christmas had always meant stacks of presents heaped under the tree, paper and ribbons spilling onto the floor, while baby dolls, Chinese checkers and paint-by-number sets burst out of their wrappings. Now Mother was asking us to forgo all of that, pare our expectations down to one gift. The request was so outrageous we knew it must be serious. Without argument, we miserably nodded our heads and agreed.

Taking a sheet of paper from a tablet, Mother tore it up into strips and handed them to my sister. One by one, we each took a piece and wrote our name on it in pencil, then dropped it into the crown of Daddy's black Stetson hat. Stirring them up, Mother silently passed the hat to my brother, my sister and my other brother. I watched while they withdrew a name, checked quickly to make sure it wasn't their own and secreted it away in their pants pockets. When my turn came, I closed my eyes, stuck my hand into the satin lining and felt for one ragged edge. As old as I was, I could hardly keep from bawling.

Christmas morning we arose glum and silent. Instead of rushing loudly down the stairs to tear into presents, we silently filed into the living room and settled around the lonely, store-bought tree. Mother and Daddy took their seats behind us while my brother knelt down and began sorting through the gifts. Reading each tag aloud, he handed the box to its owner and then turned to get another.

Mine wasn't even a box, just an envelope with its flap licked shut.

What is this? I wondered. *This isn't even a present; it's just a card.*

I could hardly keep my disappointment from showing as I slipped my finger under the edge, slit it open and pulled out a Christmas card showing a church lit up at evening. Bits of red and yellow light spilled out on the snow through the stained-glass windows, and buggies stood tied up beside the big evergreen trees.

Inside was a golden coin. A little bit bigger than a quarter, it profiled a Grecian woman with her hair pulled back in a knot and tendrils escaping beneath a crown labeled "LIBERTY." Tiny stars encircled her head, thirteen in all, ending at the number 1853, which was stamped across the bottom.

Boldly written across the page in Daddy's barely legible scrawl was my name and this note:

Dear Wanda:

This coin was minted with gold dug by your Uncle Hulva, your grandmother's uncle. It is the last one I have, and I wanted you to have it for Christmas.

Merry Christmas,
Daddy

I looked up. He was watching me to see what my reaction would be. As young as I was, I knew instantly this coin was of great value to him and that it had taken a lot for him to give it up.

"Thank you, Daddy," I said.

A slight incline of his head acknowledged my thanks, and we turned to watch the next gift being opened.

Late that afternoon, I found myself drifting down the stairway to the basement. There was Daddy, standing alone by the old oil burner, almost as if he was waiting for me.

I went up to him and said once more, "Thank you so much for the golden coin, Daddy."

He looked at me quietly, then began to speak. "When you twins were born, Mommy had a really hard time. Rita was born first and she didn't have any trouble, but then you started to come. I was sitting in the waiting room when the doctor came out and said to me, 'We're having trouble with Marilee, and I have to know—which one do you want me to save, your wife or your child?'"

Long wet tears started to slide down his face; this, from my father whom I had never seen cry. Anguish pierced the sapphire blue eyes Mother had fallen in love with over twenty years before.

"Do you know what it is like," he wrenched, "to have to choose between your wife and your child?"

Great sobs wracked his body as he wept louder. I stood astonished, at my father, broken before me, and the startling news that my mother had almost died giving birth to me. I could not bear to see him hurting so, and I stepped forward and took him in my arms to comfort him. "It's all right, Daddy," I said, pressing my cheek into the dampened wool of his Pendleton shirt. His arms tightened around me, anchoring me to the steady *kerthump-kerthump* of his weakened heart.

"I told him, 'My wife,' and then I sat down in my chair and I began to pray. I asked God to let you live." Like rain pouring off a windowpane, the tears streamed down his face as he held me back from his chest and said, "It was the first time in my life I ever prayed."

In stunned surprise, I absorbed those words. My father, who lived his life separate from God, who never acknowledged his being, had prayed for me. My father, when forced to make the most awful decision a man could ever make, had turned away from me.

I struggled with the choice he made. At the time of my birth, he had six children less than five years of age, and now my twin sister had just been born. Without a wife, how could he take care of them? Who would feed them, bathe them, put shoes on their feet? Who would change their diapers and nurse them through colds and the chicken pox? How could he leave them to go to his work drilling water wells far from his home?

Without a child, his family would survive. Without his wife, they would not. But he could not bear to give me up. So on that day, just four days before Christmas 1949, when his heart was torn with the thought of losing me, his unborn child, my father, the atheist, had begged God for me.

It was a gift worth far more than gold.

Wanda Rosseland

More Chicken Soup?

Many of the stories and poems you have read in this book were submitted by readers like you who had read earlier *Chicken Soup for the Soul* books. We publish at least five or six *Chicken Soup for the Soul* books every year. We invite you to contribute a story to one of these future volumes.

Stories may be up to twelve-hundred words and must uplift or inspire. You may submit an original piece, something you have read or your favorite quotation on your refrigerator door.

To obtain a copy of our submission guidelines and a listing of upcoming *Chicken Soup* books, please write, fax or check our Web site.

Please send your submissions to:

Chicken Soup for the Soul
P.O. Box 30880, Santa Barbara, CA 93130
fax: 805-563-2945
Web site: *www.chickensoup.com*

We will be sure that both you and the author are credited for your submission.

For information about speaking engagements, other books, audiotapes, workshops and training programs, please contact any of our authors directly.

Supporting Others

In the spirit of supporting others, a portion of the proceeds from *Chicken Soup for the Father and Daughter Soul* will be donated to Dads and Daughters®.

Dads and Daughters®, the national advocacy non-profit for fathers and daughters whose mission is to inspire fathers to actively engage in the lives of daughters, has impacted the lives of tens of thousands of fathers and daughters with outstanding educational resources and advocacy work supporting fathers' involvement in girls' lives.

Dads and Daughters® is committed to promoting supportive and healthy father-daughter relationships and providing tools and advocacy to help girls increase their self-esteem and give them greater opportunities for self-fulfillment. DADs® is further committed to transforming the pervasive cultural messages that hypersexualize, devalue and degrade women and girls and is an active and effective advocate for educational equity, prevention of eating disorders, ending marketing to children and other important children's issues. Dads and Daughters® publishes the award-winning newsletter, *Daughters*[TM]: *For Parents of Girls*, the only newsletter for parents about raising healthy daughters—*www.daughters.com*—and is read by tens of thousands of parents and adults who work with girls around the world.

Learn more about DADs® by contacting:

Dads and Daughters®
P.O. Box 3110
Duluth, MN 55803
www.DadsandDaughters.org
e-mail: *info@dadsanddaughters.org*
phone: 218-722-3942

Who Is Jack Canfield?

Jack Canfield is one of America's leading experts in the development of human potential and personal effectiveness. He is both a dynamic, entertaining speaker and a highly sought-after trainer. Jack has a wonderful ability to inform and inspire audiences toward increased levels of self-esteem and peak performance.

He is the author and narrator of several bestselling audio- and videocassette programs, including *Self-Esteem and Peak Performance, How to Build High Self-Esteem, Self-Esteem in the Classroom* and *Chicken Soup for the Soul—Live.* He is regularly seen on television shows such as *Good Morning America, 20/20* and *NBC Nightly News.* Jack has co-authored numerous books, including the *Chicken Soup for the Soul* series, *Dare to Win* and *The Aladdin Factor* (all with Mark Victor Hansen), *100 Ways to Build Self-Concept in the Classroom* (with Harold C. Wells), *Heart at Work* (with Jacqueline Miller) and *The Power of Focus* (with Les Hewitt and Mark Victor Hansen).

Jack is a regularly featured speaker for professional associations, school districts, government agencies, churches, hospitals, sales organizations and corporations. His clients have included the American Dental Association, the American Management Association, AT&T, Campbell's Soup, Clairol, Domino's Pizza, GE, ITT, Hartford Insurance, Johnson & Johnson, the Million Dollar Roundtable, NCR, New England Telephone, Re/Max, Scott Paper, TRW and Virgin Records. Jack has taught on the faculty of Income Builders International, a school for entrepreneurs.

Jack conducts an annual seven-day Training of Trainers program in the areas of self-esteem and peak performance. It attracts entrepreneurs, educators, counselors, parenting trainers, corporate trainers, professional speakers, ministers and others interested in developing their speaking and seminar-leading skills.

For further information about Jack's books, tapes and training programs, or to schedule him for a presentation, please contact:

Self-Esteem Seminars
P.O. Box 30880
Santa Barbara, CA 93130
phone: 805-563-2935 • fax: 805-563-2945
Web site: *www.jackcanfield.com*

Who Is Mark Victor Hansen?

In the area of human potential, no one is more respected than Mark Victor Hansen. For more than thirty years, Mark has focused solely on helping people from all walks of life reshape their personal vision of what's possible. His powerful messages of possibility, opportunity and action have created powerful change in thousands of organizations and millions of individuals worldwide.

He is a sought-after keynote speaker, bestselling author and marketing maven. Mark's credentials include a lifetime of entrepreneurial success and an extensive academic background. He is a prolific writer with many bestselling books, such as *The One Minute Millionaire, The Power of Focus, The Aladdin Factor* and *Dare to Win,* in addition to the *Chicken Soup for the Soul* series. Mark has made a profound influence through his library of audios, videos and articles in the areas of big thinking, sales achievement, wealth building, publishing success, and personal and professional development.

Mark is the founder of the MEGA Seminar Series. MEGA Book Marketing University and Building Your MEGA Speaking Empire are annual conferences where Mark coaches and teaches new and aspiring authors, speakers and experts on building lucrative publishing and speaking careers. Other MEGA events include MEGA Marketing Magic and My MEGA Life.

He has appeared on television (*Oprah,* CNN and *The Today Show*), in print (*Time, U.S. News & World Report, USA Today, New York Times* and *Entrepreneur*) and on countless radio interviews, assuring our planet's people that "You can easily create the life you deserve."

As a philanthropist and humanitarian, Mark works tirelessly for organizations such as Habitat for Humanity, American Red Cross, March of Dimes, Childhelp USA and many others. He is the recipient of numerous awards that honor his entrepreneurial spirit, philanthropic heart and business acumen. He is a lifetime member of the Horatio Alger Association of Distinguished Americans, an organization that honored Mark with the prestigious Horatio Alger Award for his extraordinary life achievements.

Mark Victor Hansen is an enthusiastic crusader of what's possible and is driven to make the world a better place.

Mark Victor Hansen & Associates, Inc.
P.O. Box 7665
Newport Beach, CA 92658
phone: 949-764-2640
fax: 949-722-6912
Web site: *www.markvictorhansen.com*

Who Is LeAnn Thieman?

LeAnn Thieman is a nationally acclaimed professional speaker, author and nurse who was "accidentally" caught up in the Vietnam Orphan Airlift in 1975. Her book, *This Must Be My Brother*, details her daring adventure of helping to rescue 300 babies as Saigon was falling to the Communists. An ordinary person, she struggled through extraordinary circumstances and found the courage to succeed. LeAnn and her incredible story have been featured in *Newsweek Magazine*'s "Voices of the Century" issue, FOX-TV News, PAX-TV's *It's a Miracle* and countless radio and TV programs.

Today, as a renowned motivational speaker, she shares life-changing lessons learned from her airlift experience. Believing we all have individual "war zones," LeAnn inspires audiences to balance their lives, truly live their priorities and make a difference in the world.

After her story was featured in *Chicken Soup for the Mother's Soul*, LeAnn became one of Chicken Soup's most prolific writers, with stories in eleven more *Chicken Soup* books. That, and her devotion to thirty years of nursing, made her the ideal co-author of *Chicken Soup for the Nurse's Soul*. Her life-long practice of her Christian faith led her to co-author *Chicken Soup for the Christian Woman's Soul*. All of the above earned her the honor of co-authoring *Chicken Soup for the Caregiver's Soul* and now *Chicken Soup for the Father and Daughter Soul*.

LeAnn and Mark, her husband of thirty-five years, reside in Colorado where they enjoy their "empty nest." Their two daughters, Angela and Christie, and son, Mitch, have "flown the coop" but are still drawn under their mother's wing when she needs them!

For more information about LeAnn's books and tapes or to schedule her for a presentation, please contact her at:

LeAnn Thieman
6600 Thompson Drive
Fort Collins, CO 80526
phone: 970-223-1574
Web site: *www.LeAnnThieman.com*
e-mail: *LeAnn@LeAnnThieman.com*

Who Is Patty Aubery?

As the president of Chicken Soup for the Soul Enterprises and a #1 *New York Times* bestselling coauthor, Patty Aubery knows what it's like to juggle work, family and social obligations—along with the responsibility of developing and marketing the more than 80 million *Chicken Soup* books and licensed goods worldwide.

She knows because she's been with Jack Canfield's organization since the early days—before *Chicken Soup* took the country by storm. Jack was still telling these heartwarming stories then, in his trainings, workshops and keynote presentations. And it was Patty who directed the labor of love that went into compiling and editing the original 101 *Chicken Soup* stories. Later, she supported the daunting marketing effort and steadfast optimism required to bring it to millions of readers worldwide.

Today, Patty is the mother of two active boys—J.T. and Chandler—exemplifying that special combination of commitment, organization and life balance all working women want to have. She's been known to finish at the gym by 6:00 A.M., guest-host a radio show at 6:30, catch a flight by 9:00 to close a deal—and be back in time for soccer with the kids. But perhaps the most notable accolade for this special working woman is the admiration and love her friends, family, staff and peers hold for her.

Of her part in the *Chicken Soup* family, Patty says, "I'm always encouraged, amazed and humbled by the storytellers I meet when working on any *Chicken Soup* book, but by far the most poignant have been those stories of women in the working world, overcoming incredible odds and—in the face of all challenges—excelling as only women could do."

Patty is also the coauthor of several other bestselling titles: *Chicken Soup for the Christian Soul, Christian Family Soul,* and *Christian Woman's Soul, Chicken Soup for the Expectant Mother's Soul, Chicken Soup for the Sister's Soul* and *Chicken Soup for the Surviving Soul.*

She is married to a successful international entrepreneur, Jeff Aubery, and together with J.T. and Chandler, they make their home in Santa Barbara, California. Patty can be reached at:

Self-Esteem Seminars
P.O. Box 30880
Santa Barbara, CA 93130
phone: 805-563-2935
fax: 805-563-2945

Who Is Nancy Autio?

Nancy Autio graduated from Arizona State University in May 1994 with a B.S. in Nursing. After graduation, Nancy worked at Good Samaritan Regional Medical Center in Phoenix, Arizona, in the Cardiovascular Intensive Care Unit. In September 1994, Nancy moved back to her native Los Angeles and became involved with the *Chicken Soup* series. Nancy's intentions were to help finish *A 2nd Helping of Chicken Soup for the Soul* and then return to nursing. However, in December of that year, she was asked to continue on full time as part of the *Chicken Soup* team. Nancy put nursing on hold and became Director of Story Acquisitions, working closely with Jack and Mark on all *Chicken Soup for the Soul* projects.

Nancy says that what she is most thankful for is her move back to L.A., where she could be there for her mother, Linda Mitchell, during her bout with breast cancer. Out of that struggle, Nancy coauthored, along with her sister, Patty Aubery, *Chicken Soup for the Surviving Soul: 101 Stories of Courage and Inspiration from Those Who Have Survived Cancer*. Little did she know that the book would become her own inspiration when her dad was diagnosed with prostate cancer in 1999.

Nancy also coauthored *Chicken Soup for the Christian Soul, Chicken Soup for the Christian Family Soul, Chicken Soup for the Expectant Mother's Soul, Chicken Soup for the Nurse's Soul* and *Chicken Soup for the Sister's Soul*. Nancy now enjoys being a full-time mom and resides in Santa Barbara with her husband, Kirk Autio, daughter, Molly Anne, dogs, Kona and Cora, and three cats.

You may contact Nancy Autio at:

P.O. Box 30880
Santa Barbara, CA 93130
phone: 805-682-6311
fax: 805-682-0872
e-mail: *nautio@chickensoupforthesoul.com*

Contributors

Several of the stories in this book were taken from previously published sources, such as books, magazines and newspapers. These sources are acknowledged in the permissions section. If you would like to contact any of the contributors for information about their writing or would like to invite them to speak in your community, look for their contact information included in their biographies.

The remainder of the stories were submitted by readers of our previous *Chicken Soup for the Soul* books who responded to our requests for stories. We have also included information about them.

Amy Adair is a freelance writer who lives in Elmhurst, Illinois. She's married to Jonathan, and they have one son, Joshua.

Nancy C. Anderson (*www.NancyCAnderson.com*) has been writing and speaking to women and couples for twenty years. She lives in Southern California with her husband of twenty-six years and their teenage son. Nancy is the author of *Avoiding the "Greener Grass" Syndrome: Growing Affair-Proof Hedges Around Your Marriage* (Kregel Publications, 2005).

Linda Apple lives in Springdale, Arkansas, with her husband, Neal, their five children and two grandchildren. She is a speaker for Stonecroft Ministries. Linda is a contributor to *Chicken Soup for the Nurse's Soul, Chicken Soup for the Woman's Soul* and *Chicken Soup for the Soul: Living Your Dreams*. E-mail her at *psalm10218@cox-internet.com*.

Ruth Barden has a master's degree in education and taught high school family studies for twenty years. She currently runs a restaurant business with her husband. She enjoys golf, reading and travel.

Carol McClain Bassett is the editorial assistant with a company that publishes health curricula for public schools. Her young-adult children, Susie and Bobby, are her greatest joy. She is a nutrition consultant, a victorious cancer survivor and loves to be outdoors enjoying nature. Please e-mail her at *carol47b@msn.com*.

Timothy P. Bete is the author of *In the Beginning There Were No Diapers* (Sorin Books, 2005). His award-winning humor column has been published in more than a dozen parenting magazines. More of his work can be found at *www.TimBete.com*.

Janelle Breese Biagioni is a published author and national speaker. Her work includes *Head Injuries: The Silent Epidemic* and *A Change of Mind: One Family's Journey Through Brain Injury*. Her story "Remember with Courage" is published in *Chicken Soup for the Grieving Soul.* Janelle resides in Victoria, British Columbia.

Larry Bodin received his Bachelor of Business Administration degree from Lamar University (Beaumont, Texas) in 1970. Currently, he is editor of *SportsLocal.com,* a Web site devoted strictly to Texas high-school sports. He loves traveling, reading and visiting his two grandchildren in New Hampshire. Please e-mail him at *larry@sportslocal.com.*

Bobbie Bonk received her M.A. from La Salle University in Philadelphia, Pennsylvania. She has recently fulfilled a longtime dream of becoming a spiritual director. Bobbie enjoys sharing stories of faith and is writing an inspirational book based on women in the Bible. Please e-mail her at *bobbie211@juno.com.*

Ted Bosley was a traveling salesman for most of his working years until his retirement in 1993. He spent endless hours writing about his thoughts, experiences and loves for the enrichment of his own soul. Ted sadly passed away in 2001 and is sorely missed. Any comments on his story can be fowarded to his daughter at *harper3@sympatico.ca.*

Lana Brookman lives in a small town in western Wisconsin. When not busy as a communications instructor for the district technical college, she enjoys traveling, writing, reading and spending time with friends and family. Her goal is to learn something new every day.

Linda Bryant was born in England and moved to the United States in 1983. She works at a Barnes & Noble bookstore and has run a book discussion group there for seven years. After her husband and children, her passion is the theater. Linda has been writing letters for the past twenty years.

Martin Bucella is a full-time freelance cartoonist/humorous illustrator whose work has been published over 100,000 times in magazines, newspapers, greeting cards, books and on the Internet. To see more of Marty's work, visit his Web site at *members.aol.com/mjbtoons/index.html.*

Isabel Bearman Bucher, a retired teacher, has been writing, with no training, since 1984. She was raising teenagers, and saying it on paper with words seemed better than committing murder. She's published dozens of articles in many genres and has completed two books: *Nonno's Monkey: An Italian American Memoir* and *Tweet Irene,* the story of a miraculous little house sparrow that lived with her family loosely for three years. Isabel and her husband, Robert, continue their honeymoon with life, changing homes throughout the world, walking mountains and finding adventures.

Freelance writer **Renie Burghardt** was born in Hungary. She has contributed to many anthologies, including *Chicken Soup for the Christian Family Soul* and *Horse Lover's Soul.* She lives in the country and loves nature, animals, gardening, reading and spending time with family and friends.

Aletheia Lee Butler earned her Bachelor of Science degree, with honors, in early childhood education from Atlanta Christian College in 2000. She is currently teaching English to Speakers of Other Languages (ESOL) in Douglasville, Georgia. You can e-mail her at *aletheiabutler@yahoo.com*.

Martha Campbell is a graduate of Washington University of St. Louis School of Fine Arts and a former writer/designer for Hallmark Cards. She has been a freelance cartoonist and book illustrator since 1973. She can be reached at P.O. Box 2538, Harrison, Arizona 72602, phone 870-741-5323 or by e-mail at *marthaf@alltel.net*.

Emily Chase is the author of *Why Say No When MY Hormones Say GO?* (Christian Publications, 2003). Each year, she speaks to thousands of teens about sexual self-control. She misses playing dominoes and doing crosswords with her father-in-law who recently died. You can reach Emily at *echase@ messiah.edu*.

Ann Clarke is an award-winning photographer, writer and speaker. Today she and her husband, Dick, live in the Colorado foothills near their son Rich, his wife, Shannon, and their daughter, Delaney. Contact Ann through her Web site at *www.AnnClarke.com*.

Harriet Cooper is a freelance humorist and essayist living in Toronto, Canada. Her humor, essays, articles, short stories and poetry have appeared in newspapers, magazines, Web sites, newsletters, anthologies, on radio and on a coffee can. She specializes in writing about family, relationships, cats, psychology and health. Please reach her at *harcoop@hotmail.com*.

Karen L. Cooper is a happiliy married mother of two grown sons and one daughter-in-law. You may e-mail her at *daka@cox.net*. She continues to speak to her father almost every day.

John Cox is a professional speaker, author and father who travels to schools, camps, conferences and churches, combining humor and compelling stories with practical skills that work in everyday life. John's recent experience on *Extreme Makeover Home Edition* makes him a crowd favorite anywhere he goes. You can reach John at 805-403-2646 or *John@Johncox.info*.

Patti Davis's book, *The Long Goodbye*, is being released in November 2005 by Knopf. She has written for numerous magazines, including *Time, Newsweek, Ladies' Home Journal, Glamour, Harper's Bazaar, Town and Country* as well as the *L.A. Times, The Washington Post* and *The New York Times*.

Lynn Dean is a writer and the mother of three. She has published more than 500 nonfiction articles that have appeared in over 100 publications in at least thirty-five states. Lynn specializes in the areas of parenting, women's issues, lifestyle and education. Write to Lynn at P.O Box 146, Timnath, CO 80547.

Dan DeVries received his Bachelor of Science degree in electronic engineering technology from the DeVry Institute of Technology in 1984 and is currently an engineering manager for the Boeing Company in Seattle, Washington. Dan enjoys fishing, camping and spending time with his wife and five children. Dan can be rached at *sheiladhh@aol.com.*

Danny Dugan received his Bachelor of Arts degree with honors in communications from Slippery Rock University in 1979. He has been a police officer in O'Hara Township, Pennsylvania, for twenty-five years and a freelance writer since 1998. Danny enjoys camping, fishing and writing for varied publications. Please e-mail him at *DDugan8184@aol.com.*

Sylvia Duncan is a former library manager, now a published author who won her first writing award when she was ten. She swims, teaches, writes and is a professional storyteller. She values memories of her dad, Fred Goodwin's encouragement, and appreciates continued support from writing-group friends and her family.

T. Suzanne Eller is the author of *Real Issues, Real Teens* and is a conference speaker to teens, parents of teens and women. She is an Oklahoma girl who loves writing and riding horses. You can find out more at *realteenfaith.com* or *tseller@daretobelieve.org.* Suzie's dad is doing well. He just returned from Canada where he fished for pike and hung out with the bears.

Gail Eynon (Diaz) lives in Hilo, Hawaii, and is the mother of two, grandmother of four, and a writer and motivational speaker on domestic violence. She has a story in *Chicken Soup to Inspire the Body & Soul* and has been published in many magazines. Visit her at *www.uhavecourage.com.*

Linda Ferris is a registered nurse practicing in Michigan. She enjoys quilting, traveling and writing. She has published stories in the book *Heartwarmers, Venice Golf Coast Magazine* and *Today's Christian Woman.* Her son has been married to Carrie for two years, and they just bought their first new home. Linda can be reached at *lafrn10@aol.com.*

Cynthia Fonk is owner and president of a national health and safety consulting and training company. Cindy lives on a ranch in Colorado with her husband, John. Together they raise alpacas and Appaloosa horses. Visit their live Web site, "BarnCam," at *www.alpaca.net.*

LaDonna Gatlin left a promising musical career to follow her heart and "sing a different song" apart from her brothers (country music's legendary Gatlin Brothers). She inspires audiences to live life from the inside out and stay true to their core values. Her unique style blends music, humor and personal stories that entertain while driving home a powerful message. She can be contacted at *www.ladonnagatlin.com.*

Nancy B. Gibbs is a weekly religion columnist, author and motivational speaker. Nancy has had over a dozen stories published in various *Chicken Soup for the Soul* books. Her writings have appeared in numerous magazines, anthologies and devotional guides. Visit her Web site at *www.nancybgibbs.com.* You can contact her at P.O. Box 53, Cordele, GA 31010 or via e-mail at *Daiseydood@aol.com.*

Ron Gold has been a professional writer for some forty years. He specializes in inspiration stories, memoirs and poetry. He also writes résumés, personal love stories, college entry essays and ethical wills.

For **Naida Grunden**, writing is both avocation and vocation. A writer and public relations professional for over twenty years, Naida currently serves as communications director for a healthcare consortium in Pittsburgh. She spends her spare time quilting, playing piano and cello, and gardening. Please e-mail her at *naida.grunden@gmail.com.*

Donna Gudaitis is a homemaker from Pleasanton, California. She and her husband of thirty-five years, Gary, raised three great kids and now enjoy spoiling two little grandchildren. Donna finds comfort in writing about her real-life situations. Donna's e-mail address is *dgudaitis@comcast.net.*

Abigail R. Gutierrez graduated from the University of Nevada with a degree in film production. She has completed several romantic comedy screenplays, one of which won her the "Best Achievement in Screenwriting" honor from her professors. Please e-mail her at *screenwriter1230@yahoo.com.*

Deb Haggerty is an author and speaker who lives in Orlando, Florida, with her husband, Roy. Deb is a breast cancer "victor" and is active with the Florida Breast Cancer Coalition. She speaks and writes on the topics of communication, networking and breast cancer. E-mail her at *deb@DebHaggerty.com.*

Ruth A. Hancock has been published in magazines, hospice journals and books, including *Guideposts, Chicken Soup for the Volunteer Soul, Chicken Soup for the Grieving Soul* and *Chicken Soup for the Caregiver's Soul.* Her stories are based on her interests as a hospice volunteer, wife of an Episcopal priest, mother and her career in the fashion industry. E-mail her at *Rahancock@worldnet.att.net.*

Bonnie Compton Hanson, a writer and speaker, is author of several books for adults and children, including the *Ponytail Girls* series for girls. Her hundreds of published poems and articles include those in several *Chicken Soup for the Soul* books. You can contact Bonnie at 3330 S. Lowell St., Santa Ana, CA 92707; 714-751-7824; or *bonnieh1@worldnet.att.net.*

Carol D. Haynes, a 1968 graduate of Oswego State University, has been employed in pre-press at Speedway Press in Oswego for thirty-three years. She is also an auto-racing journalist and public-relations spokesperson for that sport. She enjoys photography, traveling and reading. Carol's daughter, Jennifer, resides in Florida and works for Borders/Waldenbooks.

Stephanie Marlow James is a freelance writer who writes nonfiction and poetry. A book of poetry and a novel are in the works. She resides in Kansas City, Missouri, with her husband and daughter, who are prime sources of her inspiration. Please contact her at *smjames2@kc.rr.com.*

Louise Tucker Jones is an award-winning author and inspirational speaker. Her books include *Dance from the Heart* and *Extraordinary Kids* (coauthored), along with contributions to over a dozen compilation books and numerous magazines, including *Guideposts*. Louise has an M.A. in creative writing and resides in Edmond, Oklahoma. E-mail her at *LouiseTJ@aol.com*.

Marna Malag Jones raised a family and retired early from the personnel placement field. She has presented career-fulfillment seminars and is researching information for a new seminar about caring for aging parents. This story is part of a book she's writing about her father's life. Contact her at *marnakj@ hotmail.com*.

Sally Kelly-Engeman is a freelance writer who's had numerous short stories and articles published. In addition to reading, researching and writing, she enjoys ballroom dancing and traveling with her husband. She can be reached at *sallyfk@juno.com*.

Nancy Julien Kopp began writing late in life. She has been a teacher, wife, mother and grandmother, and still enjoys teaching through the written word. Nancy writes stories for children, nonfiction and poetry. Her work has been published in magazines and several Web e-zines. Writing feeds her soul.

Margaret Lang received her Bachelor of Arts degree from Brown University in 1963. She teaches women and children's groups in California. Margaret has one story accepted for publication and three under consideration. Her daughter is a physician/missionary, and her son is a youth pastor. Margaret has one granddaughter.

Patricia Lorenz is an art-of-living writer and speaker and the author of five books, including her latest three: *Life's Too Short to Fold Your Underwear, Grab the Extinguisher: My Birthday Cake's on Fire* (Guidepost Books, 800-431-2344) and *Great American Outhouse Stories: The Hole Truth and Nothing Butt* (Infinity Publishing, 877-289-2665). Patricia is one of the top contributors to the *Chicken Soup for the Soul* books with twenty-six stories in twenty-two of them so far. For information about hiring her as a speaker, visit her Web site at *www. patricialorenz.com* or e-mail her at *patricialorenz@juno.com*.

Al D. Luebbers has a Bachelor of Arts degree in behavioral science. He is currently working as a prison warden for the State of Missouri and is an avid golfer. Al has been married for seventeen years and is heavily involved with raising two children. His daughter is currently enrolled in elementary school in southeast Missouri.

The father of three beautiful children, **Steven H. Manchester** is the published author of *The Unexpected Storm: The Gulf War Legacy, A Father's Love, Jacob Evans* and *At the Stroke of Midnight,* as well as several books under the pseudonym Steven Herberts. Three of his screenplays have also been produced as films. Visit his Web site at *www.StevenManchester.com*.

Judith Marks-White is a columnist for the *Westport News* (Westport, Connecticut), where her weekly column, "The Light Touch," has appeared every Wednesday for the past twenty years. Ms. Marks-White is a freelance writer, lecturer and adjunct professor of English at Norwalk Community College in Connecticut as well as an instructor in humor writing. Her work has appeared nationally in newspapers and magazines. She is presently working on a novel.

Bettye Martin-McRae, a freelance writer and speaker for forty years, cared for her aging cowboy-farmer father for thirteen years. At seventy-one, this great-grandmother plows with mules, drives them to a wagon and self-publishes "books from the heart of an ol' Texas gal." (Her books are illustrated by Western humorist and cowpoke cartoonist Ace Reid.) Visit her Web site at *www.bunkhousebooks.com*. Contact Bettye at *bunkhouse@wtconnect.com* or 325-235-9969.

Janet Lynn Mitchell is a wife, mother, author and inspirational speaker. She is the coauthor of *A Special Kind of Love: For Those Who Love Children with Special Needs*, published by Broadman and Holman and Focus on the Family, 2004. Janet can be reached at *JanetLM@prodigy.net* or faxed at 714-633-6309.

Raymond L. Morehead is of Scottish descent by birth, a philosopher by inclination, a romantic sentimentalist at heart and a Pacific Northwest mountain man by choice. He believes in God, family, freedom, loyalty and honor. He lives by the mottos: "Remembering the men and women from whence I came so that they may live on"; "Can't never did anything, you have only to try and try again!" and "By the help of God try again." His ancestral motto is: *"Auxilio Dei"* [by or with the help of God].

Mark Parisi's "Off the Mark" comic panel has been syndicated since 1987 and is distributed by United Media. Mark's humor also graces greeting cards, T-shirts, calendars, magazines, newsletters and books. Please visit his Web site at *www.offthemark.com*. Lynn is his wife/business partner and their daughter, Jenny, contributes with inspiration (as do three cats).

Debra Ann Pawlak, a freelance writer from Farmington, Michigan, lives with her husband, Michael, and has two children, Rachel and Jonathon. She published a book on Farmington history and completed a screenplay about Clara Bow. Debra contributes regularly to *The Mediadrome (www.themediadrome.com)*, an online magazine for thinking people. E-mail her at *pawlakmail@sbcglobal.net*.

Donna Pennington specialized in psychiatric nursing before becoming a full-time mom. Now that her children are older, she has written two novels and is pursuing a freelance writing career. Her dad is still a big part of her life, and they are currently restoring a classic boat together.

Tom Prisk has been a published cartoonist since 1977. His work has appeared in the *Saturday Evening Post, The Best Cartoons from the Saturday Evening Post, Woman's World, Reader's Digest, Yankee Magazine, Writer's Digest, The Best Cartoons from Leadership* and more. He may be e-mailed at *cartoonist@tomprisk.com*. Visit his Web site at *www.tomprisk.com*.

Joyce Rapier, a native of Van Buren, Arkansas, is the author of two books:

Windy John's Me 'N Tut and *Windy John's Rainbow and the Pot o' Gold*. Her third book, *Whisper My Name*, was released in 2004. You may view Joyce's works at *www.authorsden.com/joycelrapier*.

Michelle Bazan Reed is a magazine editor and writer of fiction, nonfiction and haiku. She dedicates "Cash Rewards" to her father, Bill Bazan, "one of the greatest storytellers and letter writers I have ever known." She and her husband, Bill Reed, are the parents of two and live on the shore of Lake Ontario.

Carol McAdoo Rehme, one of *Chicken Soup*'s most prolific contributors, believes daddies are God's blessings to daughters of any age. Carol directs a nonprofit, Vintage Voices, Inc., which brings interactive programming to the vulnerable elderly. Contact her at *carol@rehme.com; www.rehme.com*.

Kimberly A. Ripley is a freelance writer from New Hampshire. A wife and mother of five, as well as a homeschooling parent, her family provides lots of antics about which she writes. Visit Kim at *www.kimberlyripley.writergazette.com*.

Isabel Corr Rizzo writes children's books, poetry and short stories. For many years, Isabel has been a storyteller at local schools, using Irish children's stories that she wrote. Isabel enjoys writing, cooking, music and painting. She studied journalism, writing a column and articles for a newspaper. Please reach her at *cvagg@netzero.net*.

Christie Lyn Rogers credits her story to her mom, who is the author of the family! Christie Lyn Rogers is blessed to live so close to her mother and her perfectly amazing dad! They truly are chicken soup for her soul.

Tracy Ryzan Ross is an aspiring author, public speaker and entreprenuer from Orlando, Florida. She is working on her first book, due out in 2005, entitled *My Life As a Zebra*, which addresses growing up interracial. Tracy plans to write a series of *Zebra* books. Please e-mail her at *thetalkingzebra@yahoo.com*.

Wanda Rosseland has been published in the anthologies *Woven on the Wind* and *Crazy Woman Creek*, and is currently working on a book about Montanans who have seen angels. She has written many articles and writes for *Guideposts* magazine. You may e-mail her at *wjross@midrivers.com*.

Linda Saslow is a contributing reporter for *The New York Times* on Long Island. She is also the author of three published nonfiction books, and just completed her first novel, inspired by a true story. When she is not writing, she enjoys yoga, jogging and just hanging out with her family.

Elaine Ernst Schneider is a freelance writer who has published articles, songs and children's work. Presently, Elaine is a freelance curriculum author for Group Publishing and Pearson/Prentice-Hall. She is the managing editor of Lesson Tutor, a lesson-plan Web site that can be found at *www.lessontutor.com*. Her latest book, *Taking Hearing Impairment to School*, was released in February 2004 by JayJo Books, a Guidance Channel company. She can be reached by e-mail at *julius@ionet.net*.

Maity Schrecengost is a retired elementary school teacher. She is the author of two award-winning historical fiction books for young readers, *Tasso of Tarpon Springs* and *Panther Girl,* as well as eductional materials for teachers. Maity loves making author visits to schools. Please e-mail her at *tomandmaity@cs.com.*

JoAnn Semones, Ph.D., is a self-described "coastal critter" who lives in Half Moon Bay, California. Her stories have appeared in a variety of maritime history, health and environmental publications. She loves the sea, classical music and participating in local coastal volunteer projects. Please e-mail her at *HMBJoAnn@aol.com.*

Ilan Shamir lives in Colorado and is the author of *Advice from a Tree* and *A Thousand Things Went Right Today!* books, journals and posters available at *www.YourTrueNature.com.* He delivers empowering keynotes and trainings to organizations, conferences and events. Ilan has planted over fifty thousand trees to replace paper used in his business.

Deborah Shouse lives and writes in Prairie Village, Kansas. She is a speaker, writer and creativity catalyst. Her writing has appeared in *Reader's Digest, Newsweek, Woman's Day, Family Circle* and *Ms.* Visit her Web site at *www.the creativityconnection.com.*

Dena Smallwood says she tries to live up to the ideals her father taught her every day. She and her husband live and work on a 9,000-acre ranch in Nebraska where she's pursuing her dream of working in the outdoors with animals. She continues to write in her spare time.

Holly Smeltzer is a Christian wife and mother from Truro, Nova Scotia, Canada. She writes stories and poems from a heart filled with gratitude to God, who saved her and guides her daily. You can e-mail her at *blues@ tru.eastlink.ca.*

Pam Smith, a member of the baby-boom generation, lives in Mount Vernon, Indiana, and has been writing poetry for eleven years. She has been married for thirty-five years to John, who is her biggest fan. They have three daughters, Shannon, Jennifer and Misti, who have presented them with eight grandchildren, Nicholas, Tara, Austin, Seth, Averie, Johnathan, Brandon and Zackary. She started writing poems for her grandchildren. Her oldest grandson, Nicholas, called them "story poems." The poems she writes now can still be included in this catagory. Most of her poems are from her life and the lives around her.

Jerry Snider is a veteran of the U.S. Marine Corps, a graduate of Ohio University and an avid marathon runner. He enjoys working for the American Red Cross and the Special Wish Foundation. He can be contacted at P.O. Box 1129, Lancaster, Ohio 43130.

Courtney Lynne Soucy currently lives with her mom and two sisters. She has the best boyfriend in the world, Mike. Courtney was inspired to write this story because she wanted people to read about her dad. She is honored to have her work published in this series.

John St. Augustine is the award-winning creator and host of *Power Talk Radio*. He is a sought-after speaker on human development and potential and is author of *All Are Chosen* and *Be the Change: Common Sense for Uncommon Times*. He is a proud father of Amanda Lee and Andrew John. He can be reached via e-mail at *powertalkradio@chartermi.net*.

Debi Stack is a professional speaker, media guest and the author of *Martha to the Max: Balanced Living for Perfectionists* (Moody Publishers), a humorous book for stessed-out women. She can be booked through CLASS (800-483-6633). E-mail her at *debi.stack@maxedout.net*.

Laura M. Stack, M.B.A., C.S.P. (Certified Speaking Professional), is "The Productivity Pro."® She is the president of an international consulting firm specializing in productivity improvement in high-stress industries and the author of the highly acclaimed book *Leave the Office Earlier* (Broadway Books, 2004). Contact her at *www.TheProductivityPro.com*.

Betty Stanley received her Bachelor of Science degree in occupational therapy from the University of Kansas in 1948. She enjoyed working with handicapped children and tutoring ESL students. Since her retirement, Betty enjoys walking, swimming and freelance writing. Her mailing address is 12025 Earnshaw, Overland Park, KS 66213.

Brenda K. Stevens is a homemaker and an artist. She is self-taught and has done artwork for businesses and individuals for many years. Brenda enjoys crafts, reading and writing.

Jean H. Stewart is a history, travel and parenting writer and editor. She is the wife of a retired airline pilot, mother of twin daughters and smitten grandmother of one. Jean is working on a book about letting go, with the working title, *Bungee Mama*. She can be contacted at *jstew111@earthlink.net*.

Marilyn K. Strube received her Master of Arts degree from Eastern Michigan University and teaches writing at Madonna University. She is also a regular contributor to *Guideposts* magazine and an instructor of children's literature. Please e-mail her at *mstrube@madonna.edu*.

B.J. Taylor loves getting together with family. She is also an animal lover and is writing a book titled *Find Your Dog a Job!* showing how a dog and its owner can make a difference in their community. B.J. has been published in numerous magazines and newspapers and can be reached at *bjtaylor3@earthlink.net*.

Stephanie Welcher Thompson traded suits for sweats to stay home with her two-year-old daughter, Micah. Being a wife and first-time mom at forty-one provides an abundance of material for this freelance writer. She and husband, Michael, can be reached at P.O. Box 1502, Edmond, OK 73083, *www.stateofchange.net*.

Ted A. Thompson is a former copywriter and freelance author. He presently works as a chimney sweep in Harrison, Arkansas.

John Troy has been a cartoonist for forty-nine years. He has authored eleven books and is the creator of Ben, The Hunting Retriever. John lives in northern New Jersey with his lovely wife, Doris, his golden retriever, Jesse, and two cats, Snowy and Dongo, both of whom don't know enough to go to sleep at night.

Marianne LaValle Vincent is a poet/writer with a degree in nursing. She is a practice manager in Syracuse, New York. Her first collection of poetry, "American Lie," was published in 2004. Her second collection, "Broken Me," will be available in 2005. She lives with her husband and daughter. E-mail her at *Lavs4@hotmail.com.*

Sonja Walder lives with her husband, Mike, and daughter, Kelsey, in Bismarck, North Dakota. Her hobbies include gardening, reading and spending time with her family. She works in the North Dakota Attorney General's Office in the Gaming Division. Her story was written in loving memory of her father, Jack Oster, 1929–1997.

Susan Wales is author of a dozen books, including the *Match Made in Heaven* series, *Faith in God and Generals* and *The Chase.* She is also the producer of the Annual Movieguide Awards. Susan and her husband, producer Ken Wales (CBS series, *Christy*), live in Southern California. For additional information, contact her at *www.susanwales.com.*

Margaret J. Wasilewski, a graduate of the University of California, Irvine, resides in Michigan with Ted, her husband of twenty-eight years. They have four children and seven grandchildren. She has traveled extensively throughout the United States and has fond memories of living in Alaska. She looks forward to retirement and spending time writing her memoirs. She can be reached at P.O. Box 211, Fenton, MI 48430.

Janet Hall Wigler, a former ad sales, production and layout manager for a small newspaper in Canada, now lives in Southern California with her husband, Greg. Janet loves playwriting, acting and penning short stories. She is currently working on her second novel. Please e-mail her at *actingjanet@hotmail.com.*

Arthur B. Wiknik Jr. has written over a dozen short stories that have appeared in both regional and national publications, including *Chicken Soup for the Veteran's Soul.* He served in Vietnam with the 101st Airborne Division and fought in the battle for Hamburger Hill. An active community volunteer, Arthur frequently shares his wartime experiences at Connecticut schools and civic organizations. Contact him at *mucketman@juno.com.*

Bobbie Hamlet Wilkinson is a freelance writer and artist whose creativity inspires everything from painting tractors to uniquely renovating the barn she and her husband live in. Her greatest passions are her family and appreciating the beauty that surrounds her. Contact Bobbie at *bobbiewilkinson @earthlink.net.* Visit her Web site at *artbybobbie.com.*

Ron Wutka lives in Monson, Massachusetts, with his wife, Marcy, and daughter, Aimee-Lynn. Please contact him at *rwutka@comcast.net.*

D. B. Zane is a writer, teacher and mother of three. Author of *The Great Zamboni* and *Getting the Most Out of Writing Conferences,* she currently is working on a new series for primary grades as well as a nonfiction book with her writing group.

Lanny Zechar is a writer, consultant and motivational speaker from Southern California. He writes scripts, features, commercials, speeches, poems and children's books. He is married and has three children. He can be reached at *LannyZechar@yahoo.com.*

Chicken Soup for the Father & Daughter Soul
STORY CONTEST

*Can you think of anything more beautiful than the special bond
between a father and daughter?*

*Tell us your most heartwarming, inspirational, loving, or funny story
about your father or daughter and enter to win special prizes!*

TWO GRAND PRIZES

There will be two grand prize winners:
A father's story about his daughter, and a daughter's story about her father.

♥ The winning stories will be published in the June/July 2006
Chicken Soup for the American Soul Magazine.

♥ Each winner will receive $100.00 in cash.

♥ Five signed *Chicken Soup for the Soul*® books of your choice.

Sugar and Old Spice and Everything Nice!

Please see official rules on following pages.

OFFICIAL RULES

1. Eligibility. NO PURCHASE NECESSARY. Contest is open to all legal residents of the fifty United States and the District of Columbia. Officers, directors, representatives, and employees of Health Communications, Inc., Chicken Soup for the Soul Enterprises, Inc., M.V. Hansen and Associates, Inc., and/or Self Esteem Seminars, Inc., and their respective affiliates or subsidiaries, their respective advertising, promotion, publicity, production, and judging agencies, and members of their immediate families and households, are not eligible to enter.

2. To Enter. Contest begins May 5, 2005 and ends October 15, 2005. All entries must be either submitted online or received by Chicken Soup for the Soul Enterprises, Inc. by 5:00 PM EST on October 15th, 2005. Contestant Authors may enter as many times as desired either by submitting their stories at the appropriate location in their participating bookstore, or by mailing their submission to: Chicken Soup for the Father & Daughter Soul Story Contest, Chicken Soup for the Soul Enterprises, Inc., P.O. Box 30880, Santa Barbara, California 93130, or online at *www.chickensoup.com*. Each entry must be accompanied by a fully completed Official Entry Form which may be obtained at a participating bookstore or online at *www.chickensoup.com*. Stories submitted online will not be acknowledged, nor will stories submitted by mail or to the bookstore be acknowledged or returned. Sponsors, and those working for Sponsors or on their behalf, will not be responsible for lost, late, misdirected, or damaged entries.

3. Requirements. Each submitted story must be no more than 800 words, non-fiction and authored by the Contestant. The subject matter must address the relationship between a father and a daughter; either from a father's or a daughter's point of view. (For specific information on how to write a *Chicken Soup for the Soul* story, go to *www.chickensoup.com/StorySubmission/StoryGuidelines.html*.) Each story must be wholly original and must not incorporate or include material owned by a third party, or that violates the rights of any third party. Author contestants are responsible for obtaining written permission to submit their story from anyone referenced in the story before entering the Contest, and must be able to produce that written permission upon demand from the Sponsors of this Contest. Failure to meet the terms of this paragraph will render the submitted story ineligible, and may subject the Contestant Author to liability in accordance with the indemnification obligations below. If Contestant Author is under the age of majority in the state in which Contestant resides, story submission and Official Entry Form must be accompanied by a written authorization from Contestant's parent/guardian in order to complete eligibility and to participate in the Contest.

4. Winner Selection. On or about December 1, 2005, two (2) stories will be selected as potential Contest Winners by a panel of judges consisting of book editors, marketers, publicists and authors. One (1) story authored by a daughter about her relationship with her father, and one (1) story authored by a father about his relationship with his daughter will be selected based upon the following criteria: (i) originality, (ii) adherence to *Chicken Soup* story guidelines, (iii) story construction, and (iv) ability to involve and impact the reader. Potential Contest Winners will be notified by e-mail and/or telephone on or about December 3, 2005. The decision of the judges is final and binding in all regards.

5. Winner Validation. In order for the Contestant Authors of the selected stories to become validated Contest Winners, each Contestant Author of the selected stories (or parent/guardian of Contestant Author if Contestant is under the age of majority in the state which Contestant resides) must sign and return the Chicken Soup for the Soul Enterprises, Inc. standard Contributing Author Release within twenty one (21) days after notification of winning story selection. Failure of any potential winner (or parent or guardian of Contestant Author if Contestant is under the age of majority in the state which Contestant resides) to complete, sign, and return any requested documents within such period, or the return of any prize notification or prize as undeliverable, will result in disqualification and selection of an alternate winner. The authors of the selected stories do not become Contest Winners until the validation process is complete.

6. Grand Prize. Two Grand Prizes will be awarded. Each Winner will receive a check for $100.00 (One Hundred Dollars) plus five (5) autographed *Chicken Soup for the Father and Daughter Soul* books or five (5) other *Chicken Soup for the Soul* books of their choice (approximate retail value of the books: $64.75; prize total approximate retail value: $164.75). Contest Winners may not substitute, assign or transfer prize(s) for cash or to another party. All federal, state, and local taxes are each Winner's sole responsibility. All prizes will be awarded. Sponsors reserve the right to substitute a prize of equal or greater value. Prizes will be sent to Winners within thirty (30) days after each Winner's validation is complete. The winning stories will be eligible to be published in the 2006 Father's Day issue of the *Chicken Soup for the American Soul Magazine*.

7. Use of Submission. By accepting a prize, each Winner (or parent/guardian of Winner if Winner is under the age of majority in the state which Winner resides) grants to Chicken Soup for the Soul Enterprises, Inc., a non-exclusive, perpetual license to print, re-print, translate, publish and otherwise exploit his/her story in the *Chicken Soup for the American Soul Magazine, Chicken Soup for the Soul* books, or other products displaying the Chicken Soup for the Soul trademark, and in any marketing and publicity in connection therewith; and to use his/her name, photograph, and likeness without any claim to further compensation, except where prohibited.

8. Restrictions. By submitting a story in the Contest, each Contestant Author (or parent/guardian of Contestant Author if Contestant is under the age of majority in the state which Contestant resides) agrees to (a) be bound by the decisions of the judges and these Official Rules; (b) comply with all federal, state, and local laws and regulations; and (c) indemnify, release and hold harmless the Sponsors, their respective directors, officers, employees, representatives, agents, successors, assigns, subsidiaries and affiliates from any liability (including attorneys' fees) from any claims, injuries, losses, damages, deaths, causes of action, actions, suits, debts, sums of money, or other liabilities, either at law or equity, whether known or unknown, asserted or non-asserted, arising from or in any way relating to the Winner's or any Contestant's participation in the Contest, the awarding, acceptance, use, or misuse of any prize, or the use of any submission. Sponsors reserve the right to utilize Winner's name for promotional and/or publicity materials and Contest entries will be deemed automatically approved of such utilization. Contestant also agrees that he/she shall have no claim (including, without limitation, claims based on invasion of privacy, defamation, or right of publicity) arising out of any use of his/her name, address (city and state only) and approved biographical information. Contestant represents and warrants that Contestant has the full right and authority to grant the rights granted herein and that Contestant's agreement to the terms hereof does not conflict with any existing commitment on Contestant's part. By participating in the Contest, each Contestant agrees that Florida law will apply to the Contest, and that any dispute with respect to the Contest will be resolved in either the federal or state courts located in the State of Florida. Sponsors are under no obligation to use submitted stories for any purpose.

9. Official Rules/Winners List. Copies of these Official Rules can be obtained at *www.chickensoup.com,* or send a self-addressed stamped envelope, to: The Chicken Soup for the Father and Daughter Soul Story Contest Official Rules, c/o Health Communications, Inc., 3201 SW 15th Street, Deerfield Beach, Florida 33442. VT residents may omit return postage. Written requests for Official Rules must be received no later than October 1, 2005. To obtain the names of the prize winners, send a self-addressed stamped envelope no later than February 1, 2006, to: The Chicken Soup for the Father and Daughter Soul Story Contest Winners List, c/o Health Communications, Inc., 3201 SW 15th Street, Deerfield Beach, Florida 33442.

10. Sponsors. Sponsors of the Contest are Health Communications, Inc., 3201 SW 15th Street, Deerfield Beach, Florida 33442, and Chicken Soup for the Soul Enterprises, Inc., 711 West 17th Street, Suite D2, Costa Mesa, California 92627.

11. Contest is void where prohibited, taxed, or otherwise restricted.

More great books